Implementing Azure DevOps Solutions

Learn about Azure DevOps Services to successfully apply DevOps strategies

Henry Been
Maik van der Gaag

BIRMINGHAM - MUMBAI

Implementing Azure DevOps Solutions

Commissioning Editor: Vijin Boricha
Acquisition Editor: Rohit Rajkumar
Content Development Editor: Carlton Borges
Senior Editor: Rahul Dsouza
Technical Editor: Sarvesh Jaywant
Copy Editor: Safis Editing
Project Coordinator: Neil Dmello
Proofreader: Safis Editing
Indexer: Rekha Nair
Production Designer: Alishon Mendonsa

First published: June 2020

Production reference: 1100620

Published by Packt Publishing Ltd.
Livery Place
35 Livery Street
Birmingham
B3 2PB, UK.

ISBN 978-1-78961-969-0

www.packt.com

Subscribe to our online digital library for full access to over 7,000 books and videos, as well as industry leading tools to help you plan your personal development and advance your career. For more information, please visit our website.

Why subscribe?

- Spend less time learning and more time coding with practical eBooks and Videos from over 4,000 industry professionals

- Improve your learning with Skill Plans built especially for you

- Get a free eBook or video every month

- Fully searchable for easy access to vital information

- Copy and paste, print, and bookmark content

Did you know that Packt offers eBook versions of every book published, with PDF and ePub files available? You can upgrade to the eBook version at www.packt.com and as a print book customer, you are entitled to a discount on the eBook copy. Get in touch with us at customercare@packtpub.com for more details.

At www.packt.com, you can also read a collection of free technical articles, sign up for a range of free newsletters, and receive exclusive discounts and offers on Packt books and eBooks.

Contributors

About the authors

Henry Been has been working in IT for over ten years. He is an independent architect, developer, and trainer in a number of companies. With many of these companies, he has embarked on a journey implementing practices such as continuous integration and deployment, infrastructure as code, trunk-based development, and implementing feedback loops.

Alongside his work, he creates online training courses for A Cloud Guru, and frequently speaks at meetups and conferences. He was awarded the Microsoft MVP award in 2019.

I am grateful to Gerald Versluis, who helped me with some specific sections in this book. I thank my wife, Gerja, for her support and patience, and for being the first pair of eyes that caught many errors before anyone else could see them.

Maik van der Gaag is an architect and trainer at 3fifty, an experienced consultancy company with a strong focus on the Microsoft cloud. He has over 15 years' experience of providing architecture, development, training, and design expertise. During his career, he has worked on a variety of projects, ranging from cloud transformations to DevOps implementations.

He loves to share his knowledge, which was also one of the reasons why he founded the Dutch Cloud meetup. Maik is a public speaker, writes blogs, and organizes events.

I wish to thank those people who have been close to me and supported me, especially my girlfriend, Charlotte, and my children, Tibbe, Fiene, and Jurre.

About the reviewer

Adin Ermie is an experienced Microsoft Azure Subject Matter Expert who brings passion and enthusiasm to everything he does. With expertise in emerging technologies and innovation, he utilizes his knowledge and insatiable drive for learning at the cutting-edge of developments in cloud operations to help his clients and their customers become market leaders rather than followers of trends.

Adin specializes in hybrid-cloud architecture and implementation technologies, including Microsoft Azure, Infrastructure-as-Code (IaC) via Azure Resource Manager and Terraform, Business Continuity and Disaster Recovery (BCDR), Cloud Governance, and Cloud Management & Security.

Packt is searching for authors like you

If you're interested in becoming an author for Packt, please visit authors.packtpub.com and apply today. We have worked with thousands of developers and tech professionals, just like you, to help them share their insight with the global tech community. You can make a general application, apply for a specific hot topic that we are recruiting an author for, or submit your own idea.

Table of Contents

Preface   1

Section 1: Getting to Continuous Delivery

Chapter 1: Introduction to DevOps   9
  Technical requirements   9
  What is DevOps?   9
    The relation between DevOps and Agile   11
      Agile work management   11
        Switching to a flow-based methodology   12
        Synchronizing work items to one system   13
        Fastlaning   13
        Decommissioning other work management tools   14
    Goals and benefits of a DevOps culture   14
      Measuring results   14
        Cycle time and lead time   15
        The amount of work in progress   15
        Mean time to recovery   16
        Change rate and change failure rate   16
  Creating your ideal DevOps organization   16
  Exploring DevOps practices and habits   17
    DevOps practices   18
      Configuration management   18
      Release management   19
      Continuous integration   19
      Continuous deployment   20
      Infrastructure as code   21
      Test automation   22
      Application performance monitoring   22
    DevOps habits   22
      Team autonomy and enterprise alignment   23
      Rigorous management of technical debt   23
      Focusing on flow of customer value   23
      Hypothesis-driven development   24
      Evidence gathered in production   24
      Live-site culture   24
      Managing infrastructure as a flexible resource   25
  Five stages of the DevOps evolution   25
    Normalizing the technology stack   25
    Standardizing and reducing variability   26
    Expanding DevOps practices   26
    Automating infrastructure delivery   26
    Providing self-service capabilities   26

Summary 27
Questions 27
Further reading 28

Chapter 2: Everything Starts with Source Control 29
Technical requirements 29
Types of source control in Azure DevOps 30
Centralized source control 30
Decentralized source control 30
Source control systems 31
Team Foundation Version Control 31
Git 32
Large File Storage 33
Migrating between control systems 33
Migrating existing Git repositories 34
Migrating from TFVC to an Azure Git repository 35
Migrating from Subversion to an Azure Git repository 36
Migrating without retaining history 36
Selecting a branching and merging strategy 37
Branching strategies 37
GitHub flow 37
GitFlow 38
Release Flow 39
Trunk-based development 39
Branching by abstraction 40
Merging strategies 41
TFVC 41
Git 41
Merge commit 42
Squash commit 42
Rebase 43
Managing repositories 43
Monorepo or multi-repo 43
Creating and removing repositories 44
Securing repositories 46
Branch policies 46
Other tools for source control 48
GitHub 48
GitLab 49
Subversion 49
Summary 49
Questions 50
Further reading 50

Chapter 3: Moving to Continuous Integration 53
Technical requirements 53
Introducing continuous integration 54

The four pillars of continuous integration   55
Creating a build definition in Azure DevOps   55
Connecting to source control   56
Configuring a job   57
Adding tasks to your job   60
Publishing build artifacts   61
Calling other tools   61
Task Marketplace   63
Creating variables and variable groups   64
Variable groups   65
Triggering the build   66
Build options   68
Build history   69
Task groups   69
Running a build   71
Viewing the build results   71
Building a pull request   72
Accessing build artifacts   73
Working with YAML pipelines   75
The reason for using build definitions as code   75
Writing a basic YAML pipeline   76
Writing the YAML file   76
Creating a YAML pipeline   78
Multi-job pipelines   79
Control options   80
Variables   81
Pipeline artifacts   81
Tips for writing YAML pipelines   82
Agents and agent queues   83
Built-in agent pools   83
Creating a private agent pool   84
Adding and removing agents   85
Agent selection   87
Finding agent capabilities   88
Other tools   89
GitLab CI   89
Jenkins   90
Summary   90
Questions   91
Further reading   92

Chapter 4: Continuous Deployment   93
Technical requirements   94
Continuous delivery and continuous deployment   94
Working with Azure DevOps releases   95
Creating artifacts and release triggers   96

Specifying the stages to deploy the release 99
Which stages do I need? 100
Stage triggers, approvals, and gates 100
Working with deployment groups 103
Managing deployment groups 104
Creating a release pipeline with a deployment group 105
Writing multi-stage YAML pipelines 106
Adding stages to YAML pipelines 106
Downloading artifacts 107
Approvals 108
Implementing continuous deployment strategies 110
Blue-green deployments 111
Immutable servers 112
Progressive exposure 112
Canary deployments 113
Ring-based deployments 113
Feature flags 114
Roll back or fail forward 115
Deploying mobile applications 116
Connecting to the app store 118
Using distribution groups 119
Publishing an app 120
App Center via Azure Pipelines 122
Automating release notes 122
Other tools 123
Octopus Deploy 124
Summary 124
Questions 125
Further reading 125

Section 2: Expanding your DevOps Pipeline

Chapter 5: Dependency Management 129
Technical requirements 129
Identifying shared components 130
Types of feeds 132
Creating a feed 132
Setting up a feed 133
Securing access 135
Managing views on a feed 136
Configuring upstream sources 137
Publishing packages 139
Uploading packages by hand 139
Publishing packages from a pipeline 140
Versioning packages 142
Consuming packages 144

Consuming packages from Visual Studio   144
Consuming packages from a pipeline   146
Working with universal packages   146
Uploading and downloading universal packages from Azure Pipelines   147
Uploading and downloading universal packages using the Azure CLI   149
Exploring other tools   150
MyGet   150
Artifactory   150
Azure Container Registry   150
Summary   151
Questions   151
Further reading   152
Chapter 6: Infrastructure and Configuration as Code   153
Technical requirements   154
Having everything as code   154
Working with ARM templates   155
Parameters   156
Parameter files   157
Variables   158
Resources   158
Dependent resources   159
Nested templates   160
Outputs   160
Functions   161
Deploying ARM templates   162
PowerShell   162
The Azure CLI   163
Azure Pipelines   163
Reverse engineering a template   164
Using the Export template   164
Using the Resource Explorer   166
Subscription-level templates   166
Azure Blueprints   167
November 2019 updates   168
Using Azure Automation   169
Automation account resources   169
Run As account   169
Schedules   170
Modules   171
Variables   171
Credentials   172
Connections   172
Runbooks   172
Runbook execution   173
Jobs   173
Runbooks gallery   174

PowerShell DSC   174
  Compiling and applying PowerShell DSC   175
  Using Powershell DSC with Azure Automation   175
Managing application settings   177
Azure app service settings from an ARM template   178
Loading settings at runtime from key vault   178
Azure App Configuration   180
Other tools   182
CloudFormation   182
Chef   183
Puppet   183
Ansible   184
Terraform   184
Summary   185
Questions   185
Further reading   186

Chapter 7: Dealing with Databases in DevOps Scenarios   187
Technical requirements   188
Managing a database schema as code   188
Migrations   189
End state   190
Applying database schema changes   192
Upgrading as part of the release   192
Upgrading by the application code   192
Adding a process   193
Going schema-less   195
Writing objects to the database   195
Reading objects from the database   197
Other approaches and concerns   198
Minimizing the influence of databases   198
Full side-by-side deployment   199
Testing database changes   199
Summary   200
Questions   200
Further reading   201

Chapter 8: Continuous Testing   203
Technical requirements   204
Defining quality   204
Metrics for quality   205
Technical debt   207
Understanding test types   208
Types of automated functional tests   210
  Unit tests   211

Integration tests   213
System tests   215
Types of manual functional tests   216
Scripted testing   217
Exploratory testing   223
Reporting manual test results   224
Strategies for deciding which types of functional tests you need   224
The testing pyramid   226
The testing trophy   227
Types of non-functional tests   228
Performance testing   228
Load testing   229
Usability testing   230
Executing tests in a pipeline   231
Running unit tests   231
Recording unit test code coverage   233
Running integration tests   234
Running external tests   235
Maintaining quality   236
Code reviews   236
Automatically gathering quality metrics   237
Visualizing quality   239
Quality gates   241
Classic releases   241
Multi-stage pipelines   242
Summary   244
Questions   245
Further reading   245

Chapter 9: Security and Compliance   247
Technical requirements   248
Applying DevOps principles to security and compliance 248
Bringing developers and security engineers together   249
Security concerns   250
Working with secrets   251
Storing secrets in service connections   252
Storing secrets in variable groups   254
Detecting unsecured secrets   256
Detecting application code vulnerabilities   258
OWASP Top 10   259
Implementing automated vulnerability scanning   259
OWASP Zed Attack Proxy   260
Working with dependencies   260
Working with WhiteSource Bolt   261
Ensuring infrastructure compliance   263
Assigning an Azure Policy or initiative   263

Writing an Azure Policy   264
Initiatives   266
Fetching audit results   266
Monitoring and detecting runtime security risks and threats   268
Other tools you can use   271
Summary   271
Questions   272
Further reading   272

Section 3: Closing the Loop

Chapter 10: Application Monitoring   277
  Technical requirements   278
  Investigating application crashes   278
    Gathering crash reports for mobile applications   278
    Gathering crash reports for desktop applications   281
  Instrumenting web applications   282
    Logging   284
      Emitting logs   284
      Searching logs   286
      Alerting on logs   286
    Metrics   289
      Emitting metrics   290
      Graphing metrics   292
      Alerting on metrics   293
    Investigating requests   295
    Optimizing alerting   297
      Optimizing alerts   298
      Alert fatigue   298
      Which metrics to capture   299
    Having an on-call schedule   300
    Live site reviews   301
  Integrating with other tools   302
    IT service management applications   302
    Azure Boards   303
    Grafana   304
  Summary   305
  Questions   305
  Further reading   306

Chapter 11: Gathering User Feedback   307
  Technical requirements   307
  Understanding continuous feedback   308
  Asking for direct feedback   309
    Advantages of in-product feedback   309
    Having a public roadmap   310

Using interviews or focus groups   311
Gathering indirect feedback   312
Sentiment analysis   313
Support requests   313
Implementing hypothesis-driven development   313
Summary   315
Questions   315
Further reading   316

Section 4: Section 4: Advanced Topics

Chapter 12: Containers   319
Technical requirements   320
An introduction to containers   320
DevOps and containers   321
Hosting options   322
Building a container image   322
Creating an application   323
Adding Docker support to an existing application   324
Creating an image with the application   326
Running the container image   329
Building images in Azure DevOps and running them in Azure   330
Creating a service endpoint   330
Creating a new pipeline   332
An introduction to Kubernetes   336
Functionalities of Kubernetes   336
Kubernetes core components and services   336
Master node   337
Regular nodes   337
Pod   337
Service   338
Deployment   338
Operation of Kubernetes   338
Azure Kubernetes Service   340
Kubernetes in action   340
Creating a Kubernetes cluster   340
Kubernetes infrastructure   341
Managing Kubernetes   342
Deploying a container image   343
Upgrading containers   346
Scaling containers and Kubernetes   347
Scaling pods manually   348
Autoscaling pods   348
Scaling nodes   349
Autoscaling nodes   350

Deploying to Kubernetes with Azure DevOps   350
Summary   353
Questions   353
Further reading   354

Chapter 13: Planning Your Azure DevOps Organization   355
  Technical requirements   356
  Setting up an Azure DevOps organization   356
    How Azure DevOps is organized   356
    Creating an Azure DevOps organization and project   358
    Azure DevOps security model   359
    Azure DevOps licensing   361
      Consumption-based costs   362
  Ensuring traceability   362
  Consolidating tools   364
    Standardizing tools   365
    Migration strategies   366
      Azure DevOps Server to Azure DevOps Services migration   367
      Big-bang migration   367
      Synchronization   368
      Rebuilding   368
    Integrating tools   369
  Accepting there is no end state   369
  Summary   371
  Questions   372
  Further reading   372

Chapter 14: AZ-400 Mock Exam   373
  Designing a DevOps Strategy   373
  Implementing DevOps Development Processes   377
  Implementing Continuous Integration   382
  Implementing Continuous Delivery   384
  Implementing Dependency Management   387
  Implementing Application Infrastructure   389
  Implementing Continuous Feedback   392
  Answers   393

Assessments   395

Other Books You May Enjoy   403

Index   407

Preface

As the speed at which IT products are being created and delivered is ever more important when it comes to companies succeeding, the demand for IT professionals with a thorough understanding of DevOps is increasing year on year. In this book, *Implementing Azure DevOps Solutions*, you will learn about the Microsoft tools that help to make this possible. Besides this, the knowledge that you acquire will help you to embrace DevOps and improve the way you continuously deliver value to your end users.

Who this book is for

This book targets software developers and operations' specialists interested in implementing DevOps practices on the Azure cloud. Application developers and IT professionals with some experience in software development and development practices will also find this book useful. Some familiarity with basic usage of Azure DevOps would be an added bonus.

In addition to this, the best part is that you can also use this book as one of your references for the AZ-400 exam, as the topics covered are along similar lines.

What this book covers

The book comprises four parts. The chapters are in the recommended reading order and each chapter builds upon the previous one. The order of the chapters is such that it matches the order in which you would implement the different aspects in the real world. However, it is possible to pick and choose, especially once you have gone through the first part in its entirety.

Chapter 1, *Introduction to DevOps*, provides you with an understanding of what DevOps is and what it is not. DevOps is defined and its relationship to the Agile way of working is described. The chapter ends with an introduction to DevOps practices and habits that are central to a DevOps culture.

Chapter 2, *Everything Starts with Source Control*, introduces different types of source control systems and how they compare. Pull requests and code reviews are introduced as the default way for ensuring that every change is reviewed before it becomes part of the source. The chapter concludes by going over a number of strategies for branching and merging that align well with a way of working that focuses on a constant flow of value.

Chapter 3, *Moving to Continuous Integration,* covers how to go from sources to build artifacts that are ready to be deployed later on. Azure Pipelines, as the most important way of doing so, is covered in depth. Alongside the classical, visual editor, YAML pipelines-as-code are also introduced.

Chapter 4, *Continuous Deployment,* is about orchestrating deployments using Azure Pipelines. Once again, the classical, visual release editor is introduced. Multi-stage YAML pipelines are also introduced as a means of also describing your deployment process as code. The chapter concludes by introducing different deployment strategies that can be used to mitigate the risks that come with continuous deployment, to balance the need for change with stability.

Chapter 5, *Dependency Management,* introduces package management. Package management can be used as a means for splitting larger software solutions into multiple components that are built and tested independently and only then put together. Packages can also be used to distribute build artifacts between different continuous integration and deployment products.

Chapter 6, *Infrastructure and Configuration as Code,* goes into how creating, managing and configuring infrastructure can be transformed from a manual, error-prone task into the automated deployment of configuration that is kept as code in source control. The chapter covers ARM templates, Azure Blueprints, Azure App Configuration services, and a number of related tools.

Chapter 7, *Dealing with Databases,* dives into the topic of managing database schemas in combination with continuous deployment.

Chapter 8, *Continuous Testing,* explains how, having everything as code, continuously deploying new versions is of little value if the quality of new versions is not high enough. This chapter introduces different types of tests and how they can be integrated within Azure DevOps Pipelines.

Chapter 9, *Security and Compliance,* talks about the integration of security and compliance concerns within DevOps practices. You will learn how security and dependency scanning can be integrated into pipelines. Azure Policy and Security Center are introduced for preventing non-compliant configurations and detecting new risks that come in over time.

Chapter 10, *Application Monitoring,* is the first chapter that goes into learning from changes deployed previously. For this purpose, Azure Monitor and Application Insights are used to create metrics, dashboards, and alerts.

Chapter 11, *Gathering User Feedback*, also involves learning, but learning from your users, instead of from your systems. You will learn how you can interact with users to drive your roadmap and maximize the value delivered to users. Hypothesis-driven development is introduced as an approach to minimize investments that do have minimal returns and find features that are in high demand and bring great value.

Chapter 12, *Containers*, introduces you to the topic of containers. While DevOps and containers are not synonyms, containers assist in the adoption of DevOps principles in situations where that might not otherwise be possible.

Chapter 13, *Planning Your Azure DevOps Organization*, goes into the final and overarching considerations regarding the setup of your Azure DevOps organization and project(s). Licensing and the cost model are covered, along with the subject of traceability. Another important subject is that of migrating between products, so as to achieve standardization on DevOps tools.

Chapter 14, *AZ-400 Mock Exam*, provides you with an opportunity to test the knowledge that you have acquired throughout this book by means of a mock exam.

To get the most out of this book

You should have an understanding of software development processes and experience in application development and operations as either a software developer or as an IT professional. Irrespective of your background, be it software development or operations, it is important to have a basic understanding of the software delivery processes and the tools involved.

If you have taken the mock exam or want to take the official exam after reading this book and find that you are struggling with specific exam objectives, you can use the following table to find the chapters you need to re-read.

Exam objective	Relevant chapters
Design a DevOps strategy	Chapters 1, 8, and 13
Implement DevOps development processes	Chapters 4, 6, and 9
Implement continuous integration	Chapters 2 and 3
Implement continuous delivery	Chapter 4
Implement dependency management	Chapter 5
Implement application infrastructure	Chapters 6, 9, and 12
Implement continuous feedback	Chapters 10 and 11

Please keep in mind that some questions may fall into more than one category and that this book is developed without any access to the official exam materials.

While large parts of this book are theory, it is recommended that you experiment with the concepts introduced if you have no hands-on experience with them. Remember, if you intend to sit the AZ-400 exam, this exam is intended for practitioners with two to three years' practical experience. To perform the practical exercises in the book you will require the following:

Software/Hardware covered in the book	OS Requirements
Azure DevOps Services	Any device with a modern browser
Azure portal	Any device with a modern browser
Azure Powershell	Windows 10
Azure CLI, Git client	Windows, Linux or MacOS
Visual Studio	Windows or MacOS

For more practical experience, links to exercises or labs are included at the end of each chapter. Many of these exercises come from Microsoft Learn and can also be searched at `https://docs.microsoft.com/en-us/learn/browse/?term=devops`. Microsoft has also published a cloud workshop that enables you to practice many of the topics covered in Chapters 1 to 6. This cloud workshop can be found at `https://github.com/microsoft/ MCW-Continuous-delivery-in-Azure-DevOps/blob/master/Hands-on%20lab/ Before%20the%20HOL.md`.

Download the color images

We also provide a PDF file that has color images of the screenshots/diagrams used in this book. You can download it here: `http://www.packtpub.com/sites/default/files/downloads/9781789619690_ColorImages .pdf`

Conventions used

There are a number of text conventions used throughout this book.

`CodeInText`: Indicates code words in text, database table names, folder names, filenames, file extensions, pathnames, dummy URLs, user input, and Twitter handles. Here is an example: "In Command Prompt, type `hostname` and press the *Enter* key."

A block of code is set as follows:

```
public class FoodClassifier : IFoodClassifier
{
        public FoodClassification Classify(Food food)
        {
```

```
                                              // Unchanged classification
algorithm
                    }
}
public class FoodClassifierToBeRemoved : IFoodClassifer
{
     public FoodClassification Classify(Food food)
            {
                                  // Unchanged classification
algorithm
                   }
}
```

When we wish to draw your attention to a particular part of a code block, the relevant lines or items are set in bold:

```
[default]
exten => s,1,Dial(Zap/1|30)
exten => s,2,Voicemail(u100)
exten => s,102,Voicemail(b100)
exten => i,1,Voicemail(s0)
```

Any command-line input or output is written as follows:

```
git lfs install
git lfs track "*.mp4"
git add .gitattributes
```

Bold: Indicates a new term, an important word, or words that you see on screen. For example, words in menus or dialog boxes appear in the text like this. Here is an example: "Select **System info** from the **Administration** panel."

Warnings or important notes appear like this.

Tips and tricks appear like this.

Get in touch

Feedback from our readers is always welcome.

General feedback: If you have questions about any aspect of this book, mention the book title in the subject of your message and email us at customercare@packtpub.com.

Errata: Although we have taken every care to ensure the accuracy of our content, mistakes do happen. If you have found a mistake in this book, we would be grateful if you would report this to us. Please visit www.packtpub.com/support/errata, selecting your book, clicking on the Errata Submission Form link, and entering the details.

Piracy: If you come across any illegal copies of our works in any form on the internet, we would be grateful if you would provide us with the location address or website name. Please contact us at copyright@packt.com with a link to the material.

If you are interested in becoming an author: If there is a topic that you have expertise in, and you are interested in either writing or contributing to a book, please visit authors.packtpub.com.

Reviews

Please leave a review. Once you have read and used this book, why not leave a review on the site that you purchased it from? Potential readers can then see and use your unbiased opinion to make purchase decisions, we at Packt can understand what you think about our products, and our authors can see your feedback on their book. Thank you!

For more information about Packt, please visit packt.com.

Section 1: Getting to Continuous Delivery

In this section, you will learn about the fundamental principles of DevOps, along with the practices that most organizations start with, namely, continuous integration and continuous deployment. This section creates the necessary foundations for our work, after which most of the other chapters can be read in any order.

This section comprises the following chapters:

- Chapter 1, *Introduction to DevOps*
- Chapter 2, *Everything Starts with Source Control*
- Chapter 3, *Moving to Continuous Integration*
- Chapter 4, *Continuous Deployment*

Introduction to DevOps 1

DevOps is not a product or tool that you can buy or install. DevOps is about culture and the way you write, release, and operate your software. DevOps is about shortening the time between a new idea and your first end user experiencing the value it delivers. In this book, you will learn about the tools and techniques to apply that philosophy to your way of working.

To enable this, you might have to change the way you work and adopt new tools or change the way you use them. In this first chapter, you will learn more about what DevOps really is and how to recognize a successful DevOps team.

The following topics will be covered in this chapter:

- What DevOps is and why you cannot simply buy or install it
- How DevOps complements Agile
- What the benefits of DevOps are and how to measure them
- Creating your ideal DevOps and organizational structure
- Exploring DevOps practices and habits of successful DevOps teams
- The five stages of DevOps evolution

Technical requirements

There are no technical requirements for this chapter.

What is DevOps?

If you were to list all of the different definitions and descriptions of DevOps, there would be many. However, as different as these might be, they will most likely share several concepts. These are collaboration, continuous delivery of business value, and breaking down silos.

With all of the technical discussion in the rest in this book, it is important not to overlook the value proposition for adopting DevOps, namely, that it will help you to improve the way that you continuously deliver value to your end users. To do this, you have to decrease the time between starting work on a new feature and the first user using it in production. This means that you not only have to write the software but also deliver and operate it.

Over the last decade, the way we write software has fundamentally changed. More and more companies are now adopting an Agile way of working to increase the efficiency of their software development. More and more teams are now working in short iterations or sprints to create new increments of a product in quick succession. However, creating potentially shippable increments faster and faster does not create any value in itself. Only when each new version of your software is also released to production and used by your end users does it start delivering value.

In traditional organizations, developers and operators are often located in different departments and taking software into production includes a hand-off, often with a formal ceremony around it. In such an organization, it can be hard to accelerate that delivery to production along with the speed at which development can create new versions.

Next to that, development and operations departments often have conflicting goals. While a development department is rewarded for creating many changes as fast as possible, operation departments are rewarded for limiting downtime and preventing issues. The latter is often best achieved by having as few changes as possible. The conflict here is clear—both departments have optimizations for one subgoal, as shown in the following diagram:

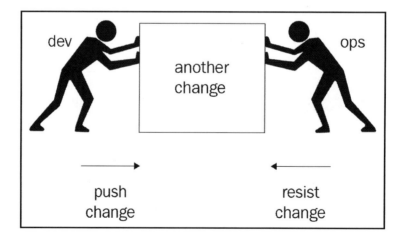

This defeats the purpose of these subgoals, which comes from the shared, overarching goal of quickly taking in new versions while maintaining stability. Precisely this conflict between developmental and operational goals is one of the things that should disappear in a DevOps culture. In such a culture, developers and operations teams should work together on delivering new versions to production in a fast and reliable manner and share responsibility for both subgoals.

While it is good to know that DevOps is a cultural movement, tools and automation are an important part of that culture. In this book, the focus will be on these tools and how to use them to implement many of the practices that come with a DevOps culture. In other words, this book will be mostly on the products and processes associated with DevOps. If you want to learn more about the cultural side of things, about the people, there are many other books to read.

The rest of this section will explore the relation between DevOps to see how they complement each other. The focus will be on Agile techniques and prices for work management. We will also discuss the goals and benefits of a DevOps culture.

The relation between DevOps and Agile

If you take a look at Agile, you might notice that part of it is the focus on business value and shortening the time between the delivery of a new business value. From that perspective, adopting DevOps is a logical next step after Agile. Agile advocates that the software development teams' responsibilities should extend forward by engaging with users and other stakeholders to more quickly deliver valuable potentially shippable products. DevOps is all about not just creating something that might be shipped, but really shipping it as well. With Agile and DevOps combined, you can create an end-to-end, continuous flow of value to your users.

One of the things you need to be able to do this is a common approach to managing the work to be done for everyone involved. In the next section, you will find some pointers on how to incorporate operational concerns in the way you manage your work.

Agile work management

When you are starting to increase the collaboration between development and operations, you will quickly notice that they have to cope with different types of work. In development, a large part of the work is planned: user stories and bugs that are picked up from a backlog. On the other hand, for operations, a large part of their work is unplanned. They respond to warnings and alerts from systems and requests or tickets from users or developers.

Integrating these two, especially if developers and operators are located on the same team, can be challenging. To see how you can deal with this, let's explore the following approach:

1. First, switch to a flow-based way of working for developers.
2. Next, allow for operations to also list their work in the same work management system as developers using synchronizations. You can also choose to implement *fastlaning*, an approach to expedite urgent work.
3. Finally, you might choose to decommission existing ticketing tools for operations if possible.

Fastlaning is an approach to organizing work that allows for both planned and unplanned work by visualizing two separate lanes of work. To do this, the Scrum board is extended with a Kanban-like board on the top. This is the fast lane. On the Kanban board, urgent but unplanned work is added. Any work added to this lane is picked up by the team with the highest priority. Only when there is no work remaining in the fast lane is work from the Scrum board with planned work picked up. Whenever new work is added to the fast lane, this takes priority again. Often, there is the agreement though that work in progress is finished before switching to work in the fast lane.

Switching to a flow-based methodology

The first thing to consider is transitioning the way developers work from batch-wise to flow-based. An example of a batch-wise way of working is Scrum. If you are using the Scrum framework, you are used to picking up a batch of work every two to four weeks and focus on completing all of that work within that time window. Only when that batch is done do you deliver a potentially shippable product.

When changing to a flow-based approach, you try to focus not on a batch, but on just one thing only. You work on that one work item and drive it completely until it's done before you start on the next. This way, there is no longer a sprint backlog, only a product backlog. The advantage of this approach is that you no longer decide which work to perform upfront, but whenever you are free to start on new work, you can pick up the next item from the backlog. In an environment where priorities quickly shift, this allows you to react to change more quickly.

These changes to the way developers organize their work make it easier to include operations in work management, but there is also another benefit. When developers are focusing on getting a single work item done instead of a whole sprint at once, you can also increase the number of times you can deliver a small portion of value to your users.

Synchronizing work items to one system

After the development team changes the way it organizes its work, it should now be easier for developers to also list their planned work on the shared backlog and pull work from that backlog when they have time to work on it. They now also have a place where they can list their unplanned work.

However, there might still be an existing ticketing system where requests for operations are dropped by users or automatically created by monitoring tools. While Azure DevOps has a great API to rework this integration to directly create work items in Azure DevOps, you might first choose to create a synchronization between your existing ticketing tool and Azure Boards. There are many integration options available and there is a lot of ongoing work in this area. This way, operators can slowly move from their old tool to the new one, since they are now in sync. Of course, the goal is for them to move over to the same tool as the developers completely.

Fastlaning

With the work of developers and operators in the same work management tool, you will notice that you have a mix of planned and unplanned, often urgent, work in the system. To ensure that urgent work gets the attention and precedence it deserves, you can introduce what is called a fastlane to your sprint board. In the following screenshot, you can see an example of an Azure Board that is set up for fastlaning production issues:

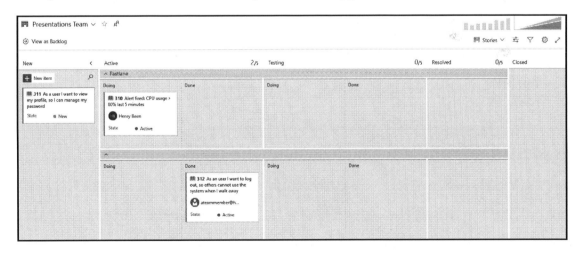

The use of this horizontal split in the board is to only work on tasks in the regular lane when there is no work to be picked up in the fast lane.

Decommissioning other work management tools

After creating a shared work management system between development and operations, there is much opportunity to increase the amount of collaboration between them. When this collaboration is taking off, old ticketing systems that were used by operations might now slowly be decommissioned over time. Integrations from monitoring tools can be shifted to the new shared tools and the number of tickets between developers and operators should slowly decrease as they find new ways of working together.

Goals and benefits of a DevOps culture

At this point, you might be wondering about the point of it all. What are the benefits of DevOps and what is there in it for you, your colleague, and your organization? The most common goal of adopting DevOps is to achieve a reduction in **cycle time**. Cycle time is the time between starting work on a new feature and the moment that the first user can use it. The way this is achieved, by automation, also serves the goals of lower change failure rate, lower **Mean Time To Repair (MTTR)** and lower planned downtime.

Next to all that, there might also be other benefits such as increased employee satisfaction, less burnout and stress, and better employee retention. This is attributed to the removal of opposing goals between developers and operators.

For a while, there was doubt whether DevOps really works, and whether these goals were really met, and whether the extra benefits were really achieved, as this was only shown using case studies. The downside of this is that case studies are often only available for successful cases and not for unsuccessful cases. This all changed in 2018 when the book *Accelerate* came out. This book shows, based on years of quantitative research, that modern development practices such as DevOps really contribute to reaching IT goals and organizational goals.

Measuring results

To measure where you currently stand as a team or organization and the impact of DevOps on you, there are several metrics that you could start recording. As always when working with metrics or **Key Performance Indicators (KPIs)**, make sure that you do not encourage people to game the system by looking only at the numbers. Several interesting metrics are detailed in the following sections and if you go over them, you will notice that they are all about encouraging flow.

Cycle time and lead time

Cycle time and **lead time** are metrics that come from Lean and Kanban and are used to measure the time needed to realize a change. Cycle time is the amount of time between starting work on a feature and users being able to use that feature in production. The lower cycle time, the quicker you can react to changing requirements or insights. Lead time is the amount of time between requesting a feature and realizing that feature. It is the time between adding work to the backlog and the start of implementation.

When you add cycle time and lead time together, you are calculating another metric, the **time to market**. This last one is often an important business metric when developing software. Minimizing both cycle time and lead time will hence have a business impact.

The amount of work in progress

Another thing you can measure is the amount of work in progress at any point in time. DevOps is focusing on the flow of value to the user. This implies that everyone should, if possible, be doing only one thing at a time and completely finish that before moving on to something else. This reduces the amount of time spent on task switching and the amount of time spent on not yet complete work. Measuring how many things a team works on in parallel and reporting on this can encourage this.

You can even go as far as putting actual limits on the amount of work that can be in progress. The following is a small part of the earlier screenshot, showing that these work-in-progress limits can even be shown in the tool:

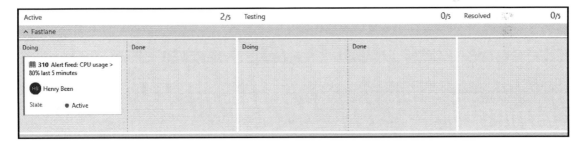

The goal is to have as little work in progress at the same time as possible.

Mean time to recovery

A third metric is the **mean time to recovery**. How long does it take you to restore service in case of a (partial) outage? In the past, companies focused on reducing the **mean time between failures**. This used to be the mean indicator of the stability of a product. However, this metric encourages limiting the number of changes going to production. The unwanted consequence often is that outages, though maybe rare, last long and are hard to fix.

Measuring the mean time to recovery shifts the attention to how quickly you can remediate an outage. If you can fix outages quickly, you achieve the same, namely, minimizing the amount of downtime without sacrificing the rate of change. The goal is to minimize the time to recovery.

Change rate and change failure rate

Finally, you can measure the number of changes delivered to production and the percentage of that which is not successful. Increasing the rate of change implies that you are more often delivering value to your users, hence realizing a flow of value. Also, by measuring not just the number of failures, but the percentage that fails, you are actually encouraging many small, successful changes instead of encouraging limiting the number of changes overall.

Your goals should be to increase the rate of change while lowering the change failure rate.

At this point, you might be wondering, how do I change my organization to foster this culture and reap all of these benefits? The next section will answer this for you.

Creating your ideal DevOps organization

Well, maybe your organizational structure does not have to change at all. DevOps has to start with a cultural change: openness, empathy, and collaboration are values that need to be encouraged. But still, changing your organizational structure might help to accelerate this.

Traditionally, developers and operators are often organized in disparate teams or even different departments—organized in teams with people that have a similar skill set and responsibility. A common change to organizations is changing this structure, by pivoting and organizing teams behind a common goal, a single product, or a group of features, for example.

Now you will need teams with different skill sets and responsibilities, teams most likely with developers and operators. It is important to realize that forcing such a change upon these people might not be the best way forward. Often, it works best to start with changing the culture, encouraging cooperation, and then this organizational change might come about in a natural way.

Finally, it is important to recognize one anti-pattern at this point. Some companies are trying to implement DevOps by hiring specialized DevOps engineers and positioning them between development and operations, interacting with both. While this, at first, might seem like a good idea, this goes against the DevOps values. If you do this, you are not breaking silos down, but you are adding a third one. You are not decreasing the number of hand-offs, you are most likely increasing them. Also, collaboration between developers and operations is often not enhanced by separating them using another organizational structure and you might not see any increase in value to your end users at all.

Now that you know what DevOps is and you have a clear understanding of how you can form a DevOps team, it is time to explore how to start achieving your goals.

Exploring DevOps practices and habits

Since you are not the first team going on this journey, you can learn from the experiences of those before you. One example is the Microsoft team that built Azure DevOps. Being in the rare position that they can use their own product for developing their product, they have learned a great deal about what makes DevOps successful. From this, they have identified seven key DevOps practices and seven DevOps habits that many successful DevOps teams share:

DevOps practices	DevOps habits
Configuration management	Team autonomy and enterprise alignment
Release management	Rigorous management of technical debt
Continuous integration	Focus on flow of customer value
Continuous deployment	Hypothesis-driven development
Infrastructure as Code	Evidence gathered in production
Test automation	Live-site culture
Application performance monitoring	Manage infrastructure as a flexible resource

Now it is important to realize that just copying the motions described will not guarantee success. Just as with Agile, you will have to spend time to really understand these practices and habits, where they come from, and what they contribute to a continuous flow of value to your end users.

The following sections explore all of these practices and habits in more detail. Keep these in the back of your mind while reading the rest of this book. While the rest of this book will mostly focus on **technical means** of **how** to do things, do not forget that these are only means. The real value comes from mindset and creating a culture that is focused on creating a continuous flow of value to your customers.

DevOps practices

This section discusses all seven DevOps practices in turn. As you will quickly see, they are highly related and it is quite hard to practice one without the other. For example, test automation is highly related to continuous integration and continuous deployment.

 In case you are planning to take the AZ-400 exam, mastering all of these practices and performing them using Azure DevOps will help you significantly.

Configuration management

Configuration management is about versioning the configuration of your application and the components it relies on, along with your application itself. Configuration is kept in source control and takes the form of, for example, JSON or YAML files that describe the desired configuration of your application. These files are the input for tools such as Ansible, Puppet, or PowerShell DSC that configure your environment and application. These tools are often invoked from a continuous deployment pipeline.

The desired state can also be reapplied at an interval, even if there are no changes made to the intended configuration. This way, it is ensured that the actual configuration stays correct and that manual changes are automatically revoked. We call this the *prevention of configuration drift*. Configuration drift occurs over time due to servers being added or removed over time, or manual, ad hoc interventions by administrators. Of course, this implies that intended updates to the configuration are done in source control and only applied using tools.

Configuration management or configuration as code is highly related to infrastructure as code. The two are often intertwined and on some platforms, the difference between the two might even feel artificial. Configuration as code will be discussed in detail in Chapter 6, *Infrastructure and Configuration as Code*.

Release management

Release management is about being in control of which version of your software is deployed to which environment. Versions are often created using continuous integration and delivery pipelines. These versions, along with all of the configuration needed, are then stored as immutable artifacts in a repository. From here on, release management tools are used to plan and control how these versions are deployed to one or more environments. Example controls are manual approvals and automated queries of open work and quality checks before allowing deployment to a new environment.

Release management is related to continuous deployment and focuses more on controlling the flow of versions through the continuous deployment pipeline. Chapter 6, *Infrastructure and Configuration as Code*, will cover configuration as code as part of release management.

Continuous integration

Continuous integration is a practice where every developer integrates their own work with that of the other developers in the team at least once a day and preferably more often. This means that every developer should push their work to the repository at least once a day and a continuous integration build verifies that their work compiles and that all unit tests run. It is important to understand that this verification should not run only on the code that the developer is working on in isolation. The real value comes when the work is also integrated with the work of others.

When integrating changes often and fast, problems with merging changes are less frequent and if they occur, are often less difficult to solve. In Chapter 2, *Everything Starts with Source Control*, you will learn more about how to set up your source control repositories to make this possible. In Chapter 3, *Moving to Continuous Integration*, you will learn about setting up a continuous integration build.

Continuous deployment

Continuous deployment is the practice of automatically deploying every new version of sufficient quality to production. When practicing continuous deployment, you have a fully automated pipeline that takes in every new version of your application (every commit), results in a new release, and starts deploying it to one or more environments. The first environment is often called test and the final environment will be production.

In this pipeline, there are multiple steps that verify the quality of the software, before letting it proceed to the next environment. If the quality is not sufficient, the release is aborted and will not propagate to the next environment. The premise behind this approach is that, in the pipeline, you try to prove that you cannot take the current version to the next environment. If you fail to prove so, you assume it is ready for further progression.

Only when a release has gone through all environments in the pipeline, it is deployed to production. Whenever a release cannot progress to the next environment, that release will be completely canceled. While you might be inclined to fix the reason for the failure and then restart deployment from the point where it failed, it is important not to do so. The changes you made at that point are after all not validated by all of the controls that the version has already passed through. The only way to validate the new version as a whole is by starting the pipeline from the start. You can see this clearly in the following diagram:

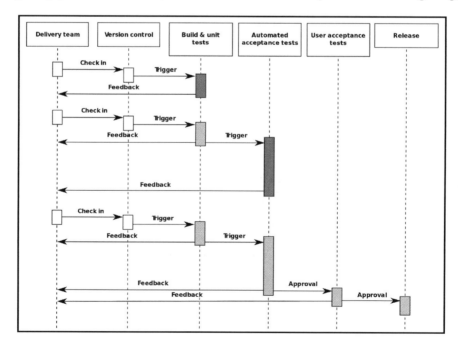

In Chapter 4, *Continuous Deployment*, you will learn about setting up continuous deployment using Azure DevOps Pipelines.

 The preceding diagram can be found at https://en.wikipedia.org/ wiki/Continuous_delivery#/media/File:Continuous_Delivery_ process_diagram.svg. The image is by Grégoire Détrez, original by Jez Humble, under CC BY-SA 4.0, at https://creativecommons.org/ licenses/by-sa/4.0/

Infrastructure as code

When writing an application, the binaries that you are building have to be running somewhere, on some application host. An example of such an application host can be a web server such as IIS or Apache. Next to an application host, we might need a database and some messaging solution. All of this together we call the infrastructure for our application. When practicing infrastructure as code, you are keeping a description of this infrastructure in your source code repository, alongside your application code.

When the time comes to release a new version of the application and you require one or more changes in the infrastructure, you are executing this description of your desired infrastructure using tools such as Chef, Puppet, PowerShell DSC, or Azure ARM templates. The execution of such a description is idempotent, which means that it can be executed more than once and the end result is the same. This is because your description of the infrastructure describes the *desired state* you want the infrastructure to be in and not a series of steps to be executed. Those steps to be executed, if there are any, are automatically determined by your tool of choice. Applying the desired state can also be done automatically in a continuous deployment pipeline and is often executed before updating the application code.

The big advantage of this is that you can now easily create a new environment, where the infrastructure is guaranteed to be the same as in your other environments. Also, the problem of configuration drift, where the infrastructure between your different environment slowly diverges, is no longer possible since every time, you apply the desired state again to every environment and they are forced.

Chapter 6, *Infrastructure and Configuration as Code*, of this book will discuss infrastructure as code in more detail.

Test automation

To continuously deliver value to your end users, you will have to release fast and often. This has implications for the way you test your application. You can no longer execute manual tests when you release your application every few minutes. This means that you have to automate as many of your tests as possible.

You will most likely want to create multiple test suites for your applications that you run at different stages of your delivery pipeline. Fast unit tests that run within a few minutes and that are executed whenever a new pull request is opened should give your team very quick feedback on the quality of their work and should catch most of the errors. Next, the team should run one or more slower test suites later in the pipeline to further increase your confidence in the quality of a version of your application.

All of this should limit the amount of manual testing to a bare minimum and allow you to automatically deploy new versions of your application with confidence.

Chapter 8, *Continuous Testing*, of this book will cover test automation in detail.

Application performance monitoring

This last practice is about learning all about how your application is doing in production. Gathering metrics such as response times and the number of requests will tell you about how the systems are performing. Capturing errors is also part of performance monitoring and allows you to start fixing problems without having to wait on your customers to contact you about them.

In addition to that, you can gather information on which parts of the application are more or less frequently used and whether new features are being picked up by users. Learning about usage patterns provides you with great insights into how customers really use your applications and common scenarios they are going through.

Chapter 9, *Security and Compliance*, and Chapter 10, *Application Monitoring*, will go into detail on learning about both your application and your users' behavior in production.

DevOps habits

The seven habits of successful DevOps teams are more concerned with culture and your attitude while developing and delivering software and less with technical means than DevOps practices are. Still, it is important to know and understand these habits since they will help to make DevOps adoption easier.

You will notice that developing these habits will reinforce the use of the practices enumerated previously and the tools you use to implement them. And of course, this holds the other way around as well.

Team autonomy and enterprise alignment

An important part of working Agile is creating teams that are largely self-directed and can make decisions without (too many) dependencies outside the team. Such a team will hence often include multiple roles, including a product owner that owns one or more features and is empowered to decide on the way forward with those.

However, this autonomy also comes with the responsibility to align the work of the team with the direction the whole product is taking. It is important to develop ways of aligning the work of tens or hundreds of teams with each other, in such a way that everyone can sail their own course, but the fleet as a whole stays together as well.

The best-case scenario is that teams take it upon themselves to align to the larger vision, instead of taking directions every now and then.

Rigorous management of technical debt

Another habit is that of rigorous management of technical debt. The term debt in itself suggests that there is a cost (interest) associated with the delay of addressing an issue. To keep moving at a constant pace and not slowly lose speed over time, it is crucial to keep the number of bugs or architectural issues to a minimum and only tolerate so much. Within some teams this is even formalized in agreements. For example, a team can agree that the number of unfixed bugs should never exceed the number of team members. This means, that if a team has four members and a ninth bug is reported that no new work will be undertaken until at least one bug should be fixed.

Focusing on flow of customer value

It is important to accept that users receive no value from code that has been written until they are actually using it. Focusing on the flow of value to a user means that code has to be written, tested, and delivered and should be running in production before you are done. Focusing on this habit can really drive cooperation between disciplines and teams.

Hypothesis-driven development

In many modern development methodologies, there is a product owner who is responsible for ordering all of the work in the backlog, based on the business value. This owner, as the expert, is responsible for maximizing the value delivered by the development team by ordering all items based on business value (divided by effort).

However, recent research has shown that, even though the product owner is an expert, they cannot correctly predict which features will bring the most value to users. Roughly one third of the work from a team actually adds value for users, and even worse while, another third actually decreases value. For this reason, you can switch your backlog from features or user stories to the hypothesis you want to prove or disprove. You create only a minimal implementation or even just a hint of a feature in the product and then measure whether it is picked up by users. Only when this happens do you expand the implementation of the feature.

Evidence gathered in production

Performance measurements should be taken in your production environment, not (just) in an artificial load test environment. There is nothing wrong with executing load tests before going to production if they deliver value to you. However, the real performance is done in the production environment. And it should be measured there and compared with previous measurements.

This holds also for usage statistics, patterns, and many, many other performance indicators. They can all be automatically gathered using production metrics.

Live-site culture

A live-site culture promotes the idea that anything that happens in the production environment takes precedence over anything else. Next, anything that threatens production, is about to go to production, or hinders going to production at any time gets priority. Only when these are all in order is the attention shifted to future work.

Also, a part of a live-site culture is ensuring that anything that disturbed the operation of the service is thoroughly analyzed—not to find out who to blame or fire but to find out how to prevent this from happening again. Prevention is preferably done by shifting left, for example, detecting an indicator of a repeat incident earlier in the pipeline.

Managing infrastructure as a flexible resource

Finally, a successful DevOps team treats its servers and infrastructure as cattle, not as pets. This means that infrastructure is spun up when needed and disregarded as soon as it is not needed anymore. The ability to do this is fueled by configuration and infrastructure as code. This might even go so far as creating a new production environment for every new deployment and just deleting the old production environment after switching all traffic from the old environment to the new one.

Besides keeping these DevOps practices and habits in mind, there are certain stages that you will go through while trying to move to a DevOps culture in your organization. The next section will take you through it.

Five stages of the DevOps evolution

When you are trying to move to a DevOps culture in your organization, this is going to take time. There are motions you have to go through while everyone in your organization embraces the changes they have to make to their individual way of working. Others that have gone before you have gone through the following five steps or stages that might help you. Knowing about them can help you to accelerate your own journey. These steps were first published in the *2018 State of DevOps Report* and are discussed in the following sections.

Normalizing the technology stack

A common first step on the road to a DevOps culture is the adoption of Agile. At a minimum, there are good tools for source control, and often a company standard and continuous integration and delivery are being rolled out. Teams are also working together to normalize the stack they develop software for. For example, one or two cloud vendors are chosen and other deployment platforms are phased out. The same goes for tools for other purposes—they are standardized where possible. Homebrewed solutions are replaced with industry standards.

Standardizing and reducing variability

In this stage, teams work on further reducing the variation between and within applications and the development and operations teams that work on them, working together on aligning operating systems, libraries, and tools. Also, in this stage, deployment processes are changed to reduce the amount of variation between them and configuration and infrastructure are often moved to source control.

Expanding DevOps practices

Remaining issues between development and operations are cleaned up, ensuring that outputs of the development team are precisely what the operations team expects. Also, collaboration starts to grow between the two and they are able to work together without external dependencies on creating and delivering changes.

Automating infrastructure delivery

In this stage, the infrastructure that is used by developers and operations becomes fully aligned. Everything is deployed from source control and the same scripts are being used by both teams.

Providing self-service capabilities

Before DevOps, virtual machines or hosting environments were often requested from operations, by developers manually or through ticketing systems. Provisioning was done manually by operators, which could take days or sometimes even weeks.

Self-service capabilities means that environments are no longer created manually, but through self-service API's that operations teams make available to developers.

This way, developers are fully able to create and destroy environments on their own. They can create and test changes on their own and send them off or schedule them for automated deployment.

Summary

In this chapter, you learned what DevOps is (and what it is not) and its relation to Agile. Moving to a DevOps culture helps you to break down conflicting targets for developers on one side and operators on the other side. This to empower them to work together on continuously delivering value to your end users, organizing their work in a single backlog and working off a single board, while respecting the differences in their ways of working. Organizing developers and operators in product-oriented teams is the next important step in creating like-minded, goal-oriented teams.

Moving to DevOps can bring many benefits and you now know how these can be measured to continuously keep improving. Next, you learned about the DevOps habits and practices that many successful DevOps team exhibit. Mastering these yourself and with your team will enable you to go through your own DevOps evaluation. All this is with the aim to continuously deliver value to your users.

The next chapter will discuss the topic of source control and how to organize your application sources to enable DevOps flows.

Questions

As we conclude, here is a list of questions for you to test your knowledge regarding this chapter's material. You will find the answers in the *Assessments* section of the Appendix:

1. True or false: Development and operations departments often have conflicting goals.
2. True or false: The seven DevOps practices discussed in this chapter are unrelated and one can be easily practiced without the other.
3. Which of the following is not a part of the five stages of DevOps evolution?
    1. Normalizing the technology stack
    2. Automating infrastructure delivery
    3. Standardizing and reducing variability
    4. Hiring a group of DevOps engineers to automate the delivery of applications
4. What is fastlaning?
5. Describe in your own words, in a few lines, what the essence of DevOps is.

Further reading

There are many other resources that you might find helpful to learn more about DevOps culture and the DevOps way of thinking. Some of them are as follows:

- *The Phoenix Project*, by Gene Kim, Kevin Behr, and George Spafford
- *Effective DevOps*, by Jennifer Davis and Katherine Daniels
- *Accelerate*, by Nicole Forsgren, Jez Humble and Gene Kim
- *Interview with Sam Guckenheimer*, available at `https://devops.com/11626/`
- *Microsoft Case Study on their DevOps Journey*, available at `http://stories.visualstudio.com/devops/`
- The *2018 State of DevOps Report*, available at `http://info.puppet.com/Eficode-Puppet-State-of-DevOps-Report.html`
- More information on assessing existing development processes can be found at `https://docs.microsoft.com/en-us/learn/modules/assess-your-development-process/index`
- More information about different Agile approaches and how to support them using Azure Boards can be found at `https://docs.microsoft.com/en-us/learn/modules/choose-an-agile-approach/index`

Everything Starts with Source Control

2

Source control is one of the most basic tools that is used in software development. Therefore, it is probably safe to assume that you have worked with source control before. For that reason, this chapter will contain only a brief introduction to source control and quickly move on to more advanced topics to help you to set up your source control to support DevOps practices.

Multiple DevOps practices rely on source control, hence, setting up your repositories to continuously deliver value to your users is a great way to get started and a prerequisite for many of the subjects in the following chapters.

The following topics will be covered in this chapter:

- The types of source control in Azure DevOps
- Source control systems
- Selecting a branching and merging strategy
- Securing source control using branch policies
- Other tools that are available for source control

Technical requirements

To practice the subjects covered in this chapter, you may need an Azure DevOps organization.

Types of source control in Azure DevOps

While there are many different source control systems in existence, they can be classified into two categories, centralized and decentralized source control, as follows:

- In a **centralized source control** system, only the server has the full history and the full set of branches that make up the repository.
- In **decentralized source control**, everyone working with the repository has a full copy of the repository, all of the branches, and its history.

Azure Repos, part of Azure DevOps services, offers both types of source control through TFVC and Git. The next two sections discuss both types of source control in more detail.

Centralized source control

In a centralized source control system, the server is the only location where the full repository, including all of the history, is stored. When you create a local version of the content, you only receive the latest version of the code. Receiving this latest version is called **checking out** the repository. In addition to this latest version, your own computer only has the changes you make locally.

Not checking out the full history obviously saves space on your local computer. However, disk space is hardly ever an issue nowadays. Yet the downside of this is that you need to be continuously connected to the server to perform operations such as viewing the history of a file, recent commits of others, or which line in a file was last changed by who.

An advantage of centralized source control systems is that that they often offer options for fine-grained control over who can access which branches, directories, and even files.

Decentralized source control

With a decentralized source control system, all files, history, and branches are also stored on a server. The difference with centralized source control comes when you **clone** the repository, to have a local copy on your own computer.

Since you have a full clone of the repository, you can now view the history of a file and other branches without connecting to the server again. This obviously lessens the load on the server and allows you to continue working even when disconnected, two advantages of decentralized source control.

The downside is that decentralized source control can be harder to learn than centralized source control. Overall, the learning curve of decentralized source control systems is steeper. Also, access control on the level of individual directories and files is often more limited.

No matter which type of source control you are using, you must put a branching and merging strategy in place to allow developers to work on different features in parallel, while always keeping your master branch in a shippable state.

Source control systems

There are many source control systems in use, but in this chapter, we will only be looking at the three currently most used. They are the following:

- **Team Foundation Version Control (TFVC)**
- Git
- Subversion

Within Azure DevOps, only TVFC and Git are available. Subversion is a centralized source control system that is created by the Apache Foundation. In the upcoming subsections, we'll take a look at TFVC and Git in more detail and learn how to migrate sources between them. Subversion is discussed at the end of this chapter in the *Other tools for source control* section.

Team Foundation Version Control

Team Foundation Version Control (**TFVC**) is a centralized source control system that was introduced by Microsoft in 2013, as part of **Team Foundation Server** (**TFS**), the product that has evolved to become Azure DevOps. TFVC is still supported in Azure DevOps but is not recommended for new projects. If you are not working with TFVC yet, there is no value in learning it. Now, TFVC is not recommended for new projects and Microsoft will most likely not release new features for it, but it isn't necessary to move away from it without other drivers.

In Azure DevOps, there is a maximum of one TFVC repository per team project.

Git

Next to TFVC, Azure DevOps also supports hosting Git repositories. Git is a form of decentralized source control that is rapidly gaining ground. Git is not specific to Azure DevOps but is a general protocol that is used by many platforms that provide source control hosting as a service. Well-known examples next to Azure DevOps are GitHub and GitLab.

To work with a Git repository, you must first clone it:

1. Open Command Prompt and navigate to the directory where you want to store the repository.
2. Execute the following command and replace the example URL with the URL to your Git repository. The example URL shows how the location of a Git repository in Azure DevOps is built up:

```
git clone
https://{organization}@dev.azure.com/{organization}/{teamProjec
t}/_git/{repository}
```

Now, you can start working on the changes you want to make. In this example, a new file, `NewFile.txt`, was added.

3. Next, this file must be staged for commit. Staging files is done to differentiate between files you want to commit and changes you want to keep for your own:

```
git add NewFile.txt
```

4. After staging all of the changes you want to group into a single commit, creating the actual `commit` is done by calling the commit command and specifying a description of the changes:

```
git commit -m "Added a new file that contains an important
text"
```

5. Finally, you can push your changes back to the central repository, the remote, by executing the following command:

```
git push
```

To make more changes, you can stage and commit changes as often as required. You can push the commits one at a time, but you can also push multiple commits at once.

You can also work with Git through the Visual Studio or VS Code interfaces. Here, you execute precisely the same steps, but instead, you can use a visual interface.

Large File Storage

Git is designed and optimized for working with plain text files and tracking changes from version to version. However, you might want to store other things than just text files into source control. Examples are images or binary files that should be included with your application at runtime. While these are valid use cases, out of the box they do not work very well with Git. To fix this, **Large File Storage (LFS)** was introduced.

Git LFS allows you to store, instead of the binary files themselves, a small text file that acts as a pointer to that file. Such a file contains a hash of the file so that the client can download the file when cloning or fetching changes and update the file when you update the binary file.

To work with Git LFS, you must install the LFS client next to the Git client. This is a separate client that every user of the repository must download. Without this client, other users will only see the pointer files instead of the actual binary files. After installing the client, you must prepare the repository for the use of LFS. The following example commands enable the use of LFS for MP4 files:

```
git lfs install
git lfs track "*.mp4"
git add .gitattributes
```

From here onward, you can work with MP4 files just as any file and behind the scenes, they will be stored separate from your text file changes.

Migrating between control systems

One of the steps on the DevOps journey is the consolidation of tools. This means that, at some point, you might be asked to migrate sources from one source control system to another. This means that companies might decide to move all of their sources from GitLab or Subversion to Azure Git Repos. There are multiple options available to you to do migrations like these.

The most likely event is that you will receive requests to move sources to one or more Azure Git repositories. Possible sources are other Git repositories, TFVC, or Subversion. There are tools and approaches available to do such a migration while retaining the change history of the original repository.

If there is no procedure available or you must import sources from another system, you can also fall back on creating a new empty repository and initialize that with an existing code base. The disadvantage of this is that all history will be a lost this way.

Migrating existing Git repositories

When it comes to migrating sources, moving to another location for hosting Git repositories is straightforward, compared to other migrations. Let's learn how to do this:

1. First, clone the existing repository to your local computer. Please note the dot at the end—this will place the repository in your current directory:

```
git clone
https://{organization}@dev.azure.com/{organization}/{teamProjec
t}/_git/{repository} .
```

2. Add another remote that refers to the new, empty repository that you want to move the sources to:

```
git remote add migrationTarget
https://{organization}@dev.azure.com/{organization}/{teamProjec
t}/_git/{newRepository}
```

3. Finally, you push the changes to this new repository. You must do this separately for every branch you want to move next to the master:

```
git push migrationTarget master
```

Meanwhile, other developers might have continued working with the existing repository.

4. To include those in the new repository as well, you must fetch them to your local computer from the original repository and then push them to the new repository. Again, repeat this for every branch:

```
git fetch origin master
git push migrationTarget master
```

5. Repeat these last two commands until there are no developers working on the source repository anymore.
6. After a successful migration, it is often best to remove the old repository. This prevents anyone from continuing to work there by accident.

The preceding steps will work for any Git-to-Git migration.

Now, if you specifically want to migrate to an Azure Git Repo, you can also use the import functionality that is included with Azure DevOps. To do this, follow these steps:

1. Navigate to Git **Repos** and optionally create a new Git repository first.
2. Choose to **Import** an existing repository.

3. Provide the requested information.
4. Click on **Import** to start importing the repository.

The following screenshot illustrates these steps:

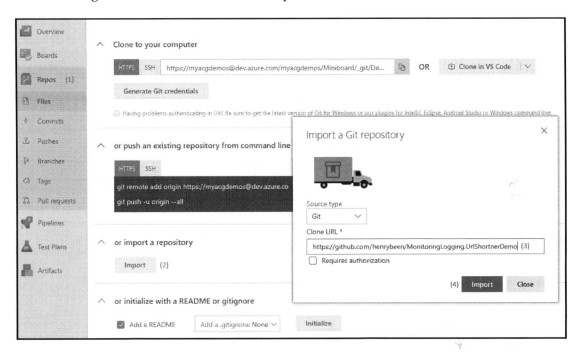

The disadvantage of this approach is that you cannot keep pushing changes from the source repository to the new repository. This means that all other developers on your team must make sure that they move their changes over on their own or do not have any pending work while you migrate the repository.

Migrating from TFVC to an Azure Git repository

For migrating from TFVC to a Git repository, you can use the same *import repository* as for moving from any Git repository to an Azure Repo. This wizard can take the history for up to 180 days when doing the import. If this is not enough and you are required to move more than 180 days' worth of history to the new repository, there are other approaches you can use but they are more involved. Links to more elaborate advice is included at the end of this chapter.

Migrating from Subversion to an Azure Git repository

A final type of request that you might receive is that of migrating from a Subversion repository to a Git repository. For this, there is no out-of-the-box solution from Microsoft available. However, Atlassian has created a tool that can be used to migrate a Subversion repository to a local Git repository while maintaining the change history.

After running this tool, the only thing left to do is to add a remote to a new empty, hosted repository and push all of the branches. These are the same as the steps for migrating from Git to Git, starting at the step that adds a new remote.

Migrating without retaining history

If you are asked to do a migration without retaining history, you can just create a new, empty repository out of sources on your local computer and push existing changes there using the following commands.

Execute the following from the directory that contains the files that should go into the master branch:

```
git init
git add
git commit -m "Initial import of existing sources"
git remote add
https://{organization}@dev.azure.com/{organization}/{teamProject}/_git/{rep
ository}
git push
```

These commands initialize a new repository, create a first commit out of all of the files already in the directory, add a reference to the target server location, and push the newly created repository there.

If you want to retain multiple branches, you must repeat the following steps for every other branch:

1. First, go to the right directory for that branch:

   ```
   Git checkout {branchName}
   ```

2. Now, copy the files that need to go into this branch into your working directory. Then, continue with the following commands:

   ```
   git add .
   git commit
   git push
   ```

This completes the migration and the latest version of the sources you had on your local computer are now available in Git. Other members of your team can now clone the repository and work with it. Next, we'll go on to learn about branching and merging.

Selecting a branching and merging strategy

Source control allows you to keep a history of all of the changes you have made to your files but also allows working separately from your team members for a while if you so desire. We call this **branching**. When you are branching in source control, you fork the line of changes currently registered. We call such a fork a **branch**. A branch allows you to temporarily isolate some work from the rest. If you at any point want to integrate the changes from a branch with the changes on the other fork, you can **merge** these changes back. Branches are often used for working on not yet complete features, proofs of concept, or hotfixes. Using branches allows you to later decide which changes to include in the next version and which not to.

Branching strategies

There are many, many branching strategies available, but the three most used nowadays are the following:

- GitHub flow
- GitFlow
- Release Flow

The following subsections will discuss these in greater detail.

 As an alternative to branching, trunk-based development is becoming more popular nowadays. To know more about this, visit `https://paulhammant.com/2013/04/05/what-is-trunk-based-development/`.

GitHub flow

GitHub flow is a simple, yet often sufficient, branching strategy. In GitHub flow, there is one **master** branch that should always be in a deployable state. No unfinished changes are allowed to go onto the master.

If you want to start work on a new feature or bugfix, you create a new topic branch of the master where you commit your work. Only when you are completely done with that work do you merge this branch back to the master. An example commit flow might look like this:

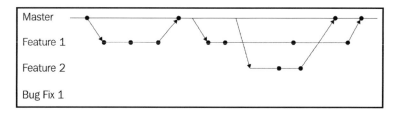

As this is the branching scheme with the least branches involved, this is probably a good strategy to start with.

GitFlow

GitFlow is another well-known elaborate branching scheme that can deal with almost any situation that might arise when working with software. GitFlow describes creating a branch, **Develop**, of the master whenever you start work on a new version. **Develop** is the integration branch where you combine new features and do integration testing. It should only contain work that you believe is ready to be released.

From **Develop**, you create one or more feature branches where you start working on new features. Only when a feature is done do you merge that branch back to the **Develop** branch.

When you want to release a new version of your application, you create a release branch of the **Develop** branch. On the code on this branch, you perform final testing and perform one or more bugfixes if needed. When you are satisfied with the quality of the code, you merge this branch to the master and tag the version. You also merge these bugfixes back to **Develop**, so they will also be incorporated in new developments. This flow is visible in the following diagram:

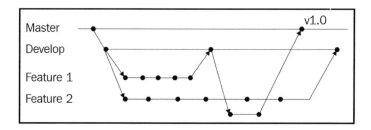

If there is ever a critical bug that you need to ship as fast as possible or you want to do a hotfix, for this is also possible. In that case, you create a new branch of the master, where you fix the bug. After testing, you merge this branch to both master and developer—just as you would with a release branch.

Release Flow

Release Flow is the branching system that is used by the Azure DevOps team to develop Azure DevOps. It is also based on working with short-lived topic branches that are made from and merged to a master branch.

The difference is that it is not the code that is on the master branch that is being deployed to production. Instead, whenever a new version of the product needs to be released, a new branch is created of **master** with the name **release-{version}**. The code from this branch is then deployed to production. Once a new release branch is deployed, the previous one can be disregarded. This results in the following flow:

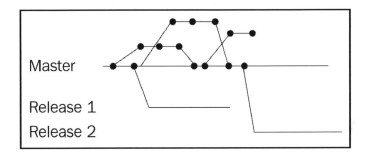

The advantage of this model is that it allows for taking a snapshot of the current state of the master branch and taking that to production. If there is ever a bug in production that needs to be fixed ahead of a new complete release then the correct commits can be merged from the master branch to the current release branch.

Trunk-based development

In many companies, branching and merging are done to retain flexibility when releasing a new version and being able to pick changes for that version only at the last moment. This flexibility comes at the cost of having to merge or integrate your changes at some point. This cost is not only the time it takes but also the risks that a merge operation introduces. Merging the changes from two different branches that contain perfectly working software might still produce non-working code.

For this reason, you might consider switching to **trunk-based development**. In trunk-based development, you are no longer using branching for picking changes that go into a version. Instead, every developer on the team continuously works from the same branch (often the master) and only creates a short-lived branch for preparing one single change, which is then merged into the master branch.

When you adopt this, you will need another way to determine which changes will and won't yet be available to your users when releasing a new version of your software. You can do this by using **branching by abstraction**.

Branching by abstraction

When branching by abstraction, you are not keeping two versions of your code side by side using branches, but you keep them side by side in your code base. For example, when you want to change the implementation of a class called `FoodClassifier`, which implements the `IFoodClassifier` interface, you go through the following steps:

1. You refactor the name of the `FoodClassifier` class to `FoodClassifierToBeRemoved`.
2. You create a copy of the complete `FoodClassifierToBeRemoved` class.
3. You name this copy back to `FoodClassifier`.

At this point, your changes should look like this:

```
public class FoodClassifier : IFoodClassifier
{
 public FoodClassification Classify(Food food)
 {
 // Unchanged classification algorithm
 }
}
public class FoodClassifierToBeRemoved : IFoodClassifer
{
 public FoodClassification Classify(Food food)
 {
 // Unchanged classification algorithm
 }
}
```

Please note that at runtime, your application will behave just as it did before. You have just added a new, yet unused, class with a change in behavior. It is safe to commit these changes and even ship the new binaries to a user. Now you can start changing the implementation of the new `FoodClassifier` class, test it, and establish trust in its implementation. Meanwhile, you can keep committing and pushing your changes, even to customers. Switching to the new implementation can be done using your dependency injection configuration, a Boolean flag, or environment variables. Just choose what makes sense in your scenario.

Only when you are fully satisfied that the new implementation is working, you remove the `FoodClassifierToBeRemoved` class and update any references back to `FoodClassifier`.

We will expand on branching by abstraction in `Chapter 4`, *Continuous Deployment*, when discussing feature toggles. While being a recommended way forward to further accelerate your delivery, branching by abstraction is a double-edged sword. If you do not have a process to keep the number of side-by-side implementations under control and clean them up after switching implementations, the quality of your code base might decline.

Merging strategies

Depending on the source control system you are working with, there might be multiple ways you can merge your changes from one branch to another.

TFVC

When you are working with TFVC, you prepare a merge locally by choosing both a source and target branch and then picking the list of changes you want to merge. TFVC will then execute the merge and show you the changes that are the consequence of this merge as local changes. You can go over these changes, correct or change them, and must resolve any conflicts. After this, you commit the changes just as you would any regular change.

Git

A merge using Git can be performed by switching to the target branch and then *merging* all of the changes from the source branch. If there are conflicting changes between the branches, you must resolve those just as you would when fetching new changes from the server. After merging the changes from the source branch and resolving any changes, you can commit the changes. This will result in a merge commit, which you push to the remote just as any change.

This can be done using the visual interface of Visual Studio or VS Code, but also using the following sequence of commands:

```
git checkout targetBranch
git merge sourceBranch
```

If there are any conflicts, you have to resolve these at this point. Otherwise, you cannot continue:

```
git commit -m "Merged changes from sourceBranch"
git push
```

As you will read in the *Securing repositories* section, it is possible to protect some branches by disallowing merging this way. Especially when it comes to changes to master, you might want to use another mechanism for merging changes, namely, pull requests. Using a pull request, you open a request for someone else to pull changes from your branch to the target branch. This way, another team member can first review your changes and only merge them when they meet all agreed standards. Others can comment on your changes or request updates before they perform the merge. This is the most common way of enforcing the four-eyes principle for source code when working with Git. The four-eyes principle says that every change or action should be viewed by at least two people.

Now, when you are approving a pull request, there are different strategies you can use for generating the merge commit. The most commonly used are a merge commit, squash commit, or a rebase.

Merge commit

A regular **merge commit** is a type of commit that maintains visibility of all previous commits. It has a reference to two parents, showing both origins of the change, namely the source and target branch. This is the same type of merge as you can perform manually using a Git merge. The advantage of this type of commit is that it clearly shows where the new state of the target branch comes from.

Squash commit

When performing a so-called **squash commit**, you are combining all of the individual commits from the source branch in one, new commit. This is useful when all of the commits on the source branch relate to one feature and you want to keep a clear, concise change history on the target branch. Especially when there are commits with bugfixes or clean-up operations on the source branch, this approach makes sense. The disadvantage is that you might lose the rationale for some incremental changes that were made on the source branch.

Rebase

Rebasing a branch means that all of the commits for which your branch is ahead of the master branch are put aside for a bit. Meanwhile, all of the commits for which the master branch is ahead of your local branch are now merged to your local branch. Finally, all of your own commits that were set aside are now reapplied. The following diagram shows a branch before and after a rebase commit:

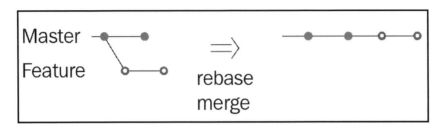

After rebasing the source branch, it is now merged into master. The advantage of this kind of merge is that you retain all individual changes in one single commit history.

Managing repositories

When working in Azure Repos, every team project can have a maximum of one TFVC repository. However, when working with Git, you can have multiple repositories in the same team project. A discussion that is gaining more attention lately is that of having a single repository for all applications or a repository per application. Other topics that are important when managing repositories are creating and removing repositories, securing them, and setting policies on them.

Monorepo or multi-repo

You are using a **monolithic repository (monorepo)** when you are storing all of the code of all of your projects and applications in one single source control repository. Opposed to this, you might be using multiple repositories where every application, library, or project is stored in its own repository. Both approaches have their own pros and cons and both approaches are used by companies from small to large.

Possible advantages of a monorepo can include the following:

- Easier reuse of existing code: If all of the code is in a single repository, it is accessible by and visible to everyone. This means that the chances of reuse are increased.
- Having all applications in one repository also means that any change affecting more than one application can be made in a single commit, in a single repository. A typical example is an API change.
- With all of the code being accessible to and maintained by everyone, there is less chance that a developer or team claims a specific repository as its own. This encourages learning from each other.

Possible advantages of multiple repositories include the following:

- A monorepo can become very, very large, even up to the point that developers checkout or clone only part of the monorepo. This effectively defeats most of the advantages of a monorepo.
- Having one repository with all of the code encourages tight coupling between components or applications. If you have multiple repositories, you could update an API and release it under a new version and upgrade clients one by one. In a monorepo, you might be tempted to upgrade the API and change all of the consumers in one commit, with all of the risks attached.

Which approach works best for you is influenced not only by the advantages and disadvantages discussed but also by the background and makeup of your team and organization. If you have a single team doing all the development for internal applications, a monorepo might make more sense. If you have multiple teams working on different applications for different clients, multiple repositories make more sense.

Creating and removing repositories

In Azure DevOps, you can have multiple Git repositories per team project. Try doing the following:

1. First, visit the **Manage repositories** interface. The following screenshot shows how to access this interface:

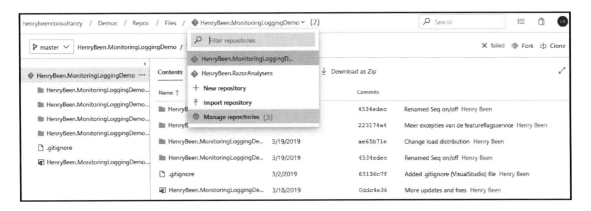

2. After opening this interface, a new interface (as shown in the following screenshot) opens up. Here, you can add new repositories by clicking on the **Add...** button with a plus sign (marked with a **1** in the following screenshot) and filling out a repository name.

3. Repositories can also be removed, by clicking on their name and then D**elete** (marked with a **2**):

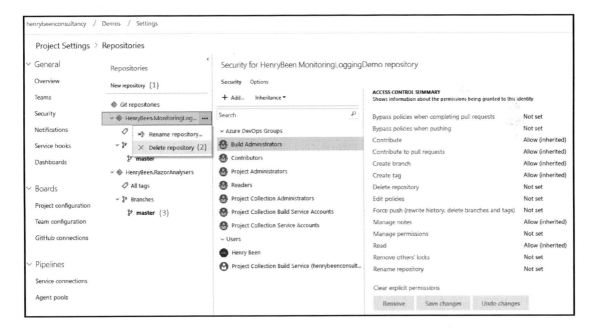

Removing repositories is not something that is often done. It might make more sense to make a no-longer-used repository read-only or remove all authorizations on it.

Now, let's learn how to secure the repositories that we create.

Securing repositories

While the security options with distributed source control are often not as broad as with centralized source control, Azure Repos offers some means to set authorizations on a repository or a server-side branch. In the last image of the previous section, you can also see how you can select a group or user in the middle column and then update the authorizations on the repository. By default, all authorizations are inherited from project defaults.

 It is recommended to only change authorizations a little as possible and if you do, it is often best to work via groups and allow authorizations.

You can also change the authorizations for a specific branch by opening the repositories branches in the drop-down menu on the left and clicking on the branch you want to override the authorizations for. In the preceding screenshot, this is marked with a **3**.

Branch policies

Finally, it is possible to enforce one or more policies on pull requests to a specific branch. The interface for branch policies is shown in the following screenshot and can be accessed by choosing the **Branch policies** option while managing the authorizations on a repository branch:

henrybeenconsultancy / Demos / Settings

Project Settings > Policies

∨ General

Overview

Teams

Security

Notifications

Service hooks

Dashboards

∨ Boards

Project configuration

Team configuration

GitHub connections

∨ Pipelines

Service connections

Agent pools

Retention and parallel jobs

Release retention

∨ Repos

Repositories

Policies

∨ Test

Retention

Policies for: Demos > HenryBeen.RazorAnalysers > master

🖫 Save changes   ⟲ Discard changes

Protect this branch
- Setting a Required policy will enforce the use of pull requests when updating the branch
- Setting a Required policy will prevent branch deletion
- Manage permissions for this branch on the Security page

☐ **Require a minimum number of reviewers**
Require approval from a specified number of reviewers on pull requests.

☐ **Check for linked work items**
Encourage traceability by checking for linked work items on pull requests.

☐ **Check for comment resolution**
Check to see that all comments have been resolved on pull requests.

☐ **Limit merge types**
Control branch history by limiting the available types of merge when pull requests are completed.

Build validation
Validate code by pre-merging and building pull request changes

＋ Add build policy

Require approval from additional services
Require other services to post successful status to complete pull requests. Learn more

＋ Add status policy

Automatically include code reviewers
Include specific users or groups in the code review based on which files changed.

＋ Add automatic reviewers

The first four checkboxes are related to default policies that can be enabled (or not) on your preference. By default, they are all disabled.

Build validation can be used to disallow the merge of any pull request if one or more of the select builds have not completed successfully. How to set up such a build is something you will learn in the next chapter.

Next to builds, you can also call external services to inspect the pull request and to allow or disallow it. An often used integration here is with a code quality tool. You might also call your own APIs here, to enforce team agreements on things such as pull request titles, relation to work items, or more complex constraints.

Finally, you can enforce that a specific user or group has to be included in the review of a pull request. This might be needed to enforce a specific level of quality, but it can also be a limiting factor on your development speed and hence flow.

Other tools for source control

Next to the source control systems available in Azure Repos, there are also some other well-known systems that you should know about:

- GitHub
- GitLab
- Subversion

We'll go over each of these in the upcoming subsections.

GitHub

GitHub is a hosted source control provider that delivers hosted Git repositories. GitHub allows anyone to create as many publicly visible repositories as they want. Only, when you create private repositories that require three or more contributors, you must switch to a paid subscription.

This model that allows unlimited, free usage of the platform if developing in public has made GitHub, by far, the largest host of open source software in the world.

GitHub was acquired by Microsoft in 2018 and since then, Microsoft and GitHub have worked together to create a great integration experience between GitHub repositories and Azure DevOps, specifically with Azure Boards and Azure Pipelines. In addition to this, Microsoft has stated that GitHub and Azure Repos will continue to exist next to each other and that there are currently no plans to terminate one of the products in favor of the other.

There is also an on-premises offering by GitHub called GitHub Enterprise.

GitLab

GitLab is another platform that delivers hosted Git repositories. Just like Azure DevOps, source control hosting is one of the services it provides.

Subversion

An older source control system is Subversion. Subversion was developed and first used in 2004 and is maintained by the Apache Software Foundation. Subversion is a centralized source control system that supports all the features that you would expect of such a system.

There are many false arguments as to where Subversion would be inferior to Git, however, most of them are not true for more recent versions of Subversion. The reality is that Subversion is a widely used type of source control system that performs well, especially for very large repositories or repositories that have very specific authorization needs.

While Azure DevOps cannot host Subversion repositories, it can connect to, and work with, sources that are stored in Subversion.

Summary

In this chapter, you have learned about source control. We saw that there are two types of source control: centralized and decentralized, both supported by Azure DevOps. TFVC is no longer recommended for new projects. You should use Git whenever starting a new project.

When using Git, you can have more than one repository in your team project. Per repository, you can assign policies to lock down specific branches and enforce the four-eyes principle. You have also learned about access control and how to provide users access to one or more repositories. Finally, you have learned about alternative tools and how to migrate sources from one tool to the other.

You can use what you have learned to make decisions on which type of source control system to use in your products. You can now professionally organize the repository or repositories you work in. You are now able to work with different branching strategies and use policies for enforcing security or quality requirements.

The next chapter will take what you have learned about source control and use that to set up continuous integration.

Questions

As we conclude, here is a list of questions for you to test your knowledge regarding this chapter's material. You will find the answers in the *Assessments* section of the Appendix:

1. What are the differences between centralized and decentralized source control and which work best in what situation?
2. True or false: Git is an example of decentralized source control.
3. Which of the following is not a common branching strategy?
    1. Release Flow
    2. Rebasing
    3. GitFlow
    4. GitHub flow

3. Many companies want a code review to be performed before code is merged into the master branch. What construct is used to do so when working with Git and how can this be enforced in Azure DevOps?
4. Which of the following are not valid merge strategies?
    1. Rebasing
    2. Trunk-based development
    3. Merge commit
    4. Squash commit

Further reading

- More information about working with Git can be found at `https://docs.microsoft.com/en-us/learn/paths/intro-to-vc-git/`.
- The original Microsoft advice on TFVC versus Git can be found at `https://docs.microsoft.com/en-us/azure/devops/repos/tfvc/comparison-git-tfvc?view=azure-devopsviewFallbackFrom=vsts`.
- More information about Git LFS can be found at `https://docs.microsoft.com/en-us/azure/devops/repos/git/manage-large-files?view=azure-devops`.
- Instructions for downloading Git LFS can be found at `https://git-lfs.github.com/`.
- More information about migrating to Git can be found at `https://docs.microsoft.com/en-us/azure/devops/repos/git/import-from-TFVC?view=azure-devops`.

- An Atlassian tool for converting an SVN repository to a local Git repository can be found at `https://www.atlassian.com/git/tutorials/migrating-convert`.
- More information about GitFlow can be found at `https://datasift.github.io/gitflow/IntroducingGitFlow.html`.
- More information about GitHub flow can be found at `https://guides.github.com/introduction/flow/`.
- Release Flow is described in more detail at `https://docs.microsoft.com/en-us/azure/devops/learn/devops-at-microsoft/release-flow`.
- Trunk-based development is discussed at `https://trunkbaseddevelopment.com/`.
- More information about GitLab can be found at `https://about.gitlab.com/`.
- More information about Subversion can be found at `https://subversion.apache.org/docs/`.

3
Moving to Continuous Integration

After setting up source control for your organization and deciding on a branching and merging strategy that supports parallel work, you are ready to move on to continuous integration. Continuous integration is a method where every developer takes their work and integrates it with the work of others, and then verifies the quality of the combined work. The value of this is an increase in quality early on in the pipeline. This reduces the risk of error later on when merging code changes and reduces the number of bugs that are found in production, thereby reducing costs and protecting your reputation.

Continuous integration is only possible when you have the proper setup with the necessary tools. In this chapter, you will learn how to use Azure DevOps pipelines to set up continuous integration.

The following topics will be covered in this chapter:

- Introducing continuous integration
- Creating a build definition
- Running a build
- Working with YAML pipelines
- Agents and agent queues
- Other tools

Technical requirements

To go through the recipes that are covered in this chapter, you will need an Azure DevOps organization.

Introducing continuous integration

Continuous integration is a methodology where you integrate your own changes with those of all of the other developers in your project and test whether the combined code still works as expected. This way, you create a fast loop that provides you with feedback on your work.

When working with extensive branching strategies for isolating code changes, it is not uncommon for one or more developers to work for days, weeks, or even months on an isolated branch. While this is great for making sure that their changes do not disrupt others, it is also a great way to make sure that there won't be merge issues later. If you have ever had to merge weeks or months of work back into a master branch, you will know how much work is involved and how often this results in bugs or other issues.

To prevent this, developers should make it a habit to integrate their changes with those of all the other developers at least once a day. Here, integrating means at least merging, compiling, and running unit tests. This way, there is a constant stream of feedback on the quality of the developer's changes and since this feedback is combined, it is a great way to prevent merge issues later.

Continuous integration also enables you to embed other concerns in your pipeline to automatically preserve the quality of your code. Testing and security scanning are two prime examples of this. These topics are discussed in later chapters, but a good continuous integration pipeline is the basis for these practices.

In the rest of this chapter, you will learn about the technical means to set up continuous integration using Azure Pipelines. But first, let's look at a common misconception and the four pillars of continuous integration.

 While an automated continuous integration build is an important ingredient for performing continuous integration, continuous integration entails more than just having a build pipeline. The important thing to remember is that continuous integration is a process where every developer integrates their work with that of their colleagues at least daily. Then, the integrated sources are compiled and tested. The value comes from compiling and testing the integrated work, not the isolated work.

The four pillars of continuous integration

There are four pillars that underpin the successful adoption of continuous integration:

- **A version control system**: Used for storing all of the changes made to a system since its inception. Version control systems were discussed in the previous chapter.
- **A package management system**: Used to store the binary packages that you use in your own application and the packages that you create. This will be discussed in detail in `Chapter 5`, *Dependency Management*.
- **A continuous integration system**: A system that can pull the changes of all developers together—several times a day—and create one integrated source version. This can be done using Azure DevOps pipelines.
- **An automated build process**: Used to compile and test the combined sources. We will look at how to implement this process using Azure DevOps Pipelines.

Continuous integration and automated builds can be set up in Azure DevOps. The next section explains how to set both up in Azure DevOps.

Creating a build definition in Azure DevOps

The main way to perform continuous integration is by using a continuous integration build. In Azure DevOps, builds can be configured as part of the Azure Pipelines offering. There are currently two approaches available for creating a build definition:

- Via the visual designer (also called **classic builds and releases**)
- Through **Yet Another Markup Language** (**YAML**) files (also called **YAML pipelines** or **multistage pipelines**)

The rest of this section focuses on the visual designer. The following section, *YAML build definitions*, will go into more detail about YAML pipelines. Both approaches support roughly the same capabilities, although there are some differences. Some features that are available in classic builds and releases are not (yet) available in YAML build definitions. Also, some new features are only provided to YAML pipelines.

If you have no experience with pipelines, the classic editor is a good way to get familiar with the workings of continuous integration/continuous development pipelines before moving on to YAML pipelines. Almost all of the concepts in classic builds translate to YAML builds as well.

In the following sections, we will start by building a classic build pipeline.

Connecting to source control

To get started with a build definition, follow these simple steps:

1. Open the **Pipelines** menu.
2. From this menu, click on **Builds**. Here, you will be presented with a button to create a new build. After clicking on this button, a new view for creating a build will open, as in the following screenshot:

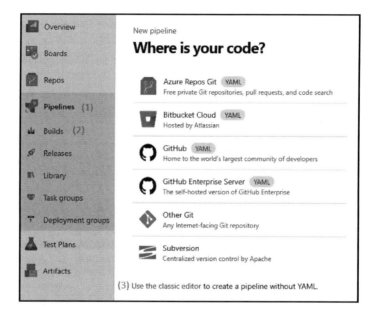

3. You will then be guided to the new YAML experience, but you can still opt to go back by choosing the classic editor.

After choosing the classic editor, you can configure how to connect to the source control. The classical editor is the editor that is visible in all of the screenshots in the following sections.

Many source control systems are supported. If you are working with a hosted Git repository, pick your specific product, if available, and only choose **Other Git** if your product is not available; currently, **GitHub**, **GitHub Enterprise Server**, and **BitBucket Cloud** are supported. The reason for this is that continuous integration using **Other Git** works by using a polling model, where all the specific products use their known integration webhooks. The following example works with a Git repository that is in the same Azure DevOps instance.

When you select the **Pipeline** header, you can set the name of the build definition and select an agent pool that the phases will run on by default. Agents take care of the actual execution of your tasks and will be looked at in more detail in the *Agents and agent queues* section of this chapter.

Below the **Pipeline** header, you can see the chronological layout of your build definition. First up is downloading sources. Here, you can once again choose to connect to a source control system. You can also specify more advanced settings that relate to the way sources are fetched, such as whether to clean the build directory first, select a branch, or add tags.

Configuring a job

Below the source's node, you can add one or more jobs that will perform the bulk of the work that you want to perform. Jobs can be added using the ellipsis on the pipeline header. There are two types of jobs available:

- **Agentless jobs**: Agentless jobs can be used to run tasks that need an agent.
- **Agent jobs**: Agent jobs are used to run tasks that require an agent to run on, which is the case for the bulk of the tasks.

Some examples of agentless tasks are as follows:

- Waiting for manual approval before continuing
- Inserting a delay before proceeding
- Calling a REST API
- Calling an Azure function

The main benefit of an agentless job is that it does not keep an agent occupied while running. This frees the agent up to do other work, meaning that you need fewer agents, which can save costs. Also, the number of agents that you can use concurrently is governed by the number of parallel pipelines that you have bought in Azure DevOps. Limiting the number of agent jobs will save money here as well.

Let's go over the process of configuring a job:

1. Select any job. You will see the view shown in the following screenshot. In this view, you can change the name of the job and, for agent jobs, override the agent pool to execute this job on:

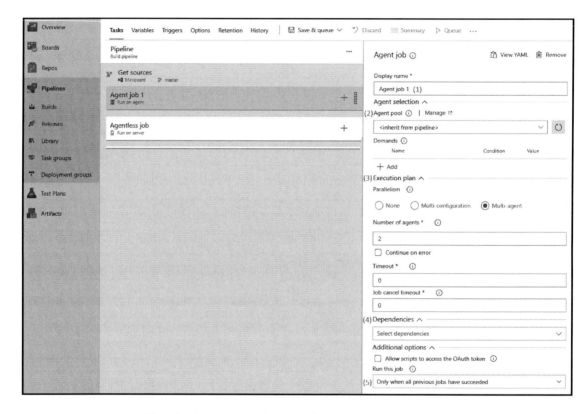

2. Next, specify which agent pool to use for running the job. Here, it also specifies the demands that you have of the agent that will execute this job. Demands will be discussed in the *Agents and agent queues* section of this chapter.

3. As part of the execution plan for an agent, you can specify **Parallelism** and choose one of three options:

   - **None**: This will just execute all the tasks you add to the agent job one after another on the same agent.
   - **Multi-configuration**: Here, you can specify a series of variables that determine the number of variations of the build to run. This is useful if you want to create, for example, x86 and x64 builds from the same code.
   - **Multi-agent**: Here, you can specify the number of agents that will run the same tasks in parallel.

4. Next, you can specify one or more dependencies. These are the other jobs that need to be completed before the selected job runs.

5. Also, for any job, you can specify how to cope with errors in previous jobs by telling it to continue or stop.

As an alternative to steps 3 and 4, you can also specify a custom expression to specify whether a job should run. This expression should evaluate to a Boolean and support rudimentary operations, such as `or()`, `and()`, or `eq()`. The following is an example condition:

```
and(succeeded(), ne(variables['Build.SourceBranch'], 'refs/heads/master'))
```

This condition specifies that the job will only run when all previous jobs have succeeded and the build is not started from the master branch. A link to a detailed description of the conditions syntax is included at the end of this chapter.

Agentless jobs have fewer options available than agent jobs. For example, it is not possible to execute the same build for multiple variable values in parallel.

Adding tasks to your job

After adding one or more jobs, you can add tasks to a job. Tasks define the actual work that is to be done during the execution of your build. The following screenshot shows you how to add a task and then configure it:

1. Click on the plus sign next to the job you want to add tasks to:

2. You will then be presented with a task picker, where you can find any task that matches your search input and add one or more tasks by clicking the **Add** button. A new screen will then open, where you can configure the individual task. The options provided here differ for each task.
3. There can be multiple versions of a task and you can switch between the major versions of the task. This means that the maintainer can push non-breaking updates and you will receive them automatically. Major or breaking updates can be pushed with a new major version number and you can upgrade them at your own discretion.

It is possible to add as many tasks as needed to a pipeline job.

Publishing build artifacts

An important part of a build definition is its outcomes. Builds are often used to produce one or more artifacts that are later used for the deployment of an application. Examples of artifacts can be executables or installer files. These files need to be made available for use after the pipeline has completed.

The **Publish Build Artifacts** task that is shown in the preceding screenshot is a task that is specifically designed to do this. It allows you to select a file or directory and publish it under an **artifact name**. The result of this is that the file(s) in the selected path is retained with every execution of the pipeline for manual download or use in a release definition later. Release definitions are discussed in the next chapter, Chapter 4, *Continuous Deployment*.

Next, we'll learn how to integrate our pipeline with other tools and configure our service connection.

Calling other tools

When building pipelines, we will often need to integrate them with other tools. For source control systems, this is part of the flow when creating a pipeline and you are limited to the built-in options. For tasks, you can create references to any tool or location you want using service connections. An example of a task that uses a service connection to an Azure app service is shown in the following screenshot.

A service connection is a pointer to a third-party system, with a name and series of properties that differ for each type of service connection. Often, you will need to put in a URL to locate the other service and a mechanism for authentication. The following steps will help you configure your service connection:

1. After defining one or more service connections, you can select the one to use from a drop-down menu:

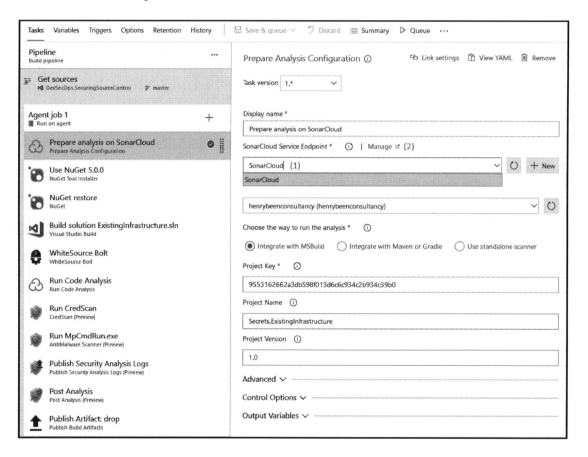

2. Service connections are managed in a central location as project settings. You can access them by going to the management view directly from the task you are currently configuring, as shown in the preceding screenshot. You can also do this by navigating to **Project Settings** and then to **Service connections**, as in the following screenshot (see label **1**):

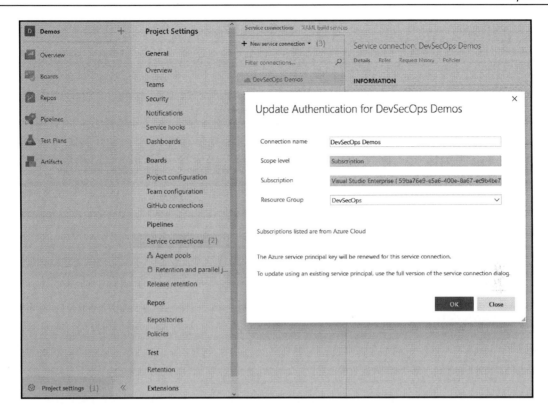

3. In this view, you can then either add a new service connection or update an existing service connection (see label **2** in the preceding screenshot).

By default, service connections are scoped to the project level, meaning they are not available for everyone in the Azure DevOps organization. To encourage the reuse of service connections, Azure has made it possible to share them between projects since mid-2019.

Task Marketplace

A set of frequently used tasks is built into Azure Pipelines; however, there are even more available using the Visual Studio marketplace for Azure DevOps. If you are an administrator, you can find and install extensions that add tasks here. If you are a regular user, you can find tasks here as well; however, you cannot install them, only request them. Your Azure DevOps administrator will then be notified and can install the extension on your behalf if they approve.

Of course, you can write and distribute extensions with tasks of your own as well.

Creating variables and variable groups

When you are configuring your build, there might be values that you need to use more than once. It is often wise to extract these values into variables, rather than just repeating those values throughout your tasks.

Variables can be used to note down values that you do not want to have stored in source control. Values such as passwords and license keys can be safely stored as non-retrievable values when locked down using the lock symbol (see label **1** in the following screenshot). After saving the build definition, these values are encrypted and can only be used by the build that they belong to. You will no longer be able to retrieve these values and they will be automatically scrubbed from logs and other output.

To learn how to work with variables in Azure Pipelines, go through the following steps:

1. In Azure Pipelines, you can add variables to your build definition by going to the **Variables | Pipeline variables** tab (see label **3** in the following screenshot). Here, you can enter them as name value, as can be seen in the following screenshot:

2. Once defined, you can use the variables in the configuration of all tasks in all jobs of the same build. For this, you can use the following notation:

```
$(variableName)
```

3. Finally, you can mark variables as **Settable at queue time** (see label **2** in the preceding screenshot), which means that their value can be changed whenever someone queues a new build. An example of a variable for which this is used is the `system.debug` built-in variable. When this variable is set to `true`, there is a verbose debug logging included in the build.

Next to your own variables, system variables are also defined. These are variables that contain information about the build that is currently running, including version numbers, agent names, build definition details, the source version, and so on. A link to the full list of system-defined variables is included at the end of this chapter.

Variable groups

As well as creating the variables that go with a specific build, you can create variable groups. These variable groups can, in turn, be linked to one or more builds. This is an effective way of sharing variables between builds; some examples of these might be the name of your company, trademark texts, product names, and so on. Let's see how we can work with variable groups:

1. Access variable groups through the menu by clicking on **Library** in the **Pipelines** menu (see label **1** in the following screenshot). This displays a list of the existing variable groups that you can edit and you can add a new group here as well, as in the following screenshot:

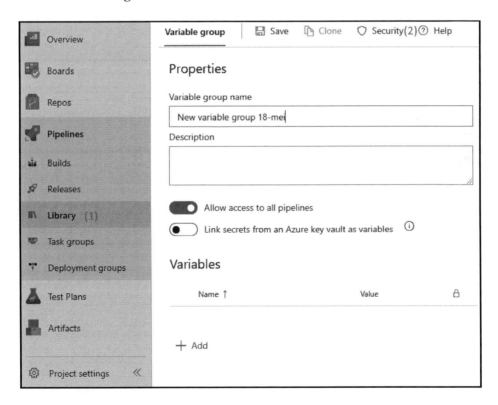

2. Here, you can work with variables in the same way that you would with the variables that come with a build. The only differences are highlighted in the following list:

- You cannot mark variables in a group as settable at queue time.
- You can allow or deny the use of this group in all pipelines. If you deny their use in all pipelines, then only you can use the variable group. You can authorize other users or groups through the **Security** option (labeled with a **2** in the preceding screenshot).
- You can reference an Azure key vault for which this variable group will act as a placeholder. After logging into Azure, you can select a key vault and select which values that are stored in the key vault you want to be accessible through the variable group.

Azure Key Vault is an Azure offering that can be used for the secure storage of secrets. Secrets in a key vault are automatically versioned, so older values are not overwritten but replaced by a newer version. In addition to this, you can specify segregated access policies that specify, per user, whether they can read, write, update, or delete values. All these actions are audited in a key vault, so you can also find who has made which change. If you are linking Azure DevOps to a key vault, then a new service principal will be created in your active directory that has access to that key vault. Now, whenever Azure DevOps needs a variable from the variable group, the actual values will be pulled from the key vault.

Variable groups can be linked to the variables of a build under the **Variable groups** tab (refer to the screenshot in the previous section).

As well as working with variable groups, you can also work with files in the library. You can upload files that are not accessible by other users but that can be used within a build. This is useful for files with private keys, license keys, and other secrets.

Just as you can with variable groups, you can specify whether each secure file can be used by any build or authorize specific users only.

Triggering the build

The next tab in a build definition governs what should start or trigger the build. To implement continuous integration, go through the following steps:

1. Click on the **Triggers** tab and select the first header on the left:

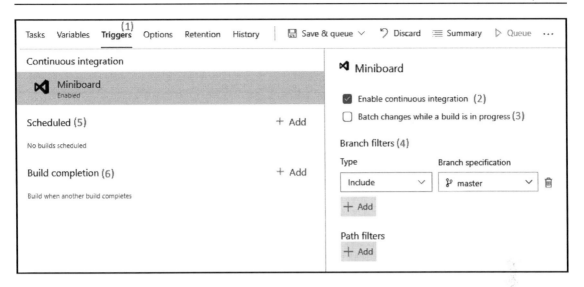

2. Check the **Enable continuous integration** box. This means that Azure DevOps will listen for changes in your repository and will queue a new build as soon as a new chance is available.

3. Next, you can choose whether you want to build every incoming change individually or batch multiple changes when more than one new change comes in while building a change. It is recommended that you build every single change separately if this is feasible.

4. Along with the continuous integration trigger, specify one or more branch and path filters. Here, you can specify which branches and files to queue a new build for. You can specify either inclusions or exclusions, depending on your needs. A common example is to limit your build to the master branch. If you have folders named `doc` and `src` in your repository and all your sources are in the latter folder, then it might make sense to limit the trigger to this path.

5. As well as choosing to have a continuous integration trigger, you can also opt to execute a build on a recurring schedule where you select one or more weekdays and a time.

6. You can also schedule a build to run whenever another build completes. This is called **chaining** builds.

Next, let's learn how to change the configurations of our build definition.

Build options

You can change the advanced configuration options for your build definition. These options include a description, the format of the build number, and the automated creation of work items on failures and times. To set this up, go through the following steps:

1. Click on the **Options** tab. You should arrive at the following screen:

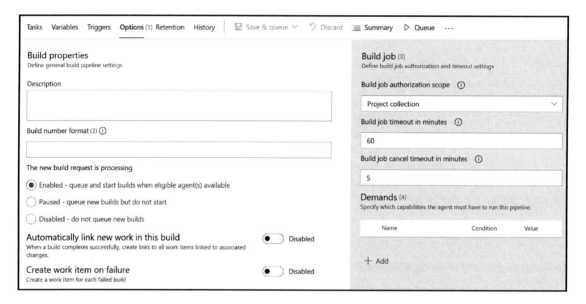

2. Now, create your build number format. If this field is left empty, then the build number for your application will be set to an ever-increasing number that will increase by 1 with every build. This number is unique within a team project and counts over all the build definitions. You can also specify a format of your own using the variables available to you. A common approach is to specify a major and minor version number manually and then add an increasing number using a variable. The following example specifies a version of 4.1.xx, where the last part is replaced by a two-digit increasing number:

```
4.1($Rev:.rr)
```

3. On the right, there are advanced (but rarely used) options for specifying the authorization scope for the **Build job** time-outs for each job in the build definition.

4. It is also possible to specify the agent demands that every agent, for every job in the build definition, should fulfill. Again, we will look further at demands in the *Agents and agent queues* section of this chapter.

Other options on the left enable you to suspend the pipeline temporarily.

Build history

The final tab, called **History**, shows you a list of every change that has been made to the build definition. Build definitions are stored in JSON format and you can pull up side-by-side comparisons for every change. The comment that you put in when saving a build is also stored here and can be used to provide the rationale for a change.

Since builds are an important means of preserving quality, it is important to keep track of who has changed them to ensure that automated quality metrics are not removed.

With this, you are now ready to run your first build. You can directly run it using the **Save & Queue** button that is visible in most of the screenshots in this section. The *Running a build* section of this chapter will teach you how to work with the results that you obtain.

Task groups

When working in a team or organization that has more than one pipeline, it often doesn't take long before multiple pipelines that take the same shape emerge. For example, in some companies, all pipelines contain tasks for security scanning, running tests, and calculating the test coverage.

Instead of repeating these tasks everywhere, they can be extracted from an existing pipeline into a task group. Task groups, in turn, can be used within multiple pipelines as if they are tasks themselves. Doing this reduces the effort needed to create a new pipeline or update all the pipelines with a new requirement. Doing this also ensures that all the pipelines using the task group have the same task configuration.

To create a new task group, open any existing build definition and go through the following steps:

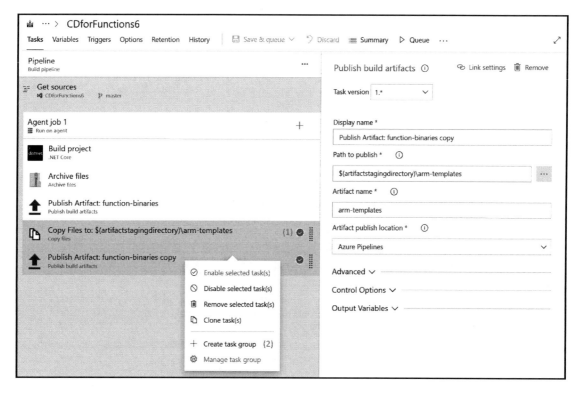

1. Select one or more tasks by clicking on them while holding down *Ctrl*, or by using the selectors that appear when hovering the mouse over a task.
2. Right-click on the selection and select **Create task group**.
3. In the popup that now appears (not shown in the screenshot), choose a name, description, and category for the task group. If any of the selected tasks have a variable value specified, you can now provide a default value and description for these parameters. These parameters will be available within the task group and need to be configured when the task group is used.
4. After clicking **Create** (not shown in the screenshot), the existing build definition is updated by removing the selected tasks and replacing them with the new task group.

Adding an already existing task group to a build or release definition is done in precisely the same way as adding regular tasks. Task groups show up in the same list of tasks to choose from.

A list of all the existing task groups can be found by navigating to the **Pipelines** menu and then **Task groups**. To edit an existing task group, select it in the list that is shown, and select the **Edit** option. Editing task groups works in precisely the same way as editing a build definition.

This section was all about creating a build definition and describing how an application should be built. The next section is about executing the build.

Running a build

In this section, you will learn how to work with the build results and use them to report and generate builds. You will also learn how to run a build with every pull request and report the quality of the changes back to that pull request to assist the reviewer.

Viewing the build results

While a build is running, an agent will perform all the configured steps one by one. Azure Pipelines will capture detailed information and logs from all these steps. As you can see in the following screenshot, a build will display a list of all the steps it has executed on the left. Clicking on any of these steps will open a detailed view that displays the logs per step:

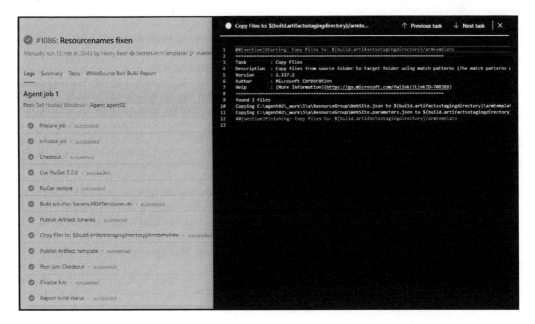

Whenever there are warnings or errors during the build, they show up in orange or red, respectively.

Building a pull request

After setting up your build definition and running your first builds, you might also see the first failures coming in—for example, when someone accidentally commits and pushes changes that do not compile or contain unit tests that do not run successfully. You can prevent this by having a build definition run automatically whenever a pull request comes in. To configure this, go through the following steps:

1. Click on **Policies** under **Project Settings**. The following screen will open. Click on **Add build policy**:

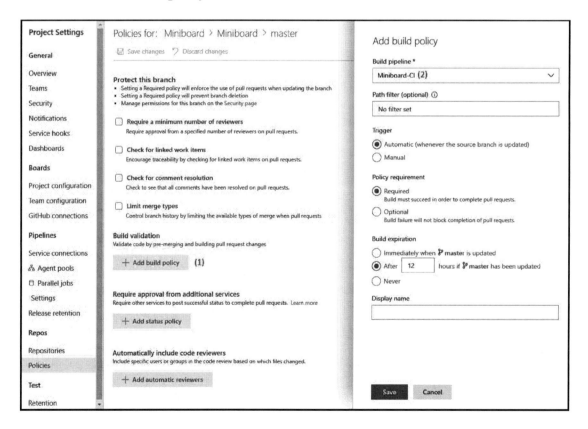

2. Select a build definition that you want to use to validate the pull request.
3. Next, there will be three more things that you can configure:
    - **Trigger**: When the build definition should start, either automatically or manually. Of course, the real value comes from running a verification build automatically.
    - **Policy requirement**: This determines whether a pull request can be completed if the build fails. In other words, this determines whether you can ignore a failing build. It is recommended that you avoid setting this to **Optional**, if possible.
    - **Build expiration**: This determines how long a positive build result is valid for. The default value is 12 hours, but you should consider changing this to **Immediately when master is updated**. The advantage of this is that you cannot merge changes without first running the build against a combination of the current state of the branch that you will merge to and the proposed changes.

You can add more than one build policy. If you have a lot of things that you can automatically validate and want to keep automated validation times to a minimum, then this is a good approach.

Accessing build artifacts

As well as compiling, testing, and validating your source code, builds can also be used to generate what are called artifacts. Artifacts are the outputs from a build and can be anything that you want to save and publish from a build, such as test results and application packages.

An application package is intended to be an immutable build of a version of your application. This package can later be picked up in a release and deployed to one or more environments:

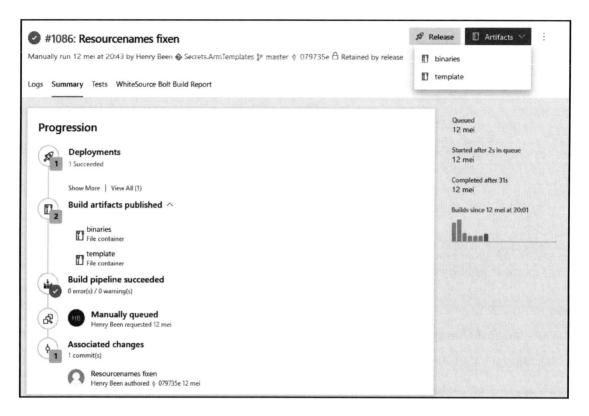

In the preceding screenshot, you can see, as part of the summary of an executed build, that there were two artifacts published. Artifacts can be accessed from either the **Artifacts** drop-down menu at the top-right corner of the screen or from the **Summary** tab. You can download and explore artifacts from this page and, in the next chapter, you will see how to work with them to set up continuous delivery.

Great! With this, you have learned how to create a definition using the visual designer. But wait—as we mentioned earlier, there is another way of doing this, which is by using YAML files. Let's see how this works in the next section.

Working with YAML pipelines

You have seen how to create a build definition using the visual designer. A new, alternative approach, which has been available since early 2019, is the use of YAML pipelines. When working with YAML pipelines, you specify your complete build definition in a YAML file and store it in source control, often next to the source code that the build is for.

While both pipeline systems coexist, using YAML pipelines is now the preferred approach for defining pipelines. This means that it is very likely that new features will only surface in YAML pipelines.

The reason for using build definitions as code

When you first start working with YAML build definitions, you might find that the learning curve is steeper than it is when working with the visual designer. This might raise the question as to why you would use YAML-defined builds. There are two main advantages that YAML build definitions have over visually designed definitions.

When you are writing your definition in YAML, it can be hosted in source control next to your code. The consequence of this is that all the policies that you have in place for changing source control now automatically apply to your build definition. This means that any change must go through a pull request, be reviewed by a peer, and can be built and verified ahead of time. Enforcing the **four-eyes principle** on your build definition, as well as your code, increases the stability of your build process. Of course, it also benefits security and compliance, topics that will be discussed in later chapters.

As well as this increase in security, having the build definition in source control also means that it is available in every branch. This means that it can be changed in every branch to build that specific branch before merging it to the master branch. When working with a visually designed build definition, this single definition is responsible for building not only your master branch but also all the branches that you want to merge through a pull request.

This means that you must do one of the following:

- Update the build definition for the change that you will merge. However, this will terminate building of the current state of the master branch.
- Merge the change, which will also result in a broken build since the build definition has not yet been updated.

Either option has the risk of allowing faulty changes to flow through the target branch, defeating the purpose of a continuous integration build. With a build definition per branch, we eradicate this problem.

While having build definitions in source control is beneficial, this is also available in classic builds. Every change is recorded and you can see who has changed what and when, along with an optional explanation from the author of the change.

Writing a basic YAML pipeline

To get started with YAML builds, there are two things you need to do:

1. First, you need to write your YAML file.
2. Then, you need to create a build definition out of it.

So, let's get started.

Writing the YAML file

The following code sample contains an example YAML definition for building a .NET Core application and running unit tests. Save a file with any name, for example, `pipeline.yaml`, in any Git repository in Azure DevOps. Then, it can be used to create a pipeline out of it later on:

```yaml
trigger:
- master

pool:
  name: Azure Pipelines
  vmImage: windows-2019

steps:
- task: DotNetCoreCLI@2
  displayName: 'dotnet build'
  inputs:
    projects: '**/*.csproj'
- task: DotNetCoreCLI@2
  displayName: 'dotnet test'
  inputs:
    command: test
    projects: '**/*.csproj'
```

This example YAML defines a basic pipeline. Every pipeline needs to be triggered in some way. Just as with classic builds, this can be done by connecting the pipeline to a change in a source code repository. The default repository for this is the repository that also contains the YAML definition. The `trigger` keyword is used to specify a push to which branches should trigger the pipeline. A good starting point is the `master` branch. As the `trigger` keyword accepts a list, multiple branches can be specified and wildcards can be used.

A trigger is not mandatory as a pipeline can also be started manually.

There are also alternative options to using the `trigger` keyword, such as to include or exclude one or more branches, tags, or paths in the repository. These options are described in detail at `https://docs.microsoft.com/en-us/azure/devops/pipelines/yaml-schema#triggers`.

As well as a trigger, every pipeline contains one or more tasks, just as in classic build definitions. All these tasks need to execute on an agent pool—again, just as in classic build definitions. The `pool` keyword is used to specify a set of key/value pairs that determine which pool the tasks will run on by specifying the name of the pool. When working with the default agents that Microsoft provides, the default name of `Azure Pipelines` can be used. When using this specific pool, a VM image has to be specified. This determines which operating system and what software is available on the agent that will execute the task.

An up-to-date list of all the VM images that are available can be found at `https://docs.microsoft.com/en-us/azure/devops/pipelines/agents/hosted#use-a-microsoft-hosted-agent`.

Finally, the definition contains a list of the steps that make up the pipeline itself. These steps correspond one-to-one with the tasks that you could drag into a classic build pipeline. A task is added by specifying the name and version—separated by the @ sign—of the task that you want to run. Next, you can optionally specify a display name for the task. This display name will later be visible in the views that show the results of an executed pipeline. Finally, specify one or more inputs for the task. These inputs relate to the task-specific configuration that you have already seen for the visual designer.

Creating a YAML pipeline

After saving your YAML file in a repository, you can create a build definition from it. When creating a new build definition (see the *Creating a build definition* section of this chapter), you should go through the following steps:

1. Choose the **Azure Repos Git YAML** option when the wizard starts.
2. From here, go through the wizard to select and review the YAML you want to build, as in the following screenshot:

3. In the first step, you locate the repository that contains the YAML file that you want to use as your pipeline.
4. Next, you configure the pipeline by choosing an example YAML file to start from or by referring to an already existing file.
5. Finally, you can review the YAML file that you have selected and start a build from it.

Your pipeline is saved automatically. Once the pipeline is saved, it can be started and you can interact with it in the same way as you would with classic build pipelines.

Multi-job pipelines

The pipeline you saw in the previous section does not specify any jobs, as you may recall from the section on classic builds. Instead, it contains a list of tasks under the `steps` keyword. This means that it implicitly contains only a single job. With YAML pipelines, it is also possible to create a definition that contains more than one job. To do this, the following structure can be used:

```
trigger:
- master

pool:
  name: Azure Pipelines
  vmImage: windows-2019

jobs:
- job: job1
  displayName: A pretty name for job1
  steps:
  - task: DotNetCoreCLI@2
    ...
- job: job2
  displayName: My second job
  pool:
    name: Azure Pipelines
    vmImage: ubuntu-18.04
  ...
```

Instead of adding the `steps` keyword directly to the pipeline, first, a list of jobs is created. Within that list, one or more `job` keywords are added, followed by the name for that job. Next to this technical name, a display name (`displayName`) can be specified for each job.

As the second job in this example shows, it is also possible to specify which agent pool to use per job. When no pool is specified for a job, the default pool specified at the top of the file is used.

 The jobs that are discussed in this section are called agent jobs. Besides agent jobs, there are also server jobs, container jobs, and deployment jobs available. More information about these types of jobs can be found at https://docs.microsoft.com/en-us/azure/devops/pipelines/process/phases#types-of-jobs.

By default, all the jobs in a pipeline run in parallel, but there are control options available to change this.

Control options

To control the order of jobs, the `dependsOn` keyword can be used on the definition of a job. This signals that the job can only be started after one or more jobs are completed. Besides this, the `condition` keyword can be used to specify a condition that a job should run under. These two keywords can be combined to realize more complex scenarios, such as the one shown here:

```
jobs:
- job: compile
  steps:
  ...
- job: test
  dependsOn: compile
  steps:
  ...
- job: build_schema
  dependsOn: compile
  steps:
  ..
- job: report
  dependsOn:
  - test
  - build_schema
  condition: or(succeeded('test'), succeeded('build_schema'))
  steps:
  ..
```

This pipeline will start by running the job named `compile`. Once this job completes, the next two jobs, `test` and `build_schema`, will run in parallel as they both depend on the `compile` task. After both of these tasks complete, the report task runs as it declares a dependency on both the `test` and `build_schema` jobs. Before this job actually starts, the condition is evaluated to determine whether the job should actually run or be skipped. Conditions can be built using a syntax that is similar to many programming languages. It checks the successful completion of a job using the `succeeded()` and `failed()` functions. There is also support for Boolean operators such as `or()`, `and()`, and `ne()`.

You can combine the `dependsOn` and `condition` keywords in any way you see fit. The only requirement is that there should be at least one job that does not depend on any other job.

Variables

Just like classic build pipelines, YAML pipelines support the use of variables. Variables can be defined at every level of a YAML pipeline (except for within a task) using the following syntax:

```
variables:
  name: value
  anotherName: otherValue
```

Variables can later be retrieved using the syntax that you already know from classic build pipelines—`$(name)` and `$(anotherName)`.

It is also possible to reference existing variable groups from within a YAML pipeline. This is done by using the `group` keyword, instead of specifying the name of a variable. To also retrieve all the variables from a variable group called `myVariableGroup`, you would extend the preceding YAML, as follows:

```
variables:
  name: value
  anotherName: otherValue
  group: myVariableGroup
```

Variables can be set at every level in a YAML pipeline, but only variables set at the root level can be overridden when queuing a new execution manually.

Pipeline artifacts

Just like classic builds, YAML pipelines can be used to build and publish artifacts. As the task used to do this is a task like any other, it can be added directly to the list of steps in a job.

However, with the introduction of YAML pipelines, a new type of artifact has become available—the so-called pipeline artifact. This comes with the benefit of improving the speed at which large artifacts can be uploaded and downloaded. When working with classic releases, pipeline artifacts are not automatically downloaded, whereas build artifacts are.

To publish a pipeline artifact, the following YAML can be used in the `steps` keyword of a job:

```
steps:
- publish: folder/to/publish
  artifact: artifactName
```

Pipeline artifacts are mainly intended to be downloaded in multi-stage YAML pipelines, which are also covered in the next chapter.

Tips for writing YAML pipelines

Writing YAML pipelines from scratch can be complicated when you are just getting started. There are two tools available that can help you.

First, there is the option to export YAML from the visual designer. For every task, there is a link with the **View YAML** title. This opens a small pop-up box that shows you the YAML corresponding to the task and configuration that you currently have open. The same can be done for jobs and, under specific conditions, for complete build definitions.

The other tool available for writing YAML is the built-in YAML editor:

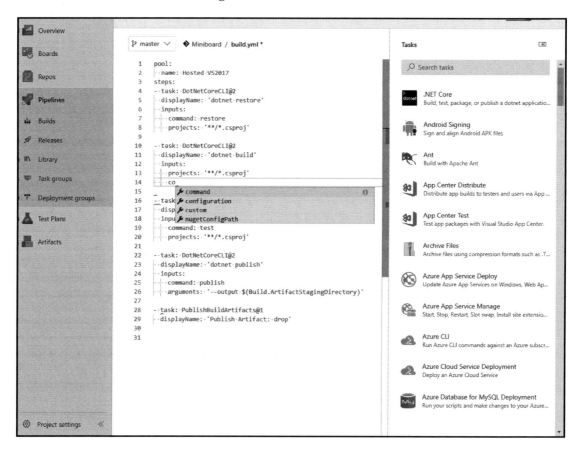

Whenever you open a YAML build definition, there are two tools available to help you. First, there is autocompletion for every location in your YAML file. This shows you the options available at that point in the file. As well as this, there are snippets available in the task picker on the right. When selecting any of the tasks on the right, you configure them visually and then click the **Add** button to add the generated YAML to your definition.

These two tools aim to bring the ease of the visual designer to the YAML build experience as well, combining the best of both worlds.

Agents and agent queues

The build definitions that you have created so far can contain agent jobs, which in turn contain tasks. These tasks are not executed within your Azure DevOps organization directly, but are executed by agents that run on VMs or in containers. In turn, agents are grouped in agent pools. There are two types of agent pools that you can work with:

- Built-in agent pools
- Self-hosted agent pools

Let's go through them one by one.

Built-in agent pools

Built-in agent pools are managed by Microsoft and are made available to you as part of the product. There are different agent pools available, depending on your needs. Pools run different versions of Windows and Visual Studio, and there are also pools available that run Linux (Ubuntu) and macOS.

The disadvantage of these managed pools is that you cannot install extra software on the machines or containers that host the agents if you need to. This means that in these cases, you have to create your own private agent pools.

Creating a private agent pool

Private pools are defined in your Azure DevOps organization and are provisioned from there to one or more of your team projects. However, you can also create your private pools at the team project level, in case they are created and provisioned in one go. To do so, go to **Project Settings** | **Agent pools.** You should see the following **Add agent pool** option:

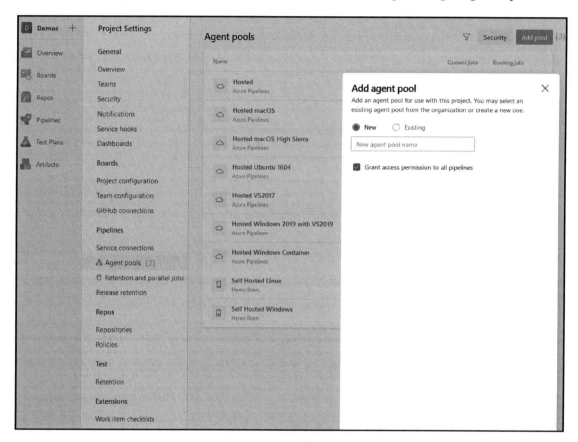

After giving the pool a name and determining whether you want to automatically provide access to all pipelines, you can save the pool. After creating the pool, you can add or remove agents.

Adding and removing agents

Adding an agent is done in two steps:

1. Download and extract the agent runtime. You can find the agent runtime by going to the section with the overview of the agent pools and opening the details of any private agent pool. After the details of the pool are opened, click on **New agent** in the top-right corner:

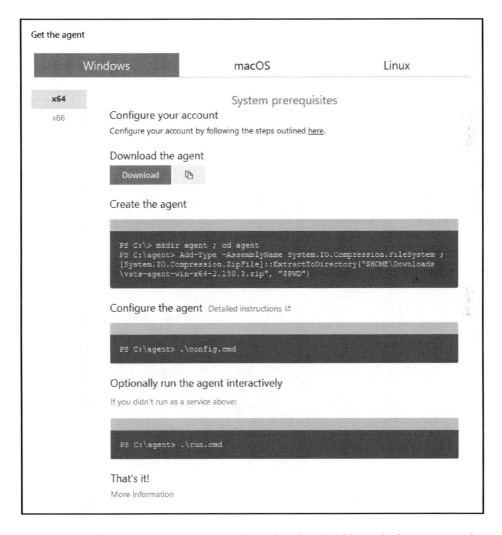

2. In the dialog that opens, you can download a ZIP file with the agent and instructions for extracting and installing the agent.

During the configuration phase, you will be prompted to authenticate with your Azure DevOps organization and to provide the name of the agent pool you want to install the agent in. While there are x86 and x64 agents available, it is recommended that you work with the x64 agent unless you have a specific reason not to.

To remove agents from the pool, you can use one of two methods:

- You can return to the PowerShell command line, just as you did for the installation, and use the following command:

  `.\remove.cmd`

- As an alternative, you can also remove agents from the agent pool overview using the **Agents** tab. Go to **Project Settings** | **Agent pools** (see label **1** in the following screenshot) | **Agents** (see label **2** in the following screenshot) and then select the options button (see label **3** in the following screenshot) on the agent you want to remove. Then, click **Delete** (see label **4** in the following screenshot):

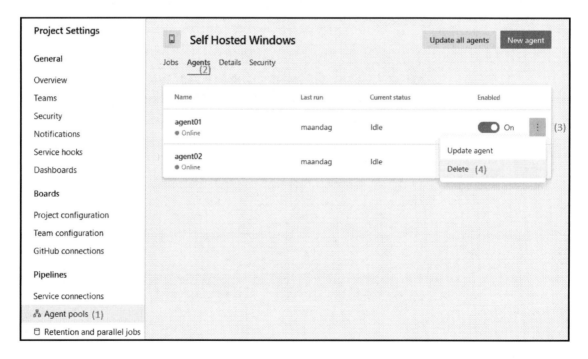

In the preceding screenshot, you can see the steps to remove an agent using the interface. Be aware that this does not clean up the binaries and any files on the host machine; however, if a machine that is hosting an agent breaks down or a VM is removed, then this is the only way to remove the agent.

Agent selection

Whenever a build job starts running, an agent is selected from the pool that will perform the tasks that you have defined in the pipeline. The selection of an agent is done in two steps:

1. Only agents that are part of the selected pool are eligible for running the tasks. This means that when working with private agent pools, it is wise to have multiple agents in a pool. If you then take one agent offline for maintenance, the agent jobs that rely on the agent pool can continue running.
2. Before an agent job can run, the demands from each job and the tasks it contains are gathered. As you learned in the *Variable groups* section, an agent job can specify the demands it has of the agent that it uses. The same goes for tasks—they can also specify demands. To run a job, only agents that meet all of these demands are used. Demands and capabilities are key–value pairs, where the value is an integer. An example capability is `msbuild=15.0` and the corresponding demand is `msbuild>15.0`.

When there is no eligible agent for a build definition, the build eventually fails after a timeout.

Finding agent capabilities

To find the capabilities that are available on the individual agents, go through the following steps:

1. Navigate to **Organization Settings** | **Agent pools**:

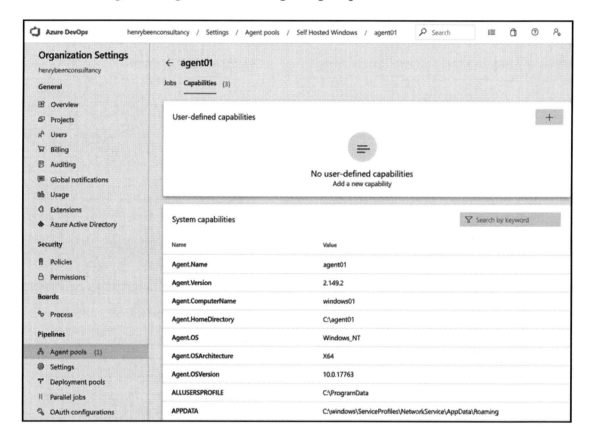

2. Navigate to the correct agent pool (either hosted or private) and then **Agents**, and then open the agent details (not shown in the preceding screenshot).
3. Open the **Capabilities** tab.

Here, you can specify one or more custom capabilities for the agent using the top block, called **User-defined capabilities**. For self-hosted (private) agents, all the capabilities that were discovered on the machine when you installed the agent are also shown.

Azure DevOps is not the only tool available for running continuous integration builds. The next section will take you through a couple of other tools.

Other tools

There are many tools available besides Azure DevOps. Two other well-known tools are GitLab CI and Jenkins. Some very basic knowledge of these tools will help you to understand how to integrate with them if that is ever necessary. Also, a limited understanding of other tools will help you to more quickly understand the concepts and generalize your knowledge of how to work with these other tools.

To highlight how these tools work with the same concepts, both examples in this section are equivalent to the Azure DevOps YAML pipeline in the *Writing a YAML build definition* section.

GitLab CI

GitLab offers build pipelines using the GitLab CI capabilities. GitLab CI is configured by putting a file with the `.gitlab-ci.yml` name in the root of a repository. In this file, you can define one or more stages and jobs, along with the tasks that they should perform. An example YAML file for GitLab CI can appear as in the following example:

```
stages:
  - build
  - test

build:
    stage: build
    script: dotnet build **/*.csproj

test:
    stage: test
    script: dotnet test **/*.csproj
```

Just as Azure DevOps uses agent pools with agents, GitLab CI relies on **runners** to perform the actual work. In GitLab CI, there is currently no support for visually creating or editing your pipelines.

Jenkins

Jenkins is another tool used to run build pipelines. Complex builds can be run using Jenkins pipelines, which get their work from a Jenkinsfile. A **Jenkinsfile** is written in a Jenkins-specific notation, as in the following code:

```
pipeline {
    agent any
    stages {
        stage('build') {
        agent any
            steps {
                dotnet build **/*.csproj
            }
        }

        stage('test') {
            agent any
            steps {
                dotnet test **/*.csproj
            }
        }
    }
}
```

Jenkins has limited support for visually creating and editing a pipeline. This is referred to as a freestyle project.

Summary

In this chapter, we looked at continuous integration and learned how it is a combination of your mindset, the process, and tools. You learned how to create build definitions using Azure Pipelines using both the graphical designer and YAML, as well as how to run builds. You learned that you can use build pipelines to compile and test your code, as well as report the outcome back to pull requests.

You learned that builds can produce outcomes, called artifacts. Artifacts are stored and retained within Azure pipelines and can be used to store reports, but are also the starting point of deployment pipelines, which you will learn about in the next chapter. You also learned about the infrastructure that you need to run builds—namely, agents and agent pools. Finally, you saw two brief examples of how to run a continuous integration build using GitLab CI and Jenkins, which are two other tools that you can use for build pipelines.

With this knowledge, you are now able to create build pipelines for your projects. You can hook up to source control and produce the builds that you will use in the next chapter to deploy your applications. With this deep knowledge of the underlying structure of tasks, jobs, stages, and pipelines, you can solve complex application-building problems.

In the next chapter, you will continue learning about pipelines, but this time for releases. You will learn how to pick up builds and release them to one or more environments.

Questions

As we conclude, here is a list of questions for you to test your knowledge regarding this chapter's material. You will find the answers in the *Assessments* section of the appendix:

1. True or false – you achieve continuous integration if you compile all the branches of your project at least daily.
2. True or false – a classic build definition is always connected to a source code repository.
3. True or false – a YAML pipeline definition is always connected to a source code repository.
4. Which of the following is needed to call an external tool from an Azure pipeline?
    1. An external service definition
    2. An Azure services connection
    3. A service connection
    4. A service locator

5. What are some common reasons for using self-hosted agents? (Choose all of the correct answers from the following:)
    1. Access to closed networks is needed.
    2. Specific extension tasks need to be available to the agent.
    3. The number of parallel pipeline executions needs to be larger than 10.
    4. Specific software needs to be installed in order for the agent to use it.

Further reading

- An in-depth definition of continuous integration by Martin Fowler is available at `https://martinfowler.com/articles/continuousIntegration.html`.
- A detailed description of the conditions syntax is available at `https://docs.microsoft.com/en-us/azure/devops/pipelines/process/conditions?view=azure-devopstabs=classic`.
- Exercises for practicing with Azure DevOps builds can be found at `https://docs.microsoft.com/en-us/learn/modules/create-a-build-pipeline/index`.
- You can find the Visual Studio marketplace for Azure DevOps at `https://marketplace.visualstudio.com/azuredevops`.
- You can find a detailed description of the Azure Pipelines YAML syntax at `https://docs.microsoft.com/en-us/azure/devops/pipelines/yaml-schema?view=azure-devopstabs=schema`.
- Details of the pricing of the Azure pipelines hosted and self-hosted agent pools are available at `https://azure.microsoft.com/en-us/pricing/details/devops/azure-pipelines/`.
- More information about GitLab CI can be found at `https://about.gitlab.com/product/continuous-integration/`.
- More information about Jenkins can be found at `https://jenkins.io/`.

Continuous Deployment

4

In the previous chapter, you learned how to use Azure DevOps pipelines for continuous integration. Due to this, you now know how to pick up a version of your sources and create artifacts that can be deployed. In this chapter, you will learn how to extend this practice with continuous delivery and continuous deployment so that you automatically deploy these artifacts to the servers or platforms your code is running on.

To do this, we will start by introducing Azure DevOps release definitions so that you can define and run the releases of your application. Next, a series of strategies will be introduced that you can use to perform deployments in a low-risk manner. Doing this makes it possible for you to automate the process of deploying new versions unattended, with a limited risk of incidents occurring. From here, we will shift our attention to automating the creation of release notes. After this, we will introduce App Center, which is used for deploying mobile applications. Finally, other tools for continuous deployment will be introduced.

The following topics will be covered in this chapter:

- Continuous delivery and continuous deployment
- Working with Azure DevOps releases
- Writing multi-stage YAML pipelines
- Implementing continuous deployment strategies
- Deploying mobile applications
- Automating release notes
- Other tools

Technical requirements

To experiment with the techniques described in this chapter, you might need one or more of the following:

- An Azure DevOps account for building release definitions and multi-stage YAML pipelines
- An App Center account for deploying mobile applications

Free trial options are available for both of these.

Continuous delivery and continuous deployment

The difference between continuous delivery and continuous deployment is a common source of confusion. Some people think these terms are interchangeable and see them as two synonyms for the same concept, but they have, in fact, two different meanings.

Continuous delivery is a practice where teams ensure that the artifacts they build are continuously validated and ready to be deployed to the production environment. Often, this is done by deploying the artifacts to a production-like environment, such as acceptance or even a staging environment, and applying a series of tests, such as verification tests, to ensure the application is working correctly.

Continuous deployment is a practice where every version that is deployed to a production-like environment and passes all tests and verifications, is also deployed to production automatically.

When working with Azure DevOps, Azure Pipelines is the tool of choice for implementing continuous delivery and deployment. This can be done using either the visual classic editor or with multi-stage YAML pipelines, both of which will be discussed in the following section.

Working with Azure DevOps releases

Continuous delivery and deployment can both be implemented in Azure DevOps by using releases. When creating a new release definition, an outline of the release process is created. This process will often start with an artifact that triggers the creation of a new release. Next, it is possible to define one or more stages that the release can be deployed to. Often, these stages correspond to the different application environments, for example, test and production, but this is not mandatory.

Let's learn how to create a new release definition and explore the various options we have. First, navigate to **Pipelines** and choose **Releases** from the menu. From here, it is possible to start creating a new release pipeline, which will take us to a screen that looks similar to the one shown in the following screenshot:

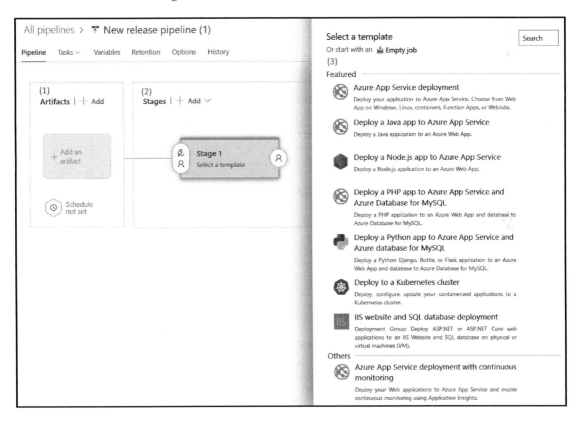

From the preceding screen, we can perform the following actions (these are numbered in the preceding screenshot):

1. First, notice that, on the left, it is possible to see the outline of the release pipeline with a box. Here, you can select one or more artifacts that can be used in the release pipeline.
2. To the right of this, there is a box where the different stages of the release can be seen. By default, one stage is created already.
3. It is possible to pick a template as a starting point for the deployment pipeline for this pre-created stage. Choosing to start with an empty job in this view allows you to craft a custom deployment pipeline from scratch.

After choosing a job template or an empty job to start with, the pane on the right will close, and it will be possible to start editing the release pipeline from left to right, starting with the artifacts.

Once a skeleton release pipeline is visible, the first things you will need to configure are the artifacts that the release should work with. This is the subject of the next section.

Creating artifacts and release triggers

The previous chapter described build definitions and YAML pipelines, which create artifacts. These artifacts are picked up in releases and form the basis for deploying an application.

To start editing a release pipeline, follow these steps:

1. Click on the **Add an artifact** button to start building the starting point of the release definition. This will open the right-hand pane shown in the following screenshot:

2. In the picker for the project, the current project will be selected by default.

3. Now, specify the artifacts that the release pipeline should pick up.

4. After this, the default version to use and the source alias will be automatically selected. The default version can always be overridden when manually starting a release, so **Latest** is a sensible default.

5. The source alias is the name of the folder where the artifacts can be located when we add jobs to the release stages at a later date. The default is often fine.

6. Finish adding the artifact by clicking **Add.**

Now that we've specified the artifacts to work with, it is time to specify when a new release should be created. Let's learn how to do this:

1. To configure the availability of a new artifact to trigger the release, click on the lightning bolt next to the artifact to open the configuration pane. This can be seen in the following screenshot:

2. In this pane, it is possible to create a new release, when one is available, using the top slider. This will expand a new section where you can define one or more filters so that you can specify conditions under which a new artifact should trigger a release.
3. Click the **Add** button to start adding a condition.
4. A common example is to only include artifacts that come from the master branch, as shown here.
5. In addition to artifacts that come from regular builds, it is possible to also allow artifacts that come from pull request builds to start a new release.
6. Finally, it is possible to create a new release on a fixed schedule.

If no schedule and no trigger are specified, a new release will only be created when someone does so manually.

Specifying the stages to deploy the release

After specifying the artifacts to release, it is time to specify one or more stages to deploy the release to. Often, every environment (test, acceptance, and production) will correspond to a stage. But it is also possible to have other stages if the situation calls for it.

Let's learn how to add a new stage and explore various options. First, click on **Pipelines** to arrive at the following screen:

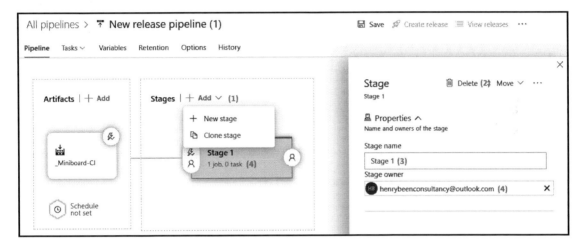

Now, complete the following steps:

1. Click the **Add** button to create a new stage. A stage can be either new or a clone of an existing one.
2. After selecting an already existing stage, it can be removed using the **Delete** button on the top right.
3. Other actions that can be performed on this screen include renaming the stage and designating a stage owner. The owner will be notified when a release is deployed to the environment.
4. After creating and naming a stage, it is possible to add jobs and tasks to a stage, just like it was possible for a build pipeline. To do this, click on the link in the box that denotes the stage.

From here on, this works exactly the same as building pipelines. There is only one addition: besides agent jobs and agentless jobs, it is also possible to use deployment group jobs. These will be discussed in the *Working with deployment groups* section later on. But first, let's understand which stages we need.

Which stages do I need?

One of the questions that frequently arises when working with releases is, *which stages do I need in my release pipeline*? According to the documentation, stages should denote the major divisions of a release pipeline. When starting out with releases, this often boils down to having one stage per environment in a release pipeline. Appropriate stages include **test**, **acceptance**, and **production**.

When working with releases for a long time, we might incorporate more automation in the pipelines and want to add extra checking stags to them. An example might be a stage called **load test** that is executed in parallel to the **test** stage. Another example might be the introduction of a stage for **automated UI tests**.

No matter which stages are added, the approach to propagating a release to production should always stay the same. When a release propagates from stage to stage and gets closer to production, this should show that there is confidence in this release, that it is working correctly, and that it can be promoted to production.

Stage triggers, approvals, and gates

After defining the required stages and adding jobs and tasks to them, it is time to configure when the release to a specific stage should be triggered. The steps for this can be seen in the following screenshot:

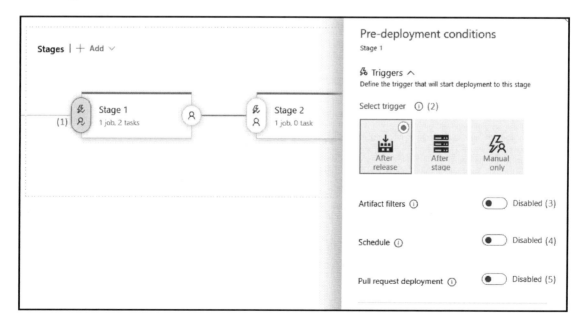

Note that the following steps need to be carried out for every stage individually:

1. To trigger a release to a specific stage, click on the button with a lightning bolt and a person icon, to the left of the square that denotes the stage.
2. The first thing to configure here is when a release should propagate to this stage. This can be either upon the availability of the release, after completing another stage, or only upon manual request. The choice you make here will also be reflected in the visual representation of the pipeline.
3. Separate from the trigger, it is possible to define one or more filters that limit which artifacts will trigger a deployment to the stage. There can be one or more include or exclude branch filters for every artifact.
4. It is also possible to redeploy on a fixed schedule.
5. Finally, if the creation of a new release is specified for builds that were started from a pull request, the release can also be allowed to propagate to the current stage using the slider.

Next to these triggers, approvers and gates can be added so that you can configure how to handle deployment queue settings. These settings can be accessed from the tabs below the section for **Triggers**, as shown in the following screenshot:

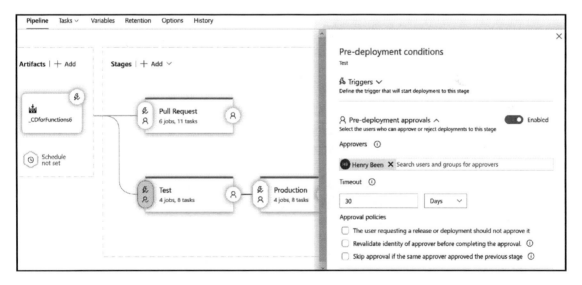

The first tab is about approvers. Here, groups or users are specified. They must give their approval before releasing to this stage can begin. Multiple people can be added and if so, an order can be defined in which they have to approve or it can be specified that a single approval is enough. By scrolling down, you will find the following options:

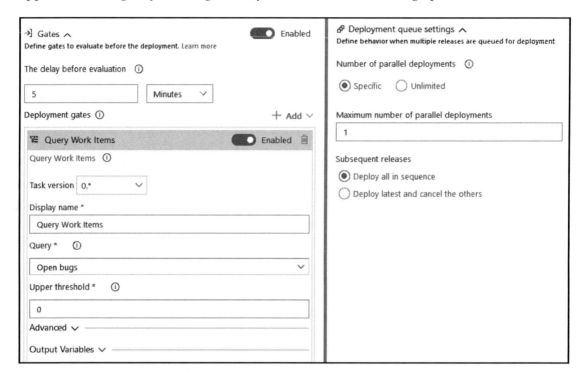

The second tab (on the left) allows you to add one or more gates. Gates are automated checks that have to succeed before the release can continue. Currently, this shows the configuration details for configuring a work item query and a threshold on the number of results, for example, to ensure that there are no open bugs before a release proceeds. There are also gates available that can call in Azure Monitor, Azure Functions, or a RESTful API. This set of gates can be extended using the Azure DevOps extension mechanisms. Some of these extensions also integrate with common change management systems.

The final tab (on the right) allows you to configure how to handle a situation where different versions of the release are ready for deployment to the same stage. Here, it is possible to specify how many releases can run in parallel. If there are even more releases coming in, you can queue them up and deploy them one after the other, or only deploy the latest.

Working with deployment groups

Another topic that you might run into at some point is deploying an application to on-premises servers or servers that are behind a firewall. You may also come across situations where it is necessary to run scripts on all of the machines hosting the application or situations where the target environment does not supply a mechanism for deploying applications.

The approach to performing releases, which was shown in the *Working with Azure DevOps releases* section of this chapter, relies on being able to connect to the target machines or services that will host the application. We call these **push-based deployments**, and this is not always possible.

When deploying to target machines that cannot be connected to, another approach needs to be taken. This approach is called **agent-based deployment**. In an agent-based deployment, an Azure DevOps agent is installed on every machine that the application will be installed on. Next, these agents must be grouped into deployment groups. Once this is done, a **deployment group job** can be added to the release.

This is very similar to an agent job, except for one thing. In an agent job, the tasks in the job will run on **one of the agents** against the target machine. In a deployment group job, all of the tasks will run on all of the agents in the release group on the target machines. This difference between both approaches can be seen in the following diagram:

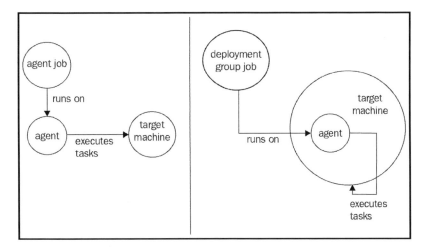

When using this approach, it is necessary to have agents on the machines that the application needs to be deployed to. These agents listen to Azure DevOps and whenever a new release is requested, they retrieve the work and execute it on the local machine.

Managing deployment groups

Before you can add a deployment group job to a release pipeline, you need to create a deployment group. To do so, perform the following steps:

1. Navigate to the **Pipelines** menu.
2. Open the **Deployment groups** menu.
3. Enter a deployment group name and description and click **Create**.

Once the new deployment group has been created, a script will appear on the right, as shown in the following screenshot:

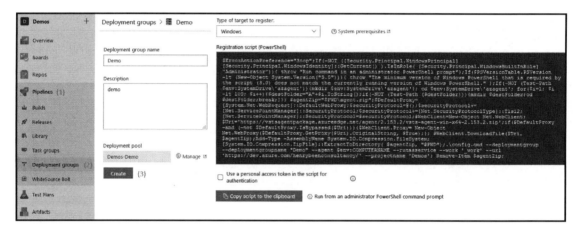

Executing this script on the target machine will install the agent and automatically register that machine as part of the newly created deployment group.

If an application must be deployed to three stages (test, acceptance, and production) using deployment groups, there will need to be three separate deployment groups, one for each environment.

Creating a release pipeline with a deployment group

After creating the necessary deployment group(s), those deployment group(s) can be used in releases from the tasks view, as shown in the following screenshot:

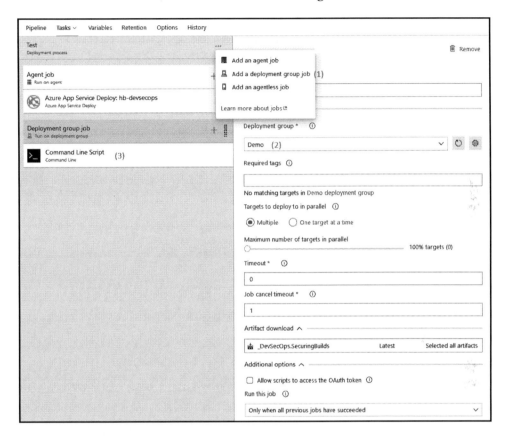

To do this, perform the following steps:

1. Add a new deployment group to the pipeline.
2. Specify which deployment group the job should run on by picking it from the drop-down menu.
3. Add one or more tasks to execute the job. The functionality of the user interface is the same as that for regular agent jobs.

Besides the different approaches to executing on all agents in a group instead of one, deployment group jobs behave the same as regular agent jobs.

Writing multi-stage YAML pipelines

In addition to the visual designer for release definitions, it is also possible to implement continuous deployment using YAML pipelines. When doing so, it is still recommended to differentiate between the build (CI) and release (CD) phases of a pipeline. The concept of stages is used to make this possible. A YAML pipeline can be divided into one or more stages. A stage can represent an environment such as test, acceptance, or production, but this isn't always true. If, in an application scenario, it makes sense to add extra stages such as pre-production or staging, this is possible. It is good practice to publish **pipeline artifacts** to earlier stages and to consume or **download artifacts** in later stages.

Multi-stage YAML pipelines are the new default for creating pipelines in Azure DevOps. Since working with YAML pipelines can have a steeper learning curve than working with classic releases, some find it easier to work with classic releases first and switch to YAML pipelines later. Just like with builds, many of the concepts of classic releases translate to multi-stage YAML pipelines as well.

Adding stages to YAML pipelines

If no stages are defined in a YAML pipeline, there is always one implicit stage that holds all the jobs. To convert a pipeline into a multi-stage pipeline, you need to add the `stages` keyword and a list of stages, as shown in the following code:

```
stages:
- stage: stage1
  displayName: My first stage
  jobs:
  - job: job1
    steps:
    - task: DotNetCoreCLI@2
      displayName: 'dotnet build'
      inputs:
        projects: '**/*.csproj'

- stage: stage2
  jobs:
  ...
```

The preceding syntax shows that a list of stages is defined at the top of the YAML file. Each stage starts by defining a name. This name can be used later on so that you can refer to this stage.

While jobs (unless otherwise specified) run in parallel by default, stages always run sequentially by default. But just like jobs, stages accept the `dependsOn` and `condition` keywords to change the ordering, parallelism, and (potentially) to skip stages.

Downloading artifacts

A common use of multi-stage pipelines it to separate the build stage and the deployment stage. To make this possible, the build stage often publishes one or more pipeline artifacts. This was discussed in the previous chapter.

All the artifacts that were published in a previous stage of the current pipeline can be downloaded using a `download` task:

```
steps:
- download: current
  artifact: artifactName
```

It is also possible to download artifacts from other pipelines. To do this, the `current` constant has to be replaced with the name of that pipeline. Pipeline artifacts are downloaded to the `$(Pipeline.Workspace)` directory.

 If you want more fine-grained control over downloading pipeline artifacts, for example, over the version of the artifact to use or the location to download the artifact to, you can also use the Download Pipeline Artifacts tasks, which are documented at `https://docs.microsoft.com/bs-cyrl-ba/azure/devops/pipelines/tasks/utility/download-pipeline-artifact?view=azure-devops`.

Publishing and downloading artifacts within a pipeline ensures that the code that is built in the first stage is also the code that is deployed in the second stage – even if the stages run days apart. In essence, each pipeline run builds a local stage of all the artifacts associated with that specific run.

Approvals

In a multi-stage pipeline, it is not possible to define approvers as it is in a classic release pipeline. The reason for this is that the pipeline – *the build and deployment process* – is viewed as code. Code is worked on by developers and operators only. Approvals are worked on by, for example, product owners. However, this does not mean that it is not possible to implement approval flows for the progression of a pipeline to the next stage.

To control whether a pipeline is allowed to proceed to a certain stage, the concept of environments needs to be introduced. An environment is defined when we give it a name and a description. One or more approvers can be attached to these environments. Once this is done, jobs can be configured to target such an environment. If there is at least one job in a stage that targets an environment, then that environment is said to be used by the stage. If an approval has been configured on that environment, the deployment to that stage will not continue until the approver has given permission.

To start working with environments, you'll need to access the list of environments. This list be found in the **Pipelines** menu, as shown in the following screenshot:

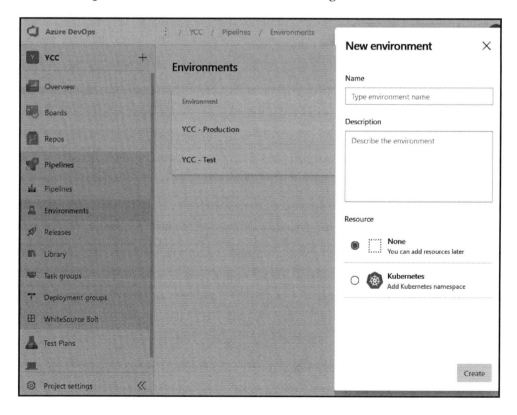

To add a new environment, perform the following steps:

1. Open the **Pipelines** menu and choose **Environments**.
2. Select **New environment** from the top right.
3. Specify a name and description.
4. Click **Create**.

It is possible to associate resources with an environment. Resources that are coupled with an environment can be used in a pipeline if, and only if, that pipeline is also targeting that environment. To protect the resources of an environment, the owner of that environment can add one or more approvers. An example of a configured approver can be seen in the following screenshot:

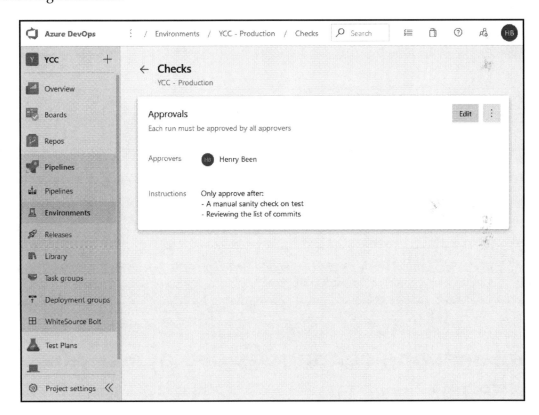

Approvers can be added to an environment as follows:

1. Navigate to the **Environments** overview pane.
2. Open an environment by clicking on it.

3. Click the top-right menu marked with the three dots, and and choose **Approvals and Checks**.
4. Click the **Create** button.
5. Pick a user or group from the list and add extra instructions if needed.
6. Click the **Create** button again.

Approvals make it possible for you to control the progression of a pipeline to the next stage if that pipeline targets the correct environment. Targeting an environment is done by specifying a specific type of job: the deployment job. The following YAML shows how to do this:

```
jobs:
- deployment: deplyoymentJobName
  displayName: Friendly name
  strategy:
  runOnce:
    deploy:
      steps:
        ...
```

Deployment jobs do not directly contain the steps to execute like an agent job does. Instead, they first have to specify an execution strategy for the tasks outlined under the `steps` keyword. At the time of writing, the only strategy supported is `runOnce`. Other strategies are expected to be announced in the future.

At the time of writing, only Kubernetes clusters are supported as environment resources, but more types of resources have been announced for the future.

Now that we know about the technical means for creating release definitions and writing multi-stage YAML pipelines, it is time to take a look at the different strategies we can use to apply this in practice. These continuous deployment strategies are designed to minimize the risk of deploying new versions of an application automatically.

Implementing continuous deployment strategies

Before we deploy an application continuously, it is important to think about the strategy we should use. Just doing deployment after deployment may have more risks associated with it than the business is willing to accept. It is important to think about how to deal with issues that might occur during or after deploying a new version of your application.

There are a few deployment strategies that can be applied to reduce the risks that might come with deployments, all of which will be covered in this section. Please note that it is possible to combine one or more of the following patterns. For example, it is perfectly possible to use a blue-green strategy for every ring in a ring-based deployment. Also, all deployment strategies can be combined with the use of feature flags.

Blue-green deployments

Blue-green deployments is a technique where a new version of an application never gets deployed to the production servers directly. Instead, it gets deployed to another set of servers first. Once this has be done successfully, users are directed to the new deployment.

Let's assume that an application runs on a total of three hosts by default. A typical setup for blue-green deployment would be two sets of three hosts: the blue group and the green group. In front of these two sets, there is a reverse proxy that functions as a load balancer and redirects the incoming requests to the blue group. The following diagram shows how this works:

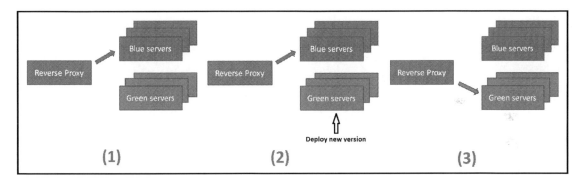

To deploy a new version of the application in this situation, it needs to be deployed to the green group of servers. Since these servers are not receiving any traffic from end users, this has no impact on them at all.

After the deployment, the new deployment can be verified to ensure it was successful and that the application is running correctly. After this verification, the load balancer is reconfigured to redirect traffic to the green group. Now, the new version of the application is served.

Should there suddenly be any unexpected issues, it is very easy to switch back to the previous deployment by reconfiguring the load balancer back to the blue group. If the deployment is successful and there are no issues, it is possible to start the deployment of the next version by going through the same procedure, but now with the roles of the green and the blue groups switched.

Immutable servers

A variation of the blue-green deployment pattern is immutable servers. With immutable servers, there is no going back and forth between two groups of servers. Instead, the group of servers that are serving the old version of the application is completely disregarded or removed. Often, this is done after a grace period.

The result of this is that there will still be means to roll back to a previous version – almost instantaneously if the old servers are kept around for a while. The other benefit is that there is now a guarantee that no remains from a previous deployment are being carried over into the newer deployments. Using immutable servers, the change of active servers over time might look as follows:

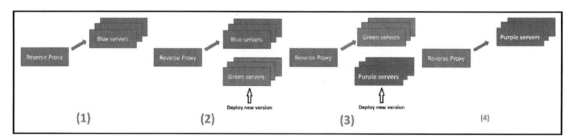

Of course, an approach like this is only feasible when using technologies such as containers or virtual machines. Nobody would expect anyone to disregard physical servers after every redeployment.

Progressive exposure

Progressive exposure is a deployment strategy in which the number of users that have access to a new deployment or a new feature is slowly increased over time. The goal of this strategy is to limit the number of users that are experiencing issues when a faulty release of a feature is made available.

We can also look at this more positively and in line with the continuous deployment way of thinking: exposing a new feature to only a few users at first and increasing that number over time allows us to increase the amount of trust in a new version or feature of an application before exposing it to all users.

Canary deployments

The first strategy for progressive exposure is to use canary deployments. In a canary deployment, not all users are routed to the new version immediately – only a limited percentage of the users get access to that version. These users are the canaries and they are monitored very closely. If they experience any issues or if degradation in performance or a service is measured, the new deployment is quickly rolled back.

A typical approach to realizing canary deployments is to use them in combination with blue-green deployments. The difference is that instead of switching all users over at the same time, only a small percentage is moved over to the new version at the start, and then the number of users that are moved over is gradually increased over time. This might look something similar to the following:

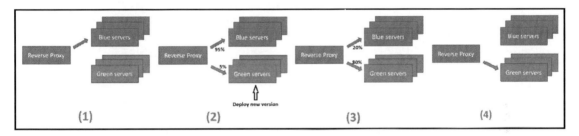

If a deployment is rolled back because errors have been observed, this is not a fun experience for users. To prevent the same small group of users running into issues repeatedly, it might be beneficial to select a different group of canary users afterward.

Ring-based deployments

In a ring-based environment, there is not just one production environment – there are multiple. Each production environment serves only a portion of the users. Its difference from a canary deployment is that, instead of just two environments, there can be as many environments as needed. Also, every new version goes to all the rings, one after the other.

So, instead of redirecting the users, in a ring-based environment, the new version is propagating to the servers used by those users. The new version just keeps propagating from one ring to the next, until they are all done:

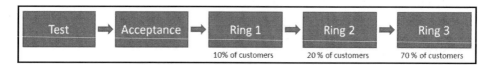

Ring-based deployment architectures are especially suitable for products that are accessed by customers from all around the world. The different rings can be positioned around the world, thus combining the deployment benefits with the added benefit of reduced latencies for users.

Feature flags

The third form of progressive deployment can be achieved using feature flags, also called feature toggles. Where canary deployments and ring-based deployments rely on slowly exposing new binaries to an increasing number of users, feature flags are used to slowly expose new features to an increasing number of users. This can be achieved even if they are all sending requests to the same server. Feature flags are used to decouple deploying a new version of the application binaries from releasing new features by enabling or disabling specific features at runtime.

The best example of a feature flag is showing or hiding a button that gives users access to a new feature. Application settings, a database, or an external service are used to keep track of which feature has been enabled for which user. Depending on that setting, the feature is shown or hidden. Examples of such external services include LaunchDarkly, Split.IO, and Prefab.cloud.

Other feature flags might toggle bug fixes or performance improvements on or off. This can help to gradually expose these to ensure there are no issues. When using feature toggles for these kinds of changes deeper in a codebase, introducing feature toggles also comes with a cost, and a process for this should be in place. This process should not only describe adding feature toggles, but also how to remove them as soon as possible. An example of such a process can be as follows.

A new feature flag is introduced by a developer as soon as the business needs to release the feature independently of the deployments that were made by the development team, or for a change that the development team qualifies as high risk and wants to be able to pull back at any time without redeploying it. Introducing a feature flag means a new database entry or a declaration of a new setting is applied in the application settings.

After introducing the feature toggle, the new feature or change is developed and tested. This means that there are one or more `if` statements in the codebase that execute different code paths, depending on the state of the feature flag. At this point, the application must maintain two code execution paths until they remove the feature flag again. It is good practice to separate these two code paths as much as possible using existing engineering practices, such as dependency injection.

While the code is continuously being shipped to users, the feature is not enabled for anyone. Only when the development team is fully satisfied with the change or the product owner feels the time is right for releasing a new feature is the feature flag turned on.

It is important not to stop here. After turning the feature flag on, it should actively be determined whether the feature or change is working properly. And if it is, the feature flag should be removed as soon as possible. This way, the time the two code paths need to be maintained for is as short as possible.

Also, note that besides maintaining an increased number of execution paths, there is now a larger number of paths to test. The impact of this consequence quickly grows if dependencies or exclusions between feature flags are introduced. Feature flags that can only be turned on or off, depending on the state of another feature flag, can be costly, and it is recommended to avoid this.

If implemented properly and removed as soon as possible, the added cost of feature flags is often worth it. As with every engineering practice, start small and evaluate what works in the given context, before adapting the practice at scale.

Roll back or fail forward

No matter which strategy is being used, it is necessary to think about the ability to roll back one or more versions and how long that will take. For example, blue-green deployments give us the ability to go back one version almost instantaneously, as long as a new version is not being deployed to the non-active servers yet. On the other hand, performing a rollback in a ring-based deployment will require a full redeploy of the previous version, which will probably take longer and comes with all the risks of deployment in itself. This may even need to be done on multiple rings, making it more challenging.

Another approach that can be adopted is that of failing forward. When adopting this approach, it is stated that there will never be a rollback to a previous version. Instead, when any issue is encountered, this will be addressed by redeploying a new version with the fix of that issue in it. This strategy is gaining traction lately since it saves time as we don't have to prepare, test, and practice rollbacks. However, there can be risks involved with this process:

- There is no guarantee that the fix will be correct. The issue might not be resolved by the new deployed version or, even worse, the new version might result in transitioning from one issue to another.
- Working out a detailed root cause of any issue takes time, just like writing a fix does. The consequence of this might be that the fix might take longer than a rollback would have taken.

No matter which approach is taken, consider the consequences and prepare for them.

So far, we have mainly focused on web-based applications. In the next section, we will shift our attention to mobile applications.

Deploying mobile applications

One type of application that needs a special approach to deployment is mobile applications. These applications are often not downloaded and installed by end users directly and are mostly consumed via an app store on their mobile device.

App Center is a Microsoft offering that can be used for distributing (deploying) mobile applications to end users via app stores, but also via private distribution lists.

After logging into App Center, you will be taken to the following screen:

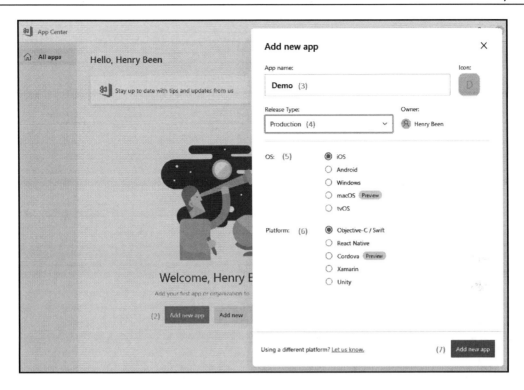

Here, you can create a new app definition. An app definition should be created for every target operating system of an application. If the same application is going to be deployed to both Android and iOS, at least two apps have to be created.

Creating an app is done by performing the following steps:

1. Log in to App Center.
2. Click the blue **Add new app** button. If there are no existing apps, this button will be on the center of the screen; otherwise, it will be at the top right (hidden under the popup shown in the preceding screenshot).
3. Enter the name of the app.
4. Select the type of release.
5. Select the operating system.
6. Select the platform to use.
7. Click **Add new app** to create the app.

Once an app has been created, it can be connected to the correct app store and distribution groups can be created.

Connecting to the app store

The app store is the main mechanism for distributing an application for all mobile platforms. Once a build is delivered to an app store, users can install and use the application. The current list of connections to app stores can be opened using the **Stores** tab, on the left-hand side of App Center. From this list, an individual store connection can be opened, which will take us to a screen similar to the one shown in the following screenshot:

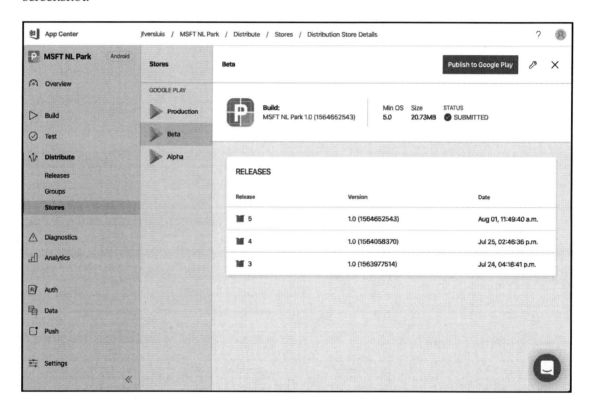

This view shows a list of all the versions of the application that have been published to the connected store account. This is also where a new version of the application can be selected for publication to the store. This is done using the blue **Publish** button at the top. This will open a popup where you can select the correct release. You only have to confirm this once to publish this version.

New connections to the store can be created by navigating back to the list of all store connections and clicking the **Add** button. This will open a wizard where two pieces of information have to be entered:

- **The type of store connection**: This list is limited to the stores that are available to apps of the type that was chosen when creating the app definition. For example, for iOS, this is limited to the Apple App Store and the Intune Company Portal.
- **Connection details**: Often, they include the means of authentication between App Center and the app store.

Once the new connection has been created, it can be found on the list shown previously and can be used to distribute the app.

Another means of distribution is using distribution groups, which we'll introduce in the next section.

Using distribution groups

Distribution groups are used to create named lists of one or more users, often testers or alpha users, that install the application through an invitation, rather than via the app store. Distribution groups can be found in the left-hand menu, under **Groups**:

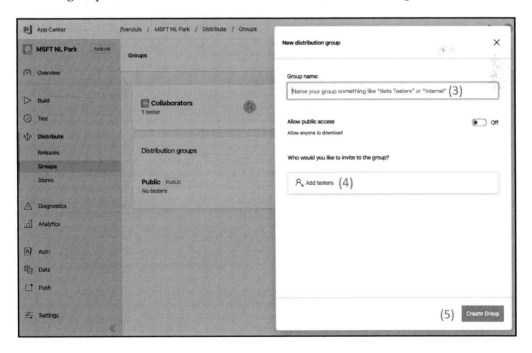

Here, a new group can be added, as follows:

1. Navigate to **Distribution groups** using the menu on the left.
2. Click the blue button labeled with a plus (**+**) sign (hidden under the popup in the preceding screenshot).
3. Choose a name for the group.
4. Add one or more members.
5. Save the new group.

Once a distribution group has been created, it can be used for publishing releases, which we will discuss in the next section.

Publishing an app

To publish the first or a new version of an app, it has to be shared with App Center. This can be done using the **Releases** tab on the left-hand side. When opening up the releases, the following view, detailing all the current releases, will appear. From here, any release can be selected so that you can view the details of that release:

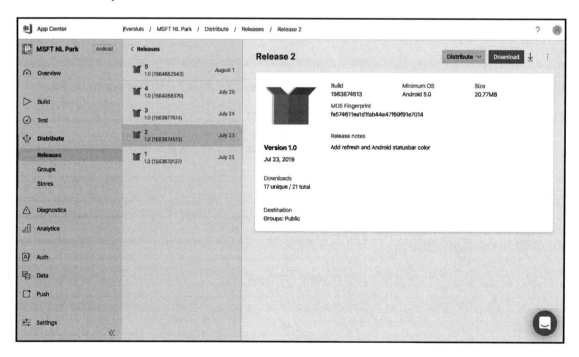

In this view, a list of the most recent releases is shown in the middle column. After selecting an individual release, the details of that version will be shown. This includes its formal version, the store(s) and/or distribution group(s) it has been shared with, and other details.

From here, it is possible to distribute this specific version to a store connection or distribution group directly using the **Distribute** bottom at the top right.

From here, a new release can also be created by uploading a new build of the app. To do this, follow these steps:

1. Click on the **New release** button, which is available from the list of all releases. (It might be necessary to close the details of a specific release first.) This will open the following view:

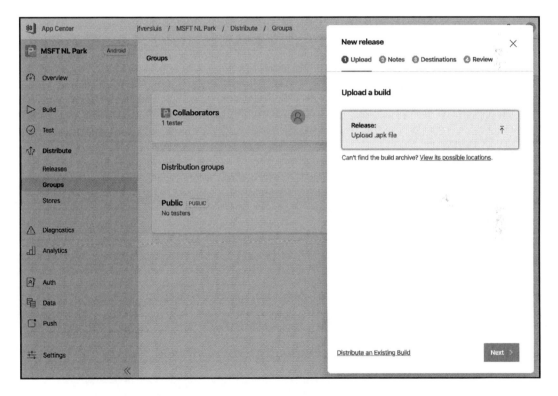

2. A new wizard will open, where a build needs to be uploaded. Depending on the type of app, the correct type of file will be requested. After uploading the binaries, click **Next**.
3. Now, the release notes have to be filled in. After detailing the changes in this release, click **Next** again.

4. Now, it is time to specify where this new build should be distributed. At least one destination – either a distribution group or a store – has to be selected. After selecting one or more destinations, click **Next** again.

5. The final wizard tab will show the selections you've made so far. Check the details and click **Distribute** to complete the creation of a new version and its initial distribution.

Often, the same version or release needs to be distributed to other groups or stores over time as well. It is not necessary (nor useful) to create a new release every time. Instead, going to the **Detail** pages of the new destination store connection or distribution group allows you to publish an existing release to that destination as well.

As an alternative to using App Center to perform release management this way, it is also possible to use Azure Pipelines for release management.

App Center via Azure Pipelines

App Center can also be integrated with Azure Pipelines. If teams are familiar with the release process in Azure Pipelines, it can be sensible to build the app in Azure Pipelines and only use App Center for deployment to stores and distribution groups.

To make this possible, there are tasks available in Azure Pipelines that allow you to upload a release and trigger the deployment of a release to a store or distribution group. That way, release management can be done in Azure Pipelines while the App Center-specific capabilities are still leveraged where applicable.

This section focused on mobile applications specifically, while the next section will apply to all types of releases. When creating releases is automated and new versions follow each other quickly, it is useful to start automating the creation and publication of release notes as well. This will be discussed in the next section.

Automating release notes

After automating the build, releasing an application, and working on increasing the flow of value to end users, many developers find that it becomes harder and harder to keep documentation and release notes up to date. As the amount of releases increases, this becomes more and more work, and eventually, the team will fall behind or even give up completely.

To combat this, it is possible to automate the creation and publication of release notes. One way to do this is by using the Azure DevOps Release Notes Generator. The generator is an Azure Functions application that is available on GitHub. To use the Release Notes Generator, the following needs to be done:

1. Download or clone the function code from GitHub.
2. Create an Azure App Service Plan, function app, and storage account in Azure.
3. Create a new blob container in the storage account called `releases`.
4. Compile the function code and deploy it to an Azure App Service.
5. Create a new Azure DevOps WebHook to call the deployed function whenever a new release is created.

After setting this up, the generator will run whenever a new release is created. It will then do the following:

1. Query the created release for its name, all associated work items, and all the commits that are new since the previous release.
2. Generate a markdown file containing all of this information.
3. Upload that file to the blob container, that is, `releases`.

Of course, the Azure DevOps Release Notes Generator is just one example of automating tasks around releases, and there are other alternatives available as well. Also, many companies create tailored, in-house automation scripts for updating and publishing documentation and other tasks.

Other tools

In addition to Azure DevOps and App Center, there are other tools that can be used for deploying and releasing software. GitLab CI/CD and Jenkins, which were discussed in the previous chapter for executing builds, can also be used for releases. Besides those, Octopus Deploy is also a commonly used tool that integrates well with Azure DevOps.

Octopus Deploy

Octopus Deploy is a deployment automation tool that is based on the concept of running a series of tasks on one or more target machines.

Octopus reaches these machines through a tentacle (an agent) that is installed on these machines. In Octopus Deploy, it is possible to define applications and environments and assign one or more machines to each of those. To do deployments, execution steps can be defined in a graphical editor, comparable to the visual release editor of Azure DevOps.

One of the main differences is that these steps are not defined per environment, only once per pipeline. Next, it is possible to specify which environments each task should run on. This way, it is easier to see where the deployment to different environments varies.

There is an integration between Azure DevOps and Octopus Deploy available, in the form of a build and release task. Using this integration, you can start a deployment using Octopus Deploy from an Azure DevOps build or release pipeline.

Summary

In this chapter, you learned about continuous delivery and deployment and how you can implement them using Azure DevOps. In addition to the visual release editor, you also learned about multi-stage YAML pipelines, which you can use for releasing your software to multiple stages, all of the way to production. Next, we discussed a series of strategies that you can use for releasing. You now know about blue-green deployments, using immutable servers, and different strategies for progressive exposure. You also learned how to choose between making sure you have rollback capabilities or accepting a fail forward strategy.

Then, you learned about automating release notes and documentation and how you can generate those automatically as part of your pipeline. After that, you learned about continuous deployment for mobile applications and how that differs from the delivery of web applications. Finally, you learned about the existence of Octopus Deploy, how it operates, and that it integrates with Azure DevOps.

In the next chapter, you will learn about topic dependency management using Azure Artifacts. Azure Artifacts can be used to host your own NuGet packages or to host build artifacts when you are using other products for building or releasing your application in combination with Azure Pipelines.

Questions

As we conclude this chapter, here is a list of questions for you to test your knowledge of this chapter's material. You will find the answers in the *Assessments* section of the Appendix:

1. True or false: An Azure DevOps Classic Release is always triggered by the availability of a new version of an artifact.
2. Which of the following platforms can App Center publish apps to? (You can choose more than one.)
    1. Google Play Store
    2. Apple App Store
    3. Microsoft Intune
3. Which of the following techniques use progressive exposure for minimizing the risks of deploying a new version? (You can choose more than one.)
    1. Feature Toggles
    2. Ring-based deployments
    3. Canary deployments
4. True or false: Deployment groups can be used for deploying software to on-premises servers when an Azure Pipelines agent is installed on the machine that will be running the software.
5. What is the advantage of integrating App Center with Azure Pipelines if you have an Azure Pipelines release definition triggering actions in App Center?

Further reading

- More information on using stages in YAML pipelines can be found at `https://docs.microsoft.com/en-us/azure/devops/pipelines/process/stages`.
- More information on the idea of immutable servers can be found at `https://martinfowler.com/bliki/ImmutableServer.html`.
- More information about LaunchDarkly can be found at `https://launchdarkly.com/`.

- More details about the build and release extension for integration with Octopus Deploy can be found at `https://marketplace.visualstudio.com/items?itemName=octopusdeploy.octopus-deploy-build-release-tasks.`
- The Azure DevOps Release Notes Generator can be found at `https://docs.microsoft.com/en-us/samples/azure-samples/azure-devops-release-notes/azure-devops-release-notes-generator/.`
- Some Microsoft hands-on labs for practicing the topics we covered in this chapter can be found at `https://docs.microsoft.com/en-us/learn/modules/create-multi-stage-pipeline/index`, `https://docs.microsoft.com/en-us/learn/modules/create-release-pipeline/index` and `https://docs.microsoft.com/en-us/learn/modules/manage-release-cadence/index.`

Section 2: Expanding your DevOps Pipeline

In part one of this book, you learned about the techniques and technologies that you can use for setting up a structured, automated delivery of your applications to your users. Using Agile work item management, source control, and continuous integration and deployment, you are now able to continuously deploy new versions of your software. With this set up, it is time to expand on that pipeline and incorporate more DevOps practices and techniques. This is what part two is about: expanding your DevOps pipelines.

This section comprises the following chapters:

- Chapter 5, *Dependency Management*
- Chapter 6, *Infrastructure and Configuration as Code*
- Chapter 7, *Dealing with Databases in DevOps Scenarios*
- Chapter 8, *Continuous Testing*
- Chapter 9, *Security and Compliance*

5
Dependency Management

In part one of this book, you learned how to continuously deploy your application. While doing so, one of the main issues you might run into is that the total time it takes to build your application is too long. Due to this, developers have to wait a long time for feedback on their changes. One way of coping with this is by splitting your solutions up into multiple builds.

One approach to this is by introducing package management. Often, you will find that you want to reuse code from a previous project in a new project. Instead of copying and pasting this code from one project to another, you can create a shared library out of it. In this chapter, you will learn how to identify shared components and how to make them reusable using Azure Artifacts. In addition to this, you will learn how you can use Azure Artifacts for storing pipeline artifacts when working in a heterogeneous architecture. Here, you will also work with other CI/CD tools than just Azure DevOps. For this, you will learn how to use Azure Artifacts for universal packages.

The following topics will be covered in this chapter:

- Identifying shared components
- Creating a feed
- Publishing packages
- Consuming packages
- Working with universal packages
- Exploring other tools

Technical requirements

To experiment with the topics mentioned in this chapter, only an Azure DevOps organization is required.

Identifying shared components

Adopting DevOps practices, such as continuous integration/continuous delivery, can greatly reduce the amount of time you have to spend on building and testing your applications. Besides building your applications, there are also many other concerns that you can address in your pipelines.

When you start adding more and more tasks to your pipelines, you might run into a situation in which a single execution of your pipeline starts taking too long, sometimes longer than 5 minutes. Note that this a general recommendation for the maximum duration of a CI pipeline. In order to battle this, you might be interested in splitting your solution up into smaller builds and maybe even repositories. To do this, you could build parts of that application in isolation and then use the results of these builds in your main application as ready-built components.

 A general recommendation for the maximum duration of a CI pipeline is 5 minutes.

Another reason for wanting to split your solution into parts is the use of shared projects. Imagine that you have two solutions that work closely together: one being a REST API and the other being a client package that you ship to your customers to work with that API. It is likely that these two solutions share at least one project with all the objects that are used for modeling the data that is sent back and forth between the two. Here, you could make a third solution with only the shared project, which you could then use as a package in your other solutions.

Or what if you work at a team that is responsible for maintaining a whole series of solutions and you find that you have complete namespaces that are copied and pasted between these solutions. It is not a desirable situation and one that probably comes with a lot of issues. What if you could write this code just once, build it, package it, and then reuse it in all of these solutions.

To summarize, three reasons for starting to work with packages and artifact feeds are as follows:

- Reducing build and CI times by splitting a larger solution into parts
- Extracting shared components into packages
- Building packages that are used by other teams

In the remainder of this chapter, you will learn techniques for doing this by building packages out of (parts of) your application code, hosting them in a centralized location, and reusing them in one or more other solutions.

In all three scenarios, you might be looking to increase the reusability of the code, but also to reduce the time taken between checking for a change and receiving feedback for that change in the form of automated test results. Before you start breaking up your application, remember that moving part of your solution to a separate component does not always achieve this.

If you break your application up into three components and one remaining main part, make sure that you can build and test these three components completely in isolation, or at least close to 100%. If you cannot test a component of your application in isolation, creating a separate repository and build for that component will actually increase the time between checking for a change and the moment of feedback to you as a developer. Both separate builds might run quicker, but now you need to wait for two builds before you receive any feedback.

> If you break your application up into separate components, make sure that each component can be built and tested in isolation to a high degree.

As well as this, you have to make sure that making a reusable component out of part of your application makes sense from a conceptual point of view. For example, components that are addressing a cross-cutting concern such as logging libraries or database abstraction layers are great candidates for factoring out to shared libraries. (On a side note, after you have done so, you might also want to consider replacing your own general-purpose libraries with off-the-shelf alternatives where possible.)

However, if splitting your solution into components makes sense, it can bring great benefits.

Types of feeds

There are many types of package feeds that can be hosted in Azure Artifacts. How you will use an Artifact feed will depend on the language and ecosystem used by the application. The following ecosystems are supported in Azure Artifacts:

- **NuGet**: When working with Microsoft .NET languages, the protocol used for package management is NuGet.
- **npm**: The npm protocol is used when building applications with JavaScript or TypeScript.
- **Maven or Gradle**: Maven and Gradle are used from the Java ecosystem.
- **Pip and Twine**: When working with Python packages, they can be obtained using these protocols.
- **Universal packages**: Universal packages are not associated with a specific ecosystem, but are a generic means for uploading and retrieving packages.

Whenever a new feed is created, no type needs to be specified. In fact, every feed can be accessed using any protocol, even with different protocols over time. However, in general, this does not make sense.

Creating a feed

Once you have identified one or more packages that you want to publish, you will need a place to store them. For this, you can use the Azure Artifacts offering. The following diagram shows the structural makeup of Azure Artifacts:

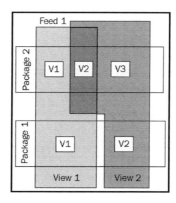

Within Azure Artifacts, you can create one or more feeds where you can store your packages. For each package, you can have multiple versions in a feed. The feed is the level on which you can set up authorizations for publishing packages. Within a feed, you can create one or more views that you can use for setting up authorizations for consuming packages. A specific version of any given package can be in more than one view at the same time. The following sections discuss all these concepts in more detail.

Setting up a feed

Within Azure Artifacts, the feed is the location where your packages are stored. Each feed is a separate and fully isolated repository. To create a new feed, follow these steps:

1. First, navigate to Azure Artifacts in the menu on the left and then click on the **Create feed** button (partially visible to access the view for creating a new feed):

2. Specify a name for the feed. It should not contain any spaces and preferably contain only letters and numbers, since it will become part of a URL.
3. Next, it is possible to specify the initial settings for visibility. This determines which users can view the feed. This will be discussed in more detail later.

4. Configure the use of upstream sources. This will also be covered in more detail later.

5. A few seconds after selecting **Create**, your feed will be available.

Once the feed is created, you can configure various settings such as hiding deleted packages, enabling package batches, and configuring retention policies. To learn how to do this, follow these steps:

1. After the feed is created, access the settings for the feed by clicking on the gearbox in the top-right corner.

2. Choose **Feed settings** in the view shown in the following screenshot. In this view, you can configure a few more things:

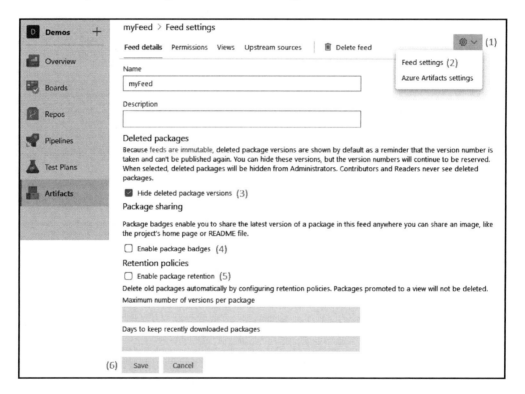

3. Besides changing the name and adding a description, you can choose to hide deleted packages. When you do this, versions of a package that have been removed are no longer visible to administrators of the feed. Regular users are never able to view or use deleted packages, but this setting enables the same view logic as administrators.

4. Another setting you can enable is that of package badges. A package badge is a visual element with the name of a package and the latest available version. If you enable this option, you can retrieve a URL for each package that will be a package badge for that package. This is useful for people who want to keep tabs on the latest version of a package.

5. Finally, you can configure a retention policy. Here, you can configure the automated removal when the number of versions of a package exceeds a certain threshold. While this helps you to save disk space and therefore costs, this can have the unintended effect of breaking downstream users of the feed. To put in a safeguard against this, you can prevent removing a package for x number of days after it has been downloaded for the last time. Next to that, keep in mind that any package version that is currently a member of a feed will not be removed.

6. Once done, click on the **Save** button.

After you have created and configured your feed, it is time to specify which users have access to the feed and what permissions they have. Let's learn how to do that next.

Securing access

There are four roles you can assign to a user or group, where the rights of each next role include the rights of the previous roles as well:

- **Readers** are able to list all packages in a feed and can download them.
- **Collaborators** are also able to use packages from upstream sources.
- **Contributors** can also publish their own packages and unlist and deprecate packages.
- Finally, **owners** have full control over the feed and can also change permissions, rename, or delete the feed.

To change the permission of a user, follow these steps:

1. Navigate to the **Permissions** view that you can see in the following screenshot. In this view, you can see a list of every user or group that has permissions assigned:

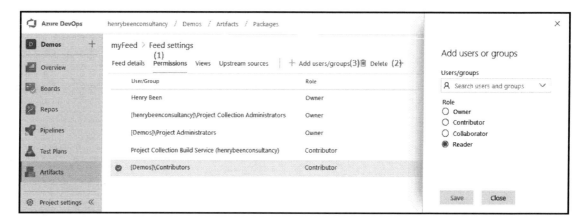

2. To remove permissions, select the row and click on **Delete**.
3. To add a new row, click on the add button. This will open the view you see to the right.

As an alternative to adding users or groups as a reader on the whole feed, it is also possible to create one or more views on the feed and set access rights per view.

Managing views on a feed

A feed is a repository of packages that you can publish and download packages to and from. However, there are many cases where you do not want every uploaded package to be available for download. Often, you might find that you want to control who can use which versions of a package; for example, when you are implementing the continuous delivery of a shared library but want to share only stable versions with the rest of your organization.

To do this, you can create views. A view is a subset of the package versions within a feed. When working with a view, as a consumer, it behaves just as if it were a feed.

Views can be managed as follows:

1. Navigate and click on **Views**; you should see something similar to the following screenshot:

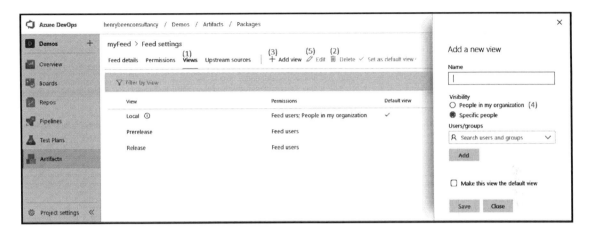

2. Here, you can see a list of all the current views and remove any views by selecting the row and clicking on **Delete**.

3. Adding new views can be done using the add button, which opens the view you see to the right.

4. You can set permissions for reading from a view here as well. You can allow read access to your whole Azure DevOps organization, or specify specific users. Any user or group you add here will get reader permissions on this view only.

5. Editing permissions can be done by selecting any row and choosing **Edit**.

Once one or more views are available, packages can be promoted to a view for consumption through the view.

Configuring upstream sources

The final thing that you can configure on your feed is the upstream sources. Azure Artifacts feeds give you a repository where you can publish your own packages for reuse from one or more locations.

However, you will probably also use packages that are publicly available on repositories such as `NuGet.org` or `npmjs.org`. In this case, you could use a combination of an Artifacts feed and `NuGet.org`, but you can also configure your feed to serve packages from `NuGet.org` as well. If you do this, `NuGet.org` is called an upstream source.

Along with simplicity, this gives you the added benefit of having one central location where you can see all the packages you are using in your solution(s). This enables you to quickly check which packages and versions you are using, which can be useful for compliance or security checks. Using the different permissions between the reader and the collaborator role, you can also configure which users are authorized to pull packages from `NuGet.org` to your feed, and which users are not.

Of course, you can do this for any repository that is accessible over the internet and implements one of the protocols that Azure Artifacts supports. To configure upstream sources, follow these steps:

1. Upstream sources can be configured after navigating to the following screen:

2. Upstream sources are configured in the same way as permissions and views. You can delete upstream sources using the **Delete** button in the menu bar.
3. Adding upstream sources is done by clicking on the **Add upstream source** button, which opens the view on the right.

 A final thing to note about the use of upstream sources is that it is not possible to have the same version of a package published to your own feed if the same version of that package is already available in an upstream source.

This section discussed how to create and connect feeds. Now that these are in place, we will learn how to publish packages to those feeds in the next section.

Publishing packages

Now that you know how to create and manage feeds, it is time to learn how to publish packages to them. If you have experience of publishing packages to public feeds, you will see that publishing to Azure Artifacts works in precisely the same way. There are two ways in which you can publish packages to a feed:

- Manually from your own computer
- By using Azure Pipelines

Both options are explored in the following sections.

Uploading packages by hand

To upload packages by hand, the following steps need to be performed:

1. First, you will have to retrieve the URL to your feed. To do this, click on **Connect to feed** for any of your feeds, as shown in the following screenshot:

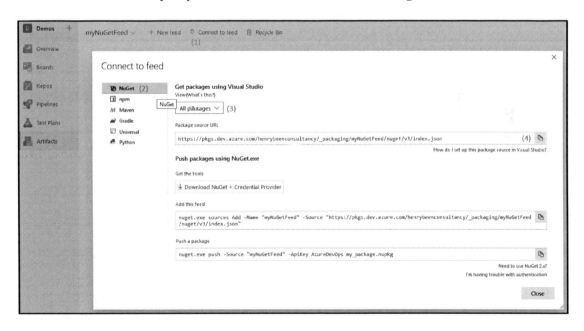

2. In the list on the left, select the protocol to use for accessing the feed.
3. Select the correct view to use. Remember that for publishing packages, the full feed URL needs to be used since views are read-only.

4. After making the correct selections, copy the correct URL to the clipboard using the **copy** button.

5. Execute the following command to create a NuGet package from a regular `.csproj` file. If you do not have the `NuGet.exe` tool already available, you can download it using the link provided at the end of this chapter:

```
nuget.exe pack DemoSolution\MyPackage.csproj -Version 1.1.0
```

6. Execute the final command for uploading the package to NuGet:

```
nuget.exe push
    -Source "{feedUrl}" "MyPackage.1.1.0.nupkg"
```

After executing the final command, the package will be published and become available in your feed.

Publishing packages from a pipeline

Uploading a package by hand is not a convenient solution if you need to do it more than once. In cases where you want to frequently generate and publish a new version of a library, you can use an Azure pipeline. As well as to the automation that this gives you, it is also a great way to introduce repeatability and reliability, since you can now use all of the benefits that pipelines offer you.

As an example, you can find a possible build definition for creating an `npm` package and publishing that as follows. The sources for this build are from an open source Microsoft GitHub repository called `tfs-cli`.

In this pipeline, there are three usages of the built-in `npm` task:

- The first occurrence is an `npm install` command. This command is used for installing the dependencies for this package:

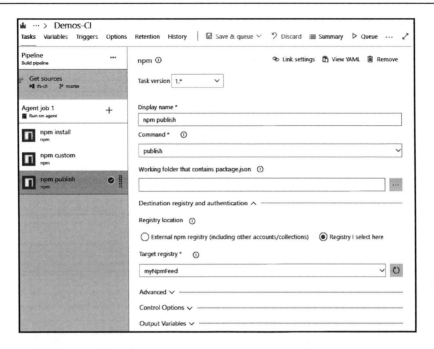

- The second occurrence is running a custom command, `build`. This command is defined in the source code itself using `package.json` and is used for transpiling the sources from TypeScript to JavaScript:

- The final and third task is running the `npm publish` command to publish the generated package to an `npm` feed. In this instance, there is no external feed selected but a built-in target registry: the Azure Artifacts feed:

After running this build, your package is available in your feed.

Versioning packages

One of the things that is not done automatically using the tasks for uploading an `npm` package, or most types of packages for that matter, is managing the version number. Of course, there are many ways in which you can make sure your packages have proper versions, but a common approach is setting (part of) the version number during the build of a package.

Expanding on the `npm` package build that we demonstrated before, three changes can be made to the build definition:

1. First, the build number format for the build definition is updated to the following: `1.0$(Rev:.rrr)`. This guarantees that a unique number is automatically generated for every build. The `Ref:.rrr` variable will generate a number with three positions, leading with zeros if needed. The first time, this number will be `000`, and it will increase by one every time the rest of the build number is not changed.

2. Second, a task is added to replace the version number that is currently specified in the source control, using the `{#Build.BuildNumber#}` token. This is a reference to the build variable with the name `Build.BuildNumber`, which contains the build number that was specified in *step 1*.

3. Finally, a **Replace Tokens** task is added to the build before all other tasks. A possible configuration to replace the magic fixed-version number with the automatic version number for this task is shown as follows:

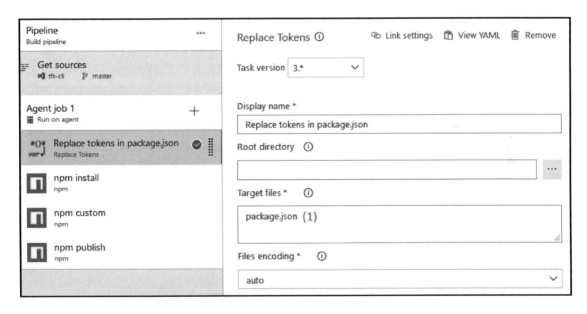

This task can be configured to replace the tokens in one or more target files (1). It will look for any series of characters starting with `{#` and ending in `#}`, take the text between these two markers, and then replace the whole text with the value of the corresponding variable.

With this in place, every package that is built using the definition will have a unique and ever-increasing patch version number. Whenever the major or minor version number needs to be updated, this can be done by updating the build number format.

As an alternative to this approach, there are many tasks available from the extensions marketplace that can help with versioning, including more complex scenarios.

This section discussed how to publish packages to a feed. With packages published to a feed, the next section will detail how these can be used with either Visual Studio or an Azure Pipeline.

Consuming packages

Uploading packages to an Azure Artifacts feed or repository makes them available for use in many different scenarios. Two common scenarios are using your own packages with Visual Studio or from Azure Pipelines. Both scenarios will be detailed in the following sections.

Consuming packages from Visual Studio

Once you have your shared libraries available as NuGet packages in an Azure Artifacts feed, you can start using them from Visual Studio. Before you can do this, you will have to register your feed in your Visual Studio instance.

To do this, you first have to grab the URL of your feed. In order to do this, refer to the *Uploading packages by hand* section. Once you have your URL ready, go to manage NuGet files for your solution, as you would do normally. If you are not familiar with working with NuGet packages in Visual Studio, you can find this option in the solution explorer on the solution and project headers:

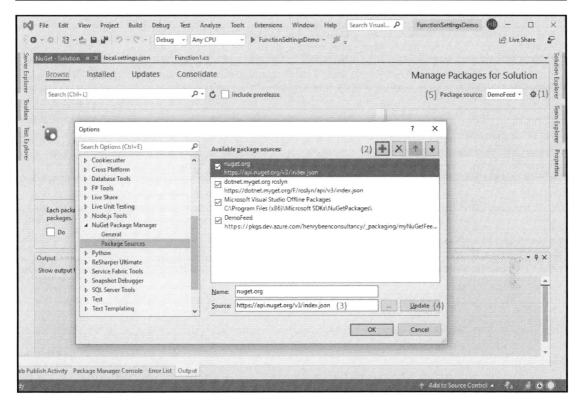

Once you are here, walk through the following steps:

1. Click on the small gearbox in the top-right corner to open the dialog where you can configure which NuGet feeds to use.
2. Add a new feed.
3. Fill in both the name and the source of your own feed.
4. After doing so, do not forget to click on **Update**; otherwise, your changes to the **Name** and **Source** fields will not be saved and there will be no warning prompting you that you have unsaved changes.
5. After you have made these changes, you can now select your feed as the package source in the top right of the screen.

From here onward, it is possible to work with these packages from your own feed just as you do with packages from NuGet.org.

Consuming packages from a pipeline

Once you start using your packages in Visual Studio, it is very likely you will need them in Azure Pipelines as well. This is in order to perform CI/CD on the dependent application that uses your packages.

Fortunately, this can be achieved with a small configuration change on your NuGet restore task, as shown in the following screenshot. The following screenshot relates to the NuGet restore task that can be used with both the Visual Studio build tasks and the .Net Core build tasks. Both contain the same interface and can be used in the same way:

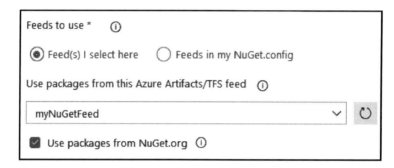

By default, only the radio button for using packages from NuGet is checked; so, to include packages from your own feeds as well, you need to select the correct feed in the drop-down list.

If you ever find the need to include packages from more than one feed, you will be forced to create one aggregator feed and use the other feeds as upstream sources for that aggregator feed.

This section covered how to consume component packages from Visual Studio. The next section will dive into working with universal packages for sharing general binary packages.

Working with universal packages

The previous sections have all concentered on using Azure Artifacts as a means for redistributing application packages such as libraries or other shared components. However, there is also another important use of Azure Artifacts, which is using a feed for storing any type of binary package. These are called universal packages.

Since a universal packages feed can be used to store any type of package, this makes it a good choice for storing build artifacts if you are working with more than one CI/CD tool. In this case, you can use universal packages for storing and serving your build artifacts to and from whichever tool you are using at that time. This can be particularly useful since the built-in storage for classic build and release pipelines cannot be accessed by other tools.

To use universal packages for staging your build artifacts in such a heterogeneous architecture, there are four basic operations you should understand: uploading and downloading universal packages from an Azure pipeline and uploading and downloading universal packages using the Azure CLI. The last one you can invoke from other tools.

Uploading and downloading universal packages from Azure Pipelines

Uploading build artifacts to a universal packages feed works in a similar way as uploading a regular build artifact. There are two changes you need to consider.

Firstly, you have to use another task for performing the upload. Instead of using the *publish build artifact* or *publish pipeline artifact* tasks, you have to use the task named **Universal Packages**. When using this task, you can still give a name to the artifact and specify a location on the filesystem of the build agent to upload it from. Next, you can specify a target feed and a version to use. This version can be either automatically incremented whenever a new package is uploaded or be specified using a build variable.

Secondly, you have to consider the fact that the uploaded package is not associated one-to-one with the build that produced it—as it is with regular build or pipeline artifacts. This means that no matter where you are using the package that has been uploaded, you have to find another way to find the correct version to download.

To perform the actual download, you can use the **Universal Packages** task again, as shown in the following screenshot:

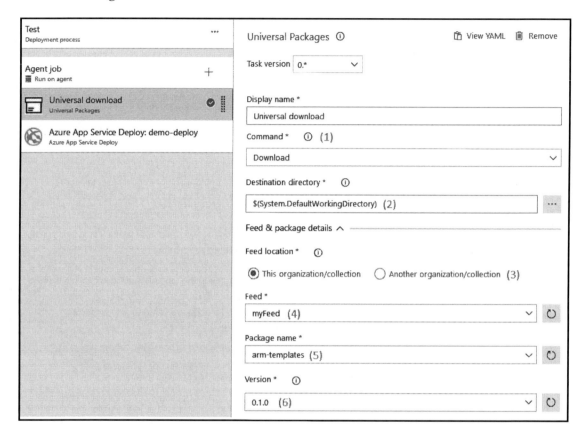

Refer to the screenshot and follow these steps:

1. After adding the task, you can toggle it between upload and download.
2. You can also specify a directory that is uploaded as the artifact.
3. Or you can specify where the artifact should be downloaded.
4. Furthermore, the name of the feed needs to be specified.
5. Also, specify the name of the package.
6. Specify the version to be either upload or download.

Note that you can also use feeds that are not part of your own organization by choosing to use another feed at step **5**. If you do so, you need to create a service endpoint for reaching that feed.

Uploading and downloading universal packages using the Azure CLI

When you want to work with universal packages from a product other than Azure Pipelines, you will have to use the Azure CLI. To do this, perform the following steps:

1. The first thing you have to do to work with universal packages using the Azure CLI is to install the CLI itself. The link to the CLI can be found at the end of this chapter.

2. Next, it is time to install the extension for Azure DevOps. This can be done using the following command:

```
az extension add –name azure-devops
```

3. After making the extension for Azure DevOps available, you have to log in using the account that you also use to work within the Azure DevOps UI. You can log in by giving the following command:

```
az login
```

4. Once logged in, you can upload a file as an artifact using the following command:

```
az artifacts universal publish
    --feed {yourFeedName}
    --name {yourPackageName}
    --version {yourVersion}
    --organization https://dev.azure.com/{yourOrganizationName}
    --path {sourceFileName}
```

5. To download a particular version of an artifact again, you can use the following:

```
az artifacts universal download
    --feed {yourFeedName}
    --name {yourPackageName}
  --version {yourVersion}
    --organization https://dev.azure.com/{yourOrganizationName}
    --path {targetFileName}
```

Using the CLI and these commands, you can use Azure Artifacts as a means for sharing build artifacts between multiple tools. When working with a number of tools on the same project, Universal Packages are a great tool for moving binaries around.

In the next section, other tools available for package management will be explored.

Exploring other tools

There are many other tools available for doing binary management. Three commonly used products are MyGet, Artifactory, and **Azure Container Registry** (**ACR**). The features they deliver do overlap, but they also have specific points at which they excel.

MyGet

MyGet is an alternative location for hosting your NuGet packages. MyGet allows you to create both public and private feeds that are managed by you. MyGet also supports defining upstream sources and delivers built-in dependency scanning to give you continuous feedback on the level of security of your dependencies.

Since MyGet is an implementation of the NuGet protocol, you can publish and use packages using the default NuGet tasks from Azure Pipelines.

Artifactory

Artifactory, a product by JFrog, is another tool that you can use for hosting your package feeds. Artifactory is originally an on-premises product, but it is now also available as a SaaS offering. Just like Azure Artifacts, it supports multiple protocols for interacting with package feeds. At the time of writing, Artifactory supports more repository protocols than Azure Artifacts. Examples of this include PHP Composer and **Red Hat Package Manager** (**RPM**).

JFrog has published an Azure Pipelines extension for downloading and uploading packages.

Azure Container Registry

Another type of storage for reusable packages is ACR. ACR is designed specifically for container images and has an understanding of the layered buildup of these images. This allows it to receive only partial uploads when a new version of an image becomes available if not all of the layers have changed. This makes ACR a very good location for storing container images. Uploads will be faster and ACR storage is cheaper than Azure Artifacts storage. This is a big benefit since container images can be large.

You can integrate with ACR from Azure Pipelines using the Docker integration extensions.

Summary

In this chapter, you learned how to identify shared components in your solutions: pieces of code that appear not only in multiple locations but are also logical units for reuse. You learned how to use Azure Artifacts feeds for hosting packages that contain these libraries. Furthermore, you learned how to use these hosted packages to build dependent solutions using both Visual Studio and Azure Pipelines. You also learned about using universal packages to share build artifacts between Azure Pipelines and other tools that you might use for CI/CD.

With this knowledge, you will now be able to identify shared components in your solution(s). Once you have identified such a component, you will also be able to isolate it in source control, build it, and publish it to an artifact feed. From here, you can distribute it to one or more consuming solutions. Finally, you are now also capable of using Artifact feeds for sharing build artifacts between different CI/CD products.

In the next chapter, you will learn about infrastructure and configuration as code. This is one of the fundamental DevOps practices that allows you to have your infrastructure definition in source control and use that as part of your release pipeline.

Questions

As we conclude, here is a list of questions for you to test your knowledge regarding this chapter's material. You will find the answers in the *Assessments* section of the Appendix:

1. True or false: Any version of a package can be deployed to only one view within a feed.
2. True or false: Pipeline artifacts can be used for sharing build outcomes (packages) from Azure DevOps to other products.
3. True or false: Azure Artifact feeds with universal packages can be used for sharing build outcomes (packages) from Azure DevOps to other products.

4. Which of the following is needed to enable building a solution that uses packages from an Azure Artifacts feed in Visual Studio? (You can select more than one option.)

      1. Adding the full package URL to your project dependencies, instead of only the package name

      2. Having at least *reader* access to the feed or one of the views in the feed

      3. Having at least *consumer* access to the feed

      4. Configuring the location of the feed as a package source for Visual Studio

5. What can be the motivators for splitting a solution into multiple parts that are separated by Azure Artifacts feeds?

Further reading

- Exercises for practicing with Azure DevOps Artifacts can be found at `https://docs.microsoft.com/en-us/learn/modules/manage-build-dependencies/`.
- You can find and download `NuGet.exe` from `https://www.nuget.org/downloads`.
- Information on downloading and installing the Azure CLI can be found at `https://docs.microsoft.com/en-us/cli/azure/install-azure-cli?view=azure-cli-latest`.
- More information about MyGet is available at `https://www.myget.org/`.
- More information about JFrog Artifactory is available at `https://jfrog.com/artifactory/`, and the extension for Azure Pipelines can be found at `https://marketplace.visualstudio.com/items?itemName=JFrog.jfrog-artifactory-vsts-extension`.
- More information about ACR is available at `https://azure.microsoft.com/en-in/services/container-registry/`.
- You can find the Docker extensions for Azure Pipelines at `https://marketplace.visualstudio.com/items?itemName=ms-vscs-rm.docker`.

6
Infrastructure and Configuration as Code

In the previous chapter, the focus was on storing and building application code and releasing the created binaries. You learned how to create a pipeline, from source control to a target environment for the automated, repeatable deployment of your applications.

In this chapter, you will learn how to apply the same principles to the infrastructure that your application runs on and the runtime configuration of your application. Doing so will help you to further increase the speed at which changes can be delivered to production, increasing the flow of value to your end users.

This chapter will start off by explaining the value of having everything, infrastructure and configuration included, as code. Next, it continues by explaining ARM templates. The syntax will be explained, as well as how to deploy ARM templates. Then, it proceeds to explain the Azure Automation offering, available in the Azure Cloud. Azure Automation can be used for running scripts on a schedule or for loading and applying PowerShell DSC modules. Next up is managing application settings for PaaS offerings, such as Azure App Service. Finally, it concludes by discussing several other tools that have similar capabilities.

The following topics will be covered in this chapter:

- Having everything as code
- Working with ARM templates
- Deploying ARM templates
- Reverse engineering a template
- Using Azure Automation
- Managing application settings
- Other tools

Technical requirements

To experiment with one or more of the technologies described in this chapter, one or more of the following may be required:

- An Azure subscription, for executing ARM templates and running Azure Automation
- PowerShell with the Azure PowerShell modules, for executing ARM templates, available from `https://docs.microsoft.com/en-us/powershell/azure/install-az-ps`
- The Azure CLI, for executing ARM templates, available from `https://docs.microsoft.com/en-us/powershell/azure/install-az-ps`
- One or more virtual machines for experimenting with the different tools discussed in this chapter

Having everything as code

If you have been responsible for creating and maintaining application infrastructure and configuration in the past, you have most likely experienced what is called **configuration drift**. Configuration drift is the name for the phenomenon where the configuration between servers in acceptance and the production environment differs. Or, even worse, when having multiple servers in the production environment, it might be the case that the configuration of these is not always the same.

The most common cause of configuration drift is manual change. When making changes manually, maybe under the pressure of a production issue, there is always the risk that you apply different settings to different servers or hosts. And if you ever need to scale out and add another server to your production environment, the chance of that server taking on the same configuration of all already existing servers is very slim.

With **Infrastructure as Code (IaC)** and **Configuration as Code (CaC)**, you no longer make changes to application configuration and infrastructure by hand, but only through automation. The first step to do this is specifying the desired state of configuration and infrastructure. The desired state is then fed into configuration management tooling that enforces this configuration on your infrastructure. Specifying only the desired state is called a *declarative* approach, which differs from an *imperative* approach, where you specify all of the steps that need to be taken.

These tools are often also capable of checking the current state of your infrastructure and configuration on a regular interval and reapplying your desired state if any deviation is detected. This is possible due to the declarative approach. This makes applying configuration an idempotent operation. An operation is idempotent if it can be repeated one or more times, while the outcome will remain the same.

When adopting IaC and CaC, you can even go so far as to recreate the complete infrastructure before deploying an application, deploy the application on that new infrastructure, and then disregard the old infrastructure after switching to the new deployment. This is an extreme form of immutable servers. The added benefit of this approach is that you are now guaranteed that there will be no traces from any configuration or binaries from the previous deployment.

In the following sections, you will learn about different IaC technologies and how to use them. It is important to understand that they are complementary and are often used together. For example, ARM templates can be used to create virtual machines in Azure and, once that is done, PowerShell DSC or Ansible can be used to configure those virtual machines.

Working with ARM templates

When working on the Azure platform, infrastructure is described using **Azure Resource Manager (ARM)** templates. ARM templates are written in JSON and a skeleton template looks as follows:

```
{
  "$schema":
"https://schema.management.azure.com/schemas/2015-01-01/deploymentTemplate.
json#",
  "contentVersion": "1.0.0.0",
  "parameters": {
  },
  "variables": {
  },
  "resources": [
  ],
  "outputs": {
  }
}
```

The template itself is, at the highest level, a JSON object. There is a mandatory property, $schema, for which the shown value is also mandatory. The contentVersion property is also mandatory and can be specified to version the contents. This version can be used by the author to version the template if necessary.

The rest of this chapter will discuss the different parts that make up ARM templates in more detail. There is also an online reference available, to which a link is added at the end of this chapter. A link to the formal, detailed breakdown of the structure and syntax of ARM templates is also added at the end of this chapter.

Parameters

Every template has to start with a parameters section. This section takes the shape of a JSON object, which can be empty but cannot be left out. The use of this section is to declare one or more parameters that can be specified by the caller of the ARM template, before deploying it. A common reason for using the parameters section is to use the same template for both the test and production environment, but varying the names of resources between the two. An example parameters section might look like this:

```
{
   "appServiceName": {
     "type": "string",
     "metadata": {
       "description": "a free to choose text"
     }
   }
}
```

For every parameter, a new key is specified with the parameter's name. The value is an object. This object has one mandatory key, type. The allowed values for type are string, int, bool, object, array, secureString, and secureObject. The secureString and secureObject variations can be used to make sure that the runtime values of these parameters are scrubbed from any log and output. They are intended to hold passwords, keys, or other secrets.

The metadata object, with the description key, is optional and can be used to add a description to the parameter for future reference.

Other properties that can be specified on a parameter object are the following:

- `minValue` and `maxValue` for specifying bounds on an integer value
- `minLength` and `maxLength` for specifying bounds on the length of a string value
- `defaultValue` for specifying a default value that will be used if no value is specified when applying the template
- `allowedValues` for specifying an array of allowed values, limiting valid inputs

Next, let's understand what parameter files are.

Parameter files

One way for specifying the parameter values when deploying a template is through a variable file. Often, a single template is accompanied by more than one parameter file, for example, one for test and one for production. The JSON for a parameter file appears as follows:

```
{
  "$schema":
"https://schema.management.azure.com/schemas/2015-01-01/deploymentParameter
s.json#",
  "contentVersion": "1.0.0.0",
  "parameters": {
    "exampleParameter": {
      "value": "exampleValue"
    }
  }
}
```

Just like an ARM template, every parameter file is a JSON object with mandatory `$schema` and `contentVersion` properties. The third property parameter is used to specify one or more parameter values. For each parameter, specify its name as the key and an object as the value. This object can hold the `value` key for providing the actual value of the parameter.

While very valuable for specifying names for resources, scaling options, and other things that have to vary between environments, this solution is not useful for secrets. Keys, passwords, and other secrets should not be stored as plaintext in source control in a parameter file. For secrets, another notation is available:

```
{
  "$schema":
"https://schema.management.azure.com/schemas/2015-01-01/deploymentParameter
s.json#",
  "contentVersion": "1.0.0.0",
```

```
    "parameters": {
      "exampleParameter": {
        "reference": {
          "keyvault": {
            "id": "/subscriptions/.../Microsoft.KeyVault/vaults/<vaultname>"
          },
          "secretName": "myKeyVaultSecret"
        }
      }
    }
  }
```

With this notation, instead of specifying the value directly, there is a pointer to a location in an Azure key vault where the correct value is stored. When deploying the template, this secret is (within Azure!) taken from the key vault and used in deployment. This is allowed only if the user or service starting the deployment has either an owner or contributor role in relation to the key vault and the key vault is enabled for template deployment.

 Strictly speaking, any role that includes the `Microsoft.KeyVault/vaults/deploy/action` permission will work. By default, these are the owner and contributor roles, but you can create custom roles that include this action as well.

Variables

The variables section is used to specify one or more values that will be used throughout the template. A common approach is building the names of all resources in the variables section, based on a single parameter called `environmentName`. This ensures that resources will have the same name between environments. Variables are also used to specify values that cannot be specified from outside the template, but should be recognized as configurable. An example might look like this:

```
{
  "appServicePlanType": "B1",
  "appServiceName": "[concat('myAppService-',
parameters('environmentName'))]"
}
```

Please note that the example for `appServiceName` contains functions that are discussed in detail in a later section called *Functions*.

Resources

The third section in any ARM template is the resources section. This is the main part of the template, where all of the resources to be created are specified. This section is the only one that is not an object, but an array. Within that array, one or more objects of the following form are specified:

```
{
    "type": "Microsoft.Sql/servers",
    "apiVersion": "2015-05-01-preview",
    "name": "mySqlServer",
    "location": "West Europe",
    "properties": {
        "administratorLogin": "myUsername",
        "administratorLoginPassword": "myPassword",
        "version": "12.0"
    }
}
```

Each resource is specified in the form of an object. The first four properties are mandatory for every type of resource:

- The type of the resource to be created or updated needs to be specified: This takes the form of the name of `resourceprovider` followed by a slash and the name of a resource type that belongs to that `resourceprovider`.
- The version of the API to use for this resource: A list of supported API versions can be retrieved from the reference.
- The name for the resource: Every resource type has its own rules for determining what a valid name is. These can also be found in the reference.
- The Azure Region where the resource is to be created: This must be a valid Azure Region.

All other properties on the object vary from resource type to resource type and are all specified in the resource.

Dependent resources

A special type of resource is the dependent resource. For example, SQL databases are hosted on a SQL Server and Service Bus Topics are located within a Service Bus namespace. For a nested resource type, the type and name reflect this nesting:

```
{
    "apiVersion": "2017-04-01",
```

```
    "name": "myNamespaceName/myTopicName",
    "type": "Microsoft.ServiceBus/namespaces/topics",
    "dependsOn": [
        "Microsoft.ServiceBus/namespaces/myNamespaceName"
    ]
}
```

Next to nesting the type and the name, the extra property, dependsOn, is also mandatory to specify that this nested resource can only be created after the containing resource exists. A location property is not necessary since this will be inherited from the containing resource.

Nested templates

A second special type of resource is template deployment. This way, one template can trigger the deployment of another. An example of defining a template deployment as a resource in a template looks as follows:

```
{
    "type": "Microsoft.Resources/deployments",
    "apiVersion": "2018-05-01",
    "name": "linkedTemplate",
    "properties": {
        "mode": "Incremental",
        "templateLink": {
            "uri":"https://.../myLinkedTemplate.json"
        },
        "parametersLink": {
            "uri":"https://.../myParameters.json"
        }
    }
}
```

The locations of the template and parameter file can be specified using both HTTP and HTTPS, but have to be publicly accessible locations. As an alternative, a single property template can be specified. This should then contain a whole template as a JSON object.

Outputs

The fourth and final section of a template is the outputs section. Here are the keys returned to the caller of the template. The caller can use these values to start another task or script and use one or more of the values created or used by the template.

The main use for this is to prevent hardcoding names in downstream automation. The outputs section is a JSON object of the following format:

```
{
    "outputName":
    {
        "type": "string",
        "value": "myValue"
    }
}
```

When specifying outputs, the same types can be used as for parameters. Of course, it does not make much sense hardcoding the values, so functions are used to retrieve values from parameters, variables, or even created resources.

Functions

Functions are used to allow for dynamic evaluation of properties in ARM templates. Calling functions uses a notation very similar to that of many programming languages: `functionName(arg1, arg2, ...)` functions can return either a value such as `string` or `int` or an object or array. When an object is returned, any property can be accessed using the `.propertyName` notation. Accessing elements in an array can be done using `[position]`. To indicate which parts of a string should be evaluated as a function, they can be enclosed in brackets:

```
"myVariable": "[concat('myAppService-', parameters('environmentName'))]"
```

The preceding example shows two example functions. First, the `concat` function is called to concatenate two string values. One is hardcoded and the other one is the result of a second function call to retrieve the value of a template parameter.

There are a fair number of functions available. They can be used for string manipulation, for retrieving details about the current subscription, resource group, or Azure Active Directory tenant, or for getting resource details.

Functions can also be used to retrieve account keys or other secrets. This is often done to automatically insert keys directly from the service that exposes the key to application settings or a key vault. This completely eliminates the need for the manual transfer of secrets.

Well, so far, we have learned the different parts that make up an ARM template, which you should be able to write on your own. Now it's time to learn how we can actually deploy them with the help of various tools.

Deploying ARM templates

Once an ARM template and its accompanying parameter files are written, they can be applied to an Azure environment. There are PowerShell Cmdlet and Azure CLI commands available for applying an ARM template from a scripting environment. When ARM templates are used for the infrastructure of an application, Azure Pipelines can be used for deploying not only code but also ARM templates.

No matter which approach is used for deployment, all of them will have a *deployment mode*. This can be either *incremental* or *complete*. In incremental mode, all resources specified in the template will be created in Azure or their properties will be updated if the resource already exists. In complete mode, all resources that are not specified in the template and already exist in Azure will also be removed. The default deployment mode is incremental.

In the next sections, several tools for executing deployments are discussed, starting with PowerShell.

PowerShell

For local development and testing of ARM templates on a local machine, Powershell has a quick command to apply an ARM template to a resource group:

```
New-AzResourceGroupDeployment -ResourceGroupName myResourceGroup -
TemplateFile "c:\my\template.json" ` -TemplateParameterFile
"c:\my\parameters.json"
```

The preceding command will pick up the specified template and parameter file and apply it to the specified resource group. This command assumes that the current session has already been logged in to Azure.

There are a few variations on the command available:

- A parameter called `-Mode` with a `Complete` or `Incremental` value is available. This can be used to specify `deploymentmode`.
- If no parameter file is specified and the template requires parameters, the cmdlet will prompt for these values on the command line.
- As an alternative, the `-TemplateUri` and `-TemplateParametersUri` options can be used to specify the location of the template and parameters to be retrieved from another location.

The next tool that we'll look into is the Azure CLI.

The Azure CLI

The Azure CLI is another way of deploying ARM templates from the command line. The benefit of the CLI is that it is completely cross-platform and runs on Windows, macOS, and Linux. The Azure CLI command for deploying an ARM template is as follows:

```
az group deployment create —resource-group myResourceGroup —template-file
"c:\my\template.json" —parameters "c:\my\parameters.json"
```

All other options that are available in PowerShell are also available in the CLI.

Azure Pipelines

A third mechanism for deploying ARM templates is from an Azure pipeline. This is particularly useful for deploying the infrastructure and configuration of an application, together with the binaries. To deploy an ARM template deployment from a pipeline, at least one service connection of the Azure Resource Manager needs to be configured. After doing this, a pipeline can be configured as shown in the following screenshot:

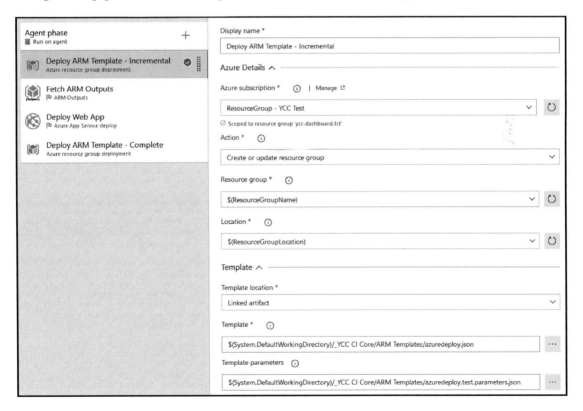

In this example, there are two deployments of an ARM template, surrounding the deployment of the application code. The first deployment is of the incremental type, while the second deployment is of the complete type. Using this approach, the first deployment will create all new infrastructure needed by the new version of the application. This deployment is done in incremental mode, so infrastructure that is no longer present in the template but still in use by the currently deployed version of the application will not yet be removed. The second deployment will take care of removing these elements after the new version of the code is deployed.

Reverse engineering a template

Writing an ARM template from scratch can be a tedious and time-consuming task. Luckily, there are two approaches available to generate an ARM template from existing infrastructure:

- Using the **Export template**
- Using the **Resource Explorer**

Let's discuss both of these in the upcoming subsections.

Using the Export template

The first approach is using the **Export template** option that can be found on every resource and resource group in the Azure portal. This will generate an ARM template of the current state of the resource (group), as shown in the following screenshot:

Please note that not every service currently supports reverse engineering an ARM template using this approach. For any service not supported, there will be a warning at the top of the screen. To work around this limitation for retrieving the JSON template for an individual resource, there is another approach, which is our next topic of discussion.

Using the Resource Explorer

For retrieving the JSON template for an individual resource, we can use the **Resource Explorer**. The Resource Explorer is shown here and can be found in the Azure portal by using the menu (*1*):

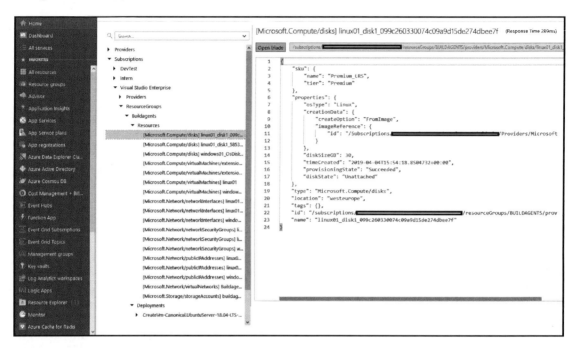

After opening the resource explorer, two new panes open up. The left pane can be used to navigate through subscriptions and drill down into the resource groups, down to the individual resources. For every element that is selected, the corresponding JSON will be displayed on the right. In the preceding example, the JSON for a hard disk is shown. This JSON is the same as the JSON that can be used in the resources array of an ARM template.

Subscription-level templates

The discussion of ARM templates up to this point has all been about ARM templates for a resource group deployment. A template describes one or more resources that are deployed to a resource group. Additionally, there are also subscription-level templates. An example ARM template for a resource group is shown as follows:

```
{
    "$schema": "https://schema.management.azure.com/schemas/2018-05-01
```

```
                                                    . . .
/subscriptionDeploymentTemplate.json#",
    "contentVersion": "1.0.0.1",
    "parameters": { },
    "variables": { },
    "resources": [
        {
            "type": "Microsoft.Resources/resourceGroups",
            "apiVersion": "2018-05-01",
            "location": "West Europe",
            "name": "myResourceGroup",
            "properties": {}
        }
    ],
    "outputs": {}
}
```

The format for a subscription template is completely the same as that for a resource group. The differences are $schema, which points to another schema location, and the types of resources that are supported. Subscription templates do not support the creation of resources directly, and support only the creation of resource groups, the initiation of template deployments, creating and assigning Azure Policies, and the creation of role assignments.

Azure Blueprints

Next to subscription level-templates, there is also another offering available: Azure Blueprints. Blueprints can be used to describe the desired state of an Azure subscription and apply that to an existing subscription.

All of the things that can be done using a blueprint can nowadays also be done using an ARM template. However, the other way around is not true. Azure Blueprints only support the following constructs, which are called artifacts:

- Policy assignments
- Role (RBAC) assignments
- Resource group creation
- Nested ARM templates at the subscription or resource group level

These are all of the elements that are needed to build the default layout, or a blueprint, for Azure subscriptions.

There are a number of key differences between blueprints and ARM templates:

- Blueprints are stored within Azure itself. A blueprint is a resource you can create and navigate to in the portal. The authoring experience is also in the portal, not in text files on a local computer.
- The relation between a subscription and the blueprint that was used to create it remains, also after the deployment completes.
- With the assignment of a blueprint to a subscription, it is possible to mark the assignment as locked. If this is done, all of the resources deployed through the blueprint cannot be deleted or edited as long as the blueprint is assigned—not even owners of the subscription that it is applied to.
- There are many built-in blueprints available that can be used to implement controls from well-known standards such as ISO, NIST, or HIPAA.

The general recommendation is to use blueprints whenever creating many new subscriptions, which should follow the same layout, and use ARM templates in all other cases. Blueprints are still in preview at the time of writing

November 2019 updates

Since November 2019, ARM templates no longer have to be pure JSON. Several other constructs are now allowed to make working with ARM templates easier.

To comment the rest of a line, `//` is used, or to comment a block, the `/* */` notation is used. This makes the following snippets both valid as part of an ARM template:

```
{
  "appServiceName": {
    // this is a single line comment
    "type": "string"
      /*
        This is a multi-line comment
      */
    }
}
```

Another deviation from JSON is that ARM templates allow for a multi-line string. When using these from the Azure CLI, this has to be enabled by specifying the `--handle-extended-json-format` switch. To use these and other new features, a new JSON schema has to be referenced from the template. This schema is `https://schema.management.azure.com/schemas/2019-04-01/deploymentTemplate.json#`.

Also, a new command has been introduced to show what changes would be made if a template wer be applied. This command is still in preview and called `New-AzDeploymentWhatIf`. A link to the documentation is included at the end of this chapter.

While ARM templates are the preferred approach in Azure for managing infrastructure, there are scenarios where it might not fit. In these cases, Azure Automation can be an alternative. Azure Automation is discussed in the next section.

Using Azure Automation

Azure Automation is a service in Azure that is designed to help users to create, manage, deploy, and maintain their Azure resources. Azure Automation contains several concepts that remove some of the complexities and low-level details from these actions. Azure Automation allows for the formulation of workflows in the form of runbooks. These runbooks can be executed against Azure resources on behalf of the user.

Automation account resources

Within an Azure Automation account, there are several resources that make this more than just a scripting engine. These resources are shared on the level of the automation account and can hence be reused within multiple runbooks.

Run As account

The first of these constructs is the *Run As* account. This account is a service principal that will be created in the Azure Active Directory that the Azure subscription containing the automation account is linked to. The credentials to authenticate as this service principal are securely stored within the automation account. These credentials are non-retrievable. The service principal is also added as a contributor to the Azure subscription. As a result, runbooks can now be set up to execute using this account.

Run As accounts can be automatically created when creating the Automation account.

Schedules

A common way of automating workflows is scheduling them to run on a specific date and time or on a fixed interval. Instead of specifying a schedule for every workflow, shared schedules can be created and reused in runbooks. To create a new schedule, first, open the list of all schedules. After that, a new schedule can be added, as shown in the following screenshot:

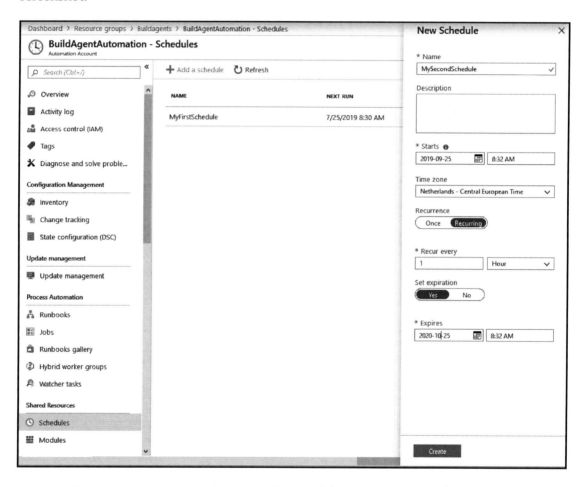

A schedule has a name and a description. These values are for the users interacting with the schedule only. Next, a starting date and time can be configured, along with an optional recurrence interval, and, if a recurrence interval is specified, an expiration date and time. Once the schedule is created, it can be used for a runbook.

Modules

The runbooks that are used in Azure Automation are written in PowerShell. PowerShell has a very rich ecosystem of modules with predefined functionalities that can be used. For using PowerShell modules from an automation account, only modules that have been uploaded to the modules section can be used. One major benefit of this is that it is possible to fix the version of a module to use. This guarantees that scripts will keep working and not break in case of updates to dependencies.

The PowerShell modules for interacting with Azure are by default installed into every automation account. Furthermore, more modules can be added, and existing modules can be upgraded or removed by administrators.

Variables

Within runbooks, a lot of variables might come into play; the names of resource groups, virtual machines, start up or shutdown times, and so on. Hardcoding these values inside a script is not good practice, but storing them together with a runbook also has downsides. For example, in the case that there are three runbooks for the same virtual machine, this would mean that a number of variable values (for example, resource group name and virtual machine name) would be repeated at least three times. To prevent this, it is possible to store variable values at the automation account level, from where they can be reused throughout every runbook that is executed in that account.

Once a variable is set, it can be accessed from a runbook using the following command:

```
$exampleVar = Get-AutomationVariable -Name 'ExampleVar'
```

In addition to reading and using variables inside a runbook, they can also be updated from within a runbook:

```
Set-AutomationVariable -name 'ExampleVar' -value 'ExampleValue'
```

While a very powerful feature, updating variables from within runbooks can have unexpected consequences. If a variable value that is used in multiple runbooks gets updated by one of them, this might break the other runbooks. Keeping track of which variables are read-only and which are written to as well is important.

Credentials

A special type of variable is the credential. Credentials contain not one but two values: a username and a password. Credentials are treated as secrets everywhere they are used. This means that they will not appear in logs and that they have to be retrieved using a specific PowerShell syntax:

```
$myCredential = Get-AutomationPSCredential -Name 'MyCredential'
```

After executing this command, the myCredential object can be used to retrieve both the username and password.

Connections

It is a very common scenario to have to connect to one or more external services from within a runbook. A common example is the Azure Resource Manager that is used to manage all resources within Azure. To avoid having to store a series of variables and build the corresponding connection in a runbook, automation accounts allow for the creation beforehand of one or more connections.

 In most scenarios, it is not necessary to create connections manually as they are provided along with a Run As account.

Once all of the shared resources are in place, it is time to start writing one or more runbooks, which is our next topic of discussion.

Runbooks

A number of types of runbooks are supported: PowerShell, Python 2, and graphical. The first two allow for writing scripts to be written in the specified language. Graphical runbooks allow for composing a runbook from all uploaded PowerShell modules, assets, and existing runbooks using drag and drop.

In addition to these three basic types of runbooks, there are PowerShell workflow and graphical workflow types available. The difference between a regular runbook and a workflow runbook is that workflow runbooks also support parallelism. Another benefit of PowerShell workflow is that it supports the use of checkpoints, which allow a script to be resumed if it encounters an exception mid-execution.

Runbook execution

Once the runbook is written, there are a number of ways to execute it:

- **Manually**: Any runbook can be run at any time by opening it in the Azure portal and pressing **Start**. Of course, these operations are also available using PowerShell or the Azure CLI.
- **By attaching a Webhook**: Once a runbook is published, one or more Webhooks can be generated for executing the runbook. Each Webhook can be enabled or disabled or given an expiration date. These tools allow a new Webhook to be generated for every user of the runbook and fine-grained control to be initiated if ever future access should not be accorded to a particular user.
- **On a schedule**: Published runbooks can be attached to one or more of the shared schedules. Being able to attach to multiple schedules means that it is easy to pre-create a series of schedules for typical reoccurrences, such as hourly, daily, or every Monday, and reuse and combine these for the appropriate runbooks.

When executing the runbook from a Webhook or on a schedule, the option to run it manually will stay available.

Jobs

Every time a runbook is executed, a new entry is created in the **Jobs** log. This log will show an entry for every time the runbook has run, no matter how execution was initiated. Every entry will contain the date and time the run was started, whether there were errors, and a full execution log.

Runbooks gallery

Runbooks are a great way of automating common tasks. Of course, there are tasks that are only for specific customers, but there are also many tasks that are applicable to all Azure customers. Examples include the automated startup of a virtual machine every Monday morning at 8 A.M. or scaling up a database every morning and back down every evening.

For these common scenarios, there is the runbooks gallery, which is enabled within every automation account. In this gallery, hundreds of pre-made runbooks can be browsed and searched. Once an appropriate runbook has been found, it can be imported directly into the account as a runbook.

Besides executing scripts on set intervals or upon the invocation of a Webhook, Azure Automation can also be used as a PowerShell DSC pull server. Let's discuss this next.

PowerShell DSC

PowerShell DSC is a notion for specifying the configuration of servers. This configuration is stored on a pull server, where it can be accessed by one or more virtual machines. These virtual machines are configured to check this server at a specified interval for the latest DSC configuration and update themselves to comply with this configuration.

PowerShell DSC is an extension to the PowerShell language specification that is used for writing desired state configurations. A configuration enables the desired state of one or more nodes to be specified. A node specifies which server, or set of servers, is to be configured. The configuration for a node is written in the form of one or more resources. An example configuration is shown as follows:

```
configuration ServerFarmConfig
{
    Node FrontEndServer
    {
        WindowsFeature IIS
        {
            Ensure = 'Present'
            Name = 'Web-Server'
            IncludeAllSubFeature = $true
        }

        File LogDirectory
        {
            Type = 'Directory'
            DestinationPath = 'C:\logs'
            Ensure = "Present"
```

```
            }
        }
    }
```

In this example, the configuration for a server farm with a single type of server is described. This server contains two resources. The first one, of the `WindowsFeature` type with the name `IIS`, ensures that `IIS` is installed together with all of its sub-features. The second resource, of the `File` type, ensures that a directory, `c:\logs`, exists. The resource types of `IIS` and `File` and many more are built into the PowerShell DSC specification. A full reference of all resources is available online and a link is included at the end of this chapter.

Compiling and applying PowerShell DSC

PowerShell DSC files are saved in plaintext, often in a `.ps1` file. These files can be compiled into MOF files. These MOF files can then be pushed to one or more servers to update the state of the server to the state described in the MOF file. This is called **push mode**.

Besides push mode, there is another model for deploying MOF files. This is called **pull mode**. In pull mode, MOF files are not directly pushed to individual servers, but stored on a central server that is called the **pull server**. This way, the pull server has a complete record of all configurations and node definitions within those configurations.

Once the pull server is up and running, individual servers are configured to fetch their DSC configuration at a fixed interval and apply that configuration. Applying a configuration means that, for every defined resource, the described state will be enacted. This can be done by doing nothing if the actual state already matches the desired state, or by running commands to achieve the desired state. In this process, all previous changes—even by administrators—will be reverted if necessary.

Using Powershell DSC with Azure Automation

Azure Automation has built-in capabilities for PowerShell DSC and can fulfill the role of pull server for one or more virtual machines.

To start using the built-in pull server capabilities, upload one or more configuration files to the automation account. This is done from the **State configuration** view that is shown in the following screenshot. Now, complete the following steps:

1. Open by clicking the menu option on the left.
2. Select **Configuration** in the tab bar at the top:

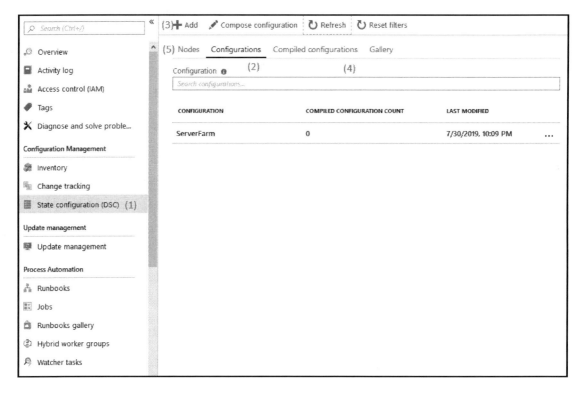

3. Once the overview of all configurations is opened, new configurations can be added using the **Add** button. In `topHere`, a local `ps1` file can be selected and that will be added to the list. Any valid configuration in the list can be clicked on and compiled in place.
4. Now, the configuration will also be shown in the tab with compiled configurations and can be applied to one or more virtual machines.
5. Once a compiled configuration is available, the **Nodes** tab can be used for adding one or more virtual machines from the subscription to a configuration node.
6. Clicking the **Add** button while this tab is shown opens the view shown as follows:

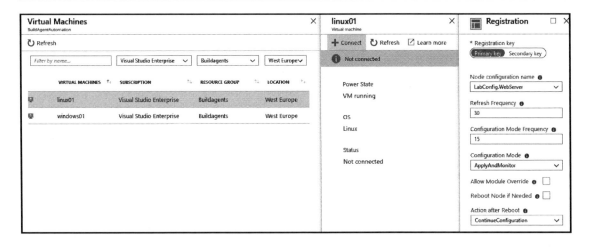

7. In this view, a virtual machine can be selected to which the selected configuration should be applied.
8. The local configuration manager on that machine will be configured to refresh the configuration at fixed intervals.
9. Whenever the configuration is refreshed, it will be reapplied to the server.

Azure Automation enables users to manage virtual machines, for example, to apply application configuration. When working with PaaS offerings, this cannot be done using techniques as PowerShell DSC and other techniques have to be used to manage application settings. These will be discussed in the next section.

Managing application settings

Another part of the infrastructure of an application is the application configuration. In this section, a number of approaches for storing and loading the application configuration for an Azure App Service are discussed. They include the following:

- Storing the configuration in the app settings
- Using a combination of Managed Identity and key vault
- Using the Azure App configuration service

The disadvantage of the first approach is that the app settings can be read by any user who has administrative (read) access to the app service that is configured. The next two approaches do not have this disadvantage.

Azure app service settings from an ARM template

The first way to configure application settings as code is by specifying app settings as a resource in an ARM template. This should be specified as a nested resource. This can be done as shown in the following screenshot:

```
{
    "name": "[concat (variables ('websiteName'), '/appsettings')]",
    "type": "config",
    "apiVersion": "2015-08-01",
    "dependsOn": [
        "[concat ('Microsoft.Web/sites/', variables ('webSiteName'))]"
    ],
    "properties": {
        "key1": " [listKeys (parameters ('storagename'),
'2018-02-01').keys[0].value]",
        "key2": "value2"
    }
}
```

The use of the `listKeys` function is especially useful in these scenarios. It allows for the direct copying of secrets from any service to the application settings without ever storing them in any intermediate solution. For secrets that do not come from Azure sources, template parameters should be used.

The configuration specified in the ARM template corresponds to the configuration of an App Service that can be found in the portal. These settings are used to override corresponding entries in the `appsettings.json` or `appsettings.config` files. Updating this configuration automatically reloads the application as well.

The downside of this approach is that secrets that are stored this way are readable through the Azure portal. Any user with read access to the app service can retrieve all secrets stored this way.

Loading settings at runtime from key vault

The next possible location for storing app service settings is in an Azure key vault, where the application loads them at runtime. To make this possible, the following has to be in place.

To be able to authorize an application with access to a key vault, the application first has to be able to authenticate itself against the **Azure Active Directory (AAD)**. Of course, this can be done by registering a service principal manually, but this would return a username and password that have to be stored somewhere. Usernames and passwords are secrets, but cannot be stored in the key vault since they are needed for accessing it. This problem of how to keep the key to the vault safe can be solved by using an Azure capability called *Managed Identity*.

 The problem of securely storing secrets but getting another secret in return for accessing them is often referred to as the problem of *turtles all the way down*. This is an old anecdote to which a link is included at the end of this chapter.

With Azure Managed Identity enabled on an app service, Azure automatically generates a service principal with a non-retrievable username and password. Only at runtime, using specific code, can an application authenticate itself as this principal. Azure will ensure that this will only work for code that is running with the app service that the Managed Identity belongs to.

Now that an application can have its own identity, that identity has to be granted access to the key vault. This can be done in the key vault description in an ARM template, using the following syntax:

```
{
    "type": "Microsoft.KeyVault/vaults",
    "name": "[parameters('keyVaultName')]",
    "apiVersion": "2015-06-01",
    "location": "[resourceGroup().location]",
    "dependsOn": [
        "[resourceId('Microsoft.Web/sites/',
parameters('appServiceName'))]"
    ],
    "properties": {
        "enabledForTemplateDeployment": false,
        "tenantId": "[subscription().tenantId]",
        "accessPolicies": [
          {
            "tenantId": "[subscription().tenantId]",
            "objectId":
[reference(concat(resourceId('Microsoft.Web/sites',parameters('appServiceNa
me')),
                    [line continued]
'/providers/Microsoft.ManagedIdentity/Idntities/default'),
                    [line continued] '2015-08-31-preview').principalId]",
            "permissions": {
              "secrets": [ "get", "list" ]
```

```
                    }
                }
            ],
            "sku": {
                "name": "standard",
                "family": "A"
            }
        }
    }
```

In this example, the `reference()` function is used to retrieve the information of the Managed Identity and uses this to create an access policy on the key vault.

Finally, with the key vault and access to it set up, the application has to retrieve the contents at start up time. To do this, config builders can be used. They are introduced with .NET Core 2.0 (and .NET Framework 4.7.1) and are used in the `StartUp` class, as shown in the following code snippet:

```
var tokenProvider = new AzureServiceTokenProvider();
var kvClient = new KeyVaultClient((authority, resource, scope) =>
tokenProvider.KeyVaultTokenCallback(authority, resource, scope));

var configurationBuilder = new ConfigurationBuilder().AddAzureKeyVault(
    $"https://{ Configuration["keyVaultName"]}.vault.azure.net/",
    kvClient,
    new DefaultKeyVaultSecretManager());

Configuration = configurationBuilder.Build();
```

All types in this code example are available in the NuGet package, `Microsoft.Configuration.ConfigurationBuilders.Azure`.

Azure App Configuration

Another location for storing the configuration of applications is Azure App Configuration. This is a new service, and at the time of writing, still in preview. App Configuration allows for the creation of a central register of key-value pairs that can be used as configuration by such a register, but also multiple applications.

App Configuration is another type of resource that can be created from the portal. The main component is a configuration explorer, as shown in the following screenshot:

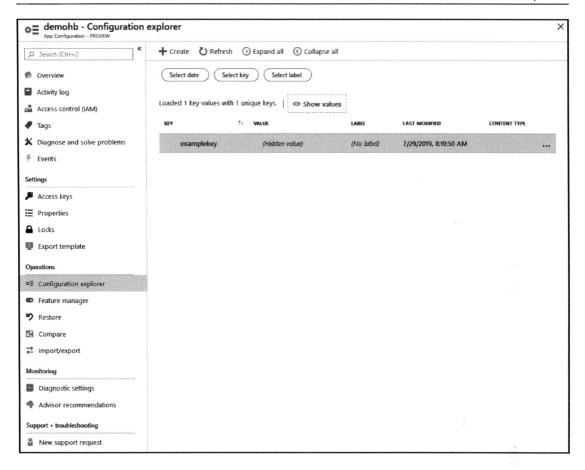

In addition to the configuration explorer, there is a keys section for retrieving access keys that applications can use to read the configuration. There are also options to view recent changes to the configuration and restore earlier versions and for importing or exporting all configuration settings.

After the App Configuration resource has been created and configuration keys added, they can be retrieved from within an application by using an extension method of the **IConfiguration** framework type:

```
config.AddAzureAppConfiguration(settings["ConnectionStrings:AppConfig"]);
```

The loader for settings from an app configuration is part of the NuGet package, `Microsoft.Azure.AppConfiguration.AspNetCore`.

Compared to storing settings in Azure key vault, App Configuration has two downsides:

- Firstly, the application needs to be configured with a connection string to the App Configuration, storing at least one new secret in the app settings.
- Secondly, App Configuration does not have access control options that are as rigid as key vault. For this reason, it might make sense to distribute configuration over both App Configuration and key vault, depending on the type of configuration value.

This concludes our discussion of Azure and Azure DevOps capabilities for infrastructure as code. The next section will discuss a series of other tools available that offer similar capabilities.

Other tools

There are many other tools available for managing infrastructure and configuration through code. Next to the native Azure and Windows options discussed in the previous sections, there are many alternatives widely in use and some of them are listed in this section. It is important to know which tool can be used for which scenarios and how to integrate with them.

CloudFormation

CloudFormation is the IaC language for the AWS Cloud. CloudFormation templates can be written in either JSON or YAML format. One example of creating an AWS S3 Storage Bucket that is publicly readable would look like this:

```
Resources:
 HelloBucket:
 Type: AWS::S3::Bucket
 Properties:
 AccessControl: PublicRead
```

There is an extension available that allows the execution of CloudFormation templates on AWS from Azure DevOps. This extension provides tasks for creating, updating, or deleting AWS Stacks. A stack has a function that is comparable to a resource group in Azure and the tasks are comparable to the tasks for applying an ARM template.

Chef

Chef is a tool for CaC, with support for describing and enforcing the configuration of servers. Chef uses a centralized server, *Chef Server*, where all configuration for all servers is saved. Here, the correct desired state for every server is determined, which is then pulled by the *Chef Client,* an agent that runs on the *node* that is being managed.

Defining the desired state for a server is done using a number of constructs. The lowest level is the recipe. A recipe contains one or more resources, built-in capabilities that can be used. An example resource is execute , which runs a bash command. Another example resource is `apt_update`, which provides the means to interact with the *apt* package manager. One or more recipes are combined in cookbooks, which describe a capability that can be assigned to a node. The assignment of one or more cookbooks to a node is done using the run list. The run list contains all cookbooks that have to be applied to a node.

Interaction with the Chef Server is done using a command-line tool called **knife**.

While the terminology is completely different, there are many conceptual parallels between PowerShell DSC and Chef.

Puppet

Puppet is a deployment and configuration management tool that operates using a server-client model. There is a centralized server called the **Puppet Master** that is responsible for taking in all of the desired state descriptions and compiling them to an intern catalog that holds the desired state for every managed server. All servers that are managed by Puppet need to have the Puppet agent installed on the local server. The agent connects to the server, to pull the state for the server it manages, and applies that locally. A managed server is called a node.

The base building block used by Puppet is called a **resource**. A resource is defined by specifying a resource type and a series of attributes. There are many resource types available, for example, for managing users and installed applications. Resources are grouped in one or more *classes*. These classes are, in turn, assigned to one or more nodes.

Puppet can be installed on any Linux VM in Azure. There is also a pre-built image with Puppet Enterprise available in the Azure marketplace.

Puppet is comparable to Chef and PowerShell DSC. All three have a comparable model for describing the desired state and they all serve the same purpose.

Ansible

Ansible is yet another configuration management tool that is mostly used on Linux but also has support for Windows. One aspect that differentiates Ansible from other tools is that it does not have a centralized server that hosts all of the desired states, nor does it work with agents. All commands executed by Ansible are executed using SSH.

Any server can initiate the deployment of a *playbook* against one or more *items* in an *inventory*. An Ansible inventory contains all of the servers that can be managed by Ansible. They can be grouped into one or more groups, which can be nested into other groups as well. Each individual server and every group is an inventory item. In Ansible, the desired state is written in playbooks. A playbook is a series of tasks or roles that need to be run at the target server. A role is a group of tasks. Roles are intended to be reused in more than one playbook and should, therefore, be general enough to be useable in multiple situations. Roles should also be idempotent. This means that the tasks in the role should ensure that the outcome of running the playbook is the same, no matter the number of times it is run.

Ansible scripts can be executed using command-line tools or an Azure DevOps extension that wraps this tool. There are also other management systems available, such as Ansible Tower, that provide a graphical user interface on top of the capabilities of the Ansible command-line tools.

Terraform

Terraform is a multi-cloud infrastructure management solution. It is comparable to ARM templates, the difference being that it also supports Amazon Web Services, Google Cloud Platform, and other clouds. Terraform uses a custom file format for specifying one or more resources to be created using one or more providers. The resources correspond to the cloud resources, and the providers are responsible for knowing how to interact with the APIs of the different vendors.

Optionally, you can use a JSON format instead of the Terraform proprietary format. Terraform also supports the use of modules for creating packages that are reusable components.

Terraform configuration files are executed using command-line interfaces.

Summary

In this chapter, you learned about the concept of infrastructure and configuration as code, its value, and how to use it in practice. For implementing these, you learned about ARM templates, the IaC mechanism for Azure. You also learned about PowerShell DSC for managing the configuration of virtual machines and about different techniques for managing the configuration of your applications. Finally, you learned about several other tools available in the market. You learned which tool can be used in which situation and whether these tools can integrate with Azure DevOps.

With this knowledge, you are now able to start describing the infrastructure and configuration of your application(s) in source control using one or more of the tools you have read about. You are also capable of setting up the means to deliver the infrastructure using automation, either from a release pipeline or using dedicated infrastructure management tools. But no matter which solution you choose, you now have the capabilities to incorporate infrastructure into your DevOps processes.

In the next chapter, you will learn about another challenge you might encounter when implementing DevOps practices: databases. When increasing the speed at which features flow to production, you may also have to change the way you manage your database schema and how you apply changes. The next chapter will discuss this subject.

Questions

As we conclude, here is a list of questions for you to test your knowledge regarding this chapter's material. You will find the answers in the *Assessments* section of the Appendix:

1. True or False: ARM templates can be used for creating, updating, and deleting Azure Resources.
2. Which of the following is not an Azure Automation Account resource?
    1. Modules
    2. Containers
    3. Run As account
    4. Variables
3. True or False: One disadvantage of infrastructure as code is that you have to put sensitive information in source control as ARM template parameter files.
4. True or False: Azure Automation Accounts allow for the execution of Powershell runbooks at a predefined schedule.
5. What are some of the benefits of using infrastructure as code?

Further reading

- A formal breakdown of the ARM template structure and syntax can be found at `https://docs.microsoft.com/en-us/azure/azure-resource-manager/templates/template-syntax`.
- The complete ARM Template reference can be found at `https://docs.microsoft.com/en-us/azure/templates/`.
- An overview of all functions that can be used in ARM templates can be found at `https://docs.microsoft.com/en-us/azure/azure-resource-manager/resource-group-template-functions`.
- More information about Azure Blueprints can be found at `https://docs.microsoft.com/en-us/azure/governance/blueprints/overview`.
- Details about the WhatIf command for ARM templates can be found at `https://docs.microsoft.com/en-us/azure/azure-resource-manager/templates/template-deploy-what-if`.
- There are many online references to the story of "turtles all the way down", but an early reference can be found digitized at `https://dspace.mit.edu/handle/1721.1/15166`.
- The reference including all Powershell DSC built-in resources can be found at `https://docs.microsoft.com/en-us/powershell/scripting/dsc/overview/overview`.
- More information about CloudFormation can be found at `https://aws.amazon.com/cloudformation/`.
- More information about Chef can be found at `https://www.chef.io/`.
- More information about Puppet can be found at `https://puppet.com/`.
- More information about Ansible can be found at `https://www.ansible.com/`.
- More information about Terraform can be found at `https://www.terraform.io/`.
- The following are links to Microsoft hands-on labs that can be used to get hands-on experience with the topics discussed in this chapter (`https://docs.microsoft.com/en-us/learn/modules/intro-to-governance/`):
    - `https://docs.microsoft.com/en-us/learn/modules/configure-infrastructure-azure-pipelines/index`
    - `https://docs.microsoft.com/en-us/learn/modules/provision-infrastructure-azure-pipelines/index`
    - `https://docs.microsoft.com/en-us/learn/modules/protect-vm-settings-with-dsc/`

7
Dealing with Databases in DevOps Scenarios

In the previous chapters, you have learned about the continuous integration and continuous deployment of your software. You also learned how the same principles can be applied to the delivery of configuration in infrastructure. Once you have adopted these principles and start increasing the flow of value delivery, you might run into another challenge: managing your database schema changes.

Applying DevOps to databases can feel like trying to change the tires on a running car. You must find some way of coordinating changes between database schema and application code without taking the system down for maintenance.

In this chapter, you will learn about different approaches for doing just that: managing these schema changes while avoiding downtime. With proper planning and a disciplined approach, this can be achieved in a way that manages risks well. You will see how you can treat your database schema as code, and you will learn about the different approaches that are available to do so. You will also see another approach that avoids database schemas altogether, namely, going schema-less.

The following topics will be covered in this chapter:

- Managing a database schema as code
- Applying database schema changes
- Going schema-less
- Other approaches and concerns

Technical requirements

In order to practice the ideas that are laid out in this chapter, you will need to have the following tools installed:

- An application with the Entity Framework Core NuGet package installed
- Visual Studio with SQL Server Data Tools
- Access to Azure Pipelines
- An Azure subscription, for accessing Cosmos DB

Managing a database schema as code

For those of you who are familiar with working with relational databases from application code, it is very likely they have been working with an **object-relational mapper (ORM)**. ORMs were introduced to fill the impedance mismatch between object-oriented programming languages and the relational database schema, which works with tables. Well-known examples are Entity Framework and NHibernate.

ORMs provide a layer of abstraction that allows for the storage and retrieval of objects from a database, without worrying about the underlying table structure when doing so. To perform automated mapping of objects to tables, or the other way around, ORMs often have built-in capabilities for describing a database schema, the corresponding object model, and the mappings between them in a markup language. Most of the time, neither of these have to be written by hand. Often, they can be generated from an object model or an existing database, and the mappings between them are often, by convention, generated or drawn in a visual editor.

While all this allows for the current database schema to be defined as code, this alone does not help with coping with schema changes, yet. For handling schema changes as code, two common approaches are available. The first one describes every change in code; the other one describes only the latest version of the schema in code. These approaches are known as migration-based and state-based approaches. Both can rely on third-party tooling to use these for applying the changes to the database.

Migrations

The first approach is based on keeping an ordered set of changes that have to be applied to the database. These changes are often called *migrations*, and they can be generated by tools such as Microsoft Entity Framework, or Redgate SQL Change Automation, or they can be written by hand.

Tools can automatically generate the migration scripts based on a comparison of the current schema of the database and the new schema definition in source control. This is called **scaffolding**. The scripts generated by tools are not always perfect, and they can be improved by applying the domain knowledge that the programmer has, but the tool does not. Once one or more new migrations are scaffolded or written, they can be applied to a database using the chosen tool. A diagram showing how that works is shown here:

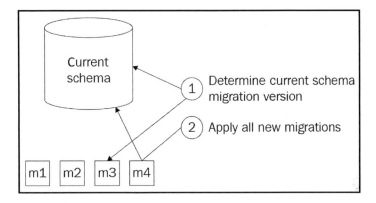

Here, we see how an ever-growing series of migrations, labeled m1 to m4, are generated to describe incremental changes to the database. To update the database to the latest version, the latest applied migration is determined and all migrations after that are added one after the other.

When editing migration scripts by hand, the following has to be kept in mind:

- The migration scripts should be ordered. Migrations describe the SQL statements that need to be executed in order to move the database from a version x to version $x+1$. Only once this is complete can the next migration be started.
- A migration script should migrate not only the schema, but also the data. This can mean that in-between steps are needed. For example, moving two columns to another table often implies that the new columns are first created, then filled with the data from the old columns, and that only then are the old columns removed.

- It is advisable to include all database objects in the migration scripts. Extra indexes and constraints should not be applied to the production database only, but also to test environments. With migrations, there is already a mechanism for delivering those from source control. Having these in the same migration scripts also ensures that indexes and constraints are applied in the same order, and cannot unexpectedly block migrations by existing only in production.
- If possible, migration scripts should be made idempotent. If there is ever an issue or the suspicion of an issue, being able to just rerun the last migration is a great way to ensure that it is fully applied.

One disadvantage of this approach is the strict ordering requirement that is imposed on generating and applying the generated migrations. This makes it hard to integrate this approach into a development workflow that relies heavily on the use of branches. Migrations created in different branches that are merged together only later might break the ordering of migrations or, even worse, merge a split in the migration path. For example, imagine the case where two migrations, b and c, in two different branches, have been created after an existing migration, a. How are these going to be merged? Neither order—a, b, c or a, c, b—is correct, since both b and c are created to be executed directly after a. The only way such an error can be fixed is by performing the following steps:

1. Remove all migrations apart from the first new one, for example, c in this case.
2. Apply all other migrations to a database that has none of the new migrations applied; in this case, only b if a was already applied, or both a and b.
3. Generate a new migration for the other migrations; in this case, a replacement for c.

An advantage of this approach is that every individual schema change will be deployed against the database in the same fashion. Irrespective of whether one—or more than one—migration is applied to the production database at the same time, they will still run one by one in a predictable order and in the same way in which they ran against the test environment, even if they were applied there one by one.

End state

A different approach to managing schema changes is to not keep track of the individual changes (or migrations), but only store the latest version of the schema in source control. External tools are then used to compare the current schema in source control with the actual schema of the database, generate migration scripts, and apply these when running. The migration scripts are not stored, and are single-use only.

Unlike writing migrations, it is not feasible to execute a task like this by hand. While tracking the newest version of the schema by hand in source control can be managed, the same is not feasible for an end-state approach. Generating a migration script while comparing the existing schema and the new schema and applying this migration script can only be done using a tool. Examples of these tools are Redgate SQL Source Control and SQL Server Data Tools. How these tools work, is shown in the here:

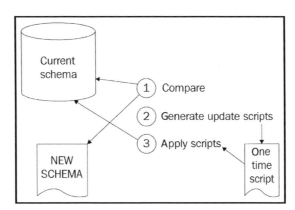

Here we see how the current actual database schema and the description of the desired database schema are compared to generate an upgrade and directly apply a script for making the changes needed to make the actual schema the same as the desired schema.

One advantage of this approach is that there is no series of scripts generated that have to be executed in a specific order. Therefore, this approach combines easily with extensive branching schemas, where changes are integrated more slowly over time. It also removes the need to write migrations by hand for simple scenarios, such as adding or deleting a column, table, or index.

The disadvantage of this approach is that it makes it harder to handle changes that need data operations as well. Again, imagine a scenario of moving two columns to another table. Since the tooling only enforces the new schema, this will lead to data loss if there is no further intervention.

One possible form of intervention to circumvent this is the addition of pre- and post-deployment scripts to the schema package. In the pre-deployment script, the current data is staged in a temporary table. Then, after applying the new schema, the data is copied from the temporary table to the new location in the post-deployment script.

This section was about managing database schema changes in a format that can be stored in source control. The next section discusses how these changes can be picked up at deploy time and then applied to a database.

Applying database schema changes

With the database schema, and optionally, a series of migrations defined in source control, it is time to start thinking about when to apply changes to the database schema. There are two methods to do so. Database schema changes can be applied prior to deployment of the new application version, or by the application code itself.

Upgrading as part of the release

The first approach to applying databases changes is as part of the release pipeline. When this is the case, the tool that is responsible for reading and executing the migration scripts is invoked using a step in the pipeline.

This invocation can be done using a custom script in PowerShell or another scripting language. However, this is error-prone, and with every change of tool, there is a risk that the scripts need to be updated. Luckily, for most of the migration-based tools, there are Azure Pipelines tasks that are readily available for starting the migration from the release.

For example, there is an Azure Pipelines extension available for applying Entity Framework Core migrations to a database directly from the `dll` file where they are defined. This task can be added to the release pipeline for updating the database, before the new application code is deployed.

Another variation is a split between the build and the release phase of an application. In this case, the migration scripts are exported as a separate build artifact, either directly from source code—if written in SQL—or after executing a tool that generates the necessary SQL scripts as output. This artifact is then downloaded again in the release phase, where it is applied to the database using an Azure Pipelines task for executing SQL.

Upgrading by the application code

Instead of applying schema changes from the release pipeline, they can also be applied by the application itself. Some of the ORMs, with migration support built in, have the capability to automatically detect whether the database schema matches the latest migration. If not, they can automatically migrate the schema to that latest version on the spot.

An example of an ORM that supports this is Entity Framework. The core version of Entity Framework does not have support for automatic migrations built in. In Entity Framework Core, a single line of application code can be used to initiate an upgrade at a time that is convenient from the perspective of the application. The code for doing so is shown in the following code snippet:

```
using (var context = new MyContext(...))
{
    context.Database.Migrate();
}
```

The advantage of this approach is that it is very simple to enable. Just a Boolean switch in the configuration of, for example, Entity Framework can enable this workflow. However, the disadvantage is that most ORMs that support this will enforce a global lock on the database—stopping all database transactions while the migrations are running. For any migration or set of migrations that take more than a few seconds, this approach might be impractical.

This approach is normally only used for migration-based approaches. Approaches that use an end-state approach require an external third-party tool that is used to generate the necessary migration scripts and apply them. This is normally done from the release pipeline and is not wrapped in the application itself.

Adding a process

As the previous section illustrated, it is important to think about how and when changes to the database schema or the application (or applications!) that use that schema are applied. But no matter how the deployment of schema changes and code deployment are scheduled, there will always be a period at which one of the following is true:

- The new application code is already running while the schema changes are not applied yet or are in the process of being applied.
- The old application code is still running while the schema changes are already applied or are in the process of being applied.
- The application code is not running while the schema changes are being applied.

The third situation is highly undesirable. This is true in general, but especially when practicing DevOps. If changes are shipped often and during working hours, it is unacceptable to take the application down for every schema change.

To prevent having to take the application down while schema changes are being applied, one of the following conditions has to be met:

- The schema changes are backward-compatible in such a way that the old version of the application code can run without errors against a database where the schema changes have already been applied, or are being applied.
- The new application code is backward-compatible in such a way that it can run against both the old and the new versions of the schema.

Meeting the first of these conditions ensures that the old application code can continue to run while the schema changes are being applied. Meeting the second of these conditions ensures that the new version of the application code can be deployed first, and once that is completed, the database can be upgraded while this code is running. While either will work, it is often desirable to aim for the first condition. The reason is that schema changes often support application code changes.

This means that the following is a safe process for deploying schema changes without downtime:

1. Create a new database.
2. Apply the database changes.
3. Verify that the changes have been applied properly, or abort the deployment pipeline.
4. Deploy the new application code.

It is important to realize that this process assumes failing forward. This means that if there ever is an issue with the deployment of schema changes, they should be resolved before going forward with the code changes.

Finally, meeting the condition of backward combability for schema changes can sometimes be impossible to fulfill for a schema change. If this is the case, the change can often be split into two partial changes that together have the same end result, while they both meet the condition of backward combability. For example, renaming a property, or changing the unit in which it stores a distance from feet to meters, can be executed as follows:

1. Generate a migration that adds a new column to a database table, storing the distance in meters.
2. Add an application code that reads from the old column, but writes to both columns.
3. Deploy these changes to production.

4. Add a new migration that migrates data from the old column to the new column for all cases where the new column is not yet filled, but the old column is.
5. Update the application code to read and write only the new column.
6. Deploy these changes to production.
7. Add a new migration that removes the old column.

Using the correct tools and a proper process, it is possible to execute effective and safe deployments of schema changes. In the next section, another approach, using schema-less databases, is introduced.

Going schema-less

In the previous sections, the focus was on relational databases, where strict schemas are applied to every table. A completely different approach to database schema management is to let go of having a database schema altogether. This can be done by using schema-less or document databases. A well-known example of a schema-less database is Azure Cosmos DB. These databases can store documents of different forms into the same table. Table is quoted here, since these types of databases often do not use the term "table", but call this a database, a container, or a collection.

Since these databases can store documents with a different schema in the same collection, schema changes no longer exist from a database's point of view. But of course, there will be changes to the structure of the corresponding objects in the application code over time. To see how to handle this, it is best to differentiate between storing objects in the database and reading them back.

Writing objects to the database

The documents that are stored in a schema-less database are often serializations of objects in application code. When working with a relational database, these objects are often stored using an **object-relational mapper (ORM)**, such as Entity Framework, Dapper, or NHibernate. When working with a document database, these objects are often serialized and stored in the database. This means that a change in the definition of that code object will also result in a different document structure when saving the object. Due to the nature of document databases, this will work fine.

As an example, take the following C# class and its JSON representation after serializing it to a document database:

```public class Person { [JsonConstructor] private Person() {} public Person(string name) { Name = name ?? throw new ArgumentNullException(); } [JsonProperty] public string Name { get; private set; } }```	```{ "Name": "Mark Anderson" }```

After this code has been running in a production environment for a while, and thousands of persons have been saved, a new requirement comes in. Next to the name of the person, the city where they live must also be recorded. For this reason, the `Person` class is extended to include another property. After performing this change and deploying the new code, whenever a person is saved, the following code is used, resulting in the JSON shown next to it:

```public class Person { [JsonConstructor] private Person() {} public Person(string name, string city) { Name = name ?? throw new ArgumentNullException(); City = city ?? throw new ArgumentNullException(); } [JsonProperty] public string Name { get; private set; } [JsonProperty] public string City { get; private set; } }```	```{ "Name": "Mark Anderson", "City": "Amsterdam" }```

While the definition of the `Person` class has changed—and the corresponding JSON has as well—both document forms can be saved into the same collection.

This shows that from the viewpoint of writing information to the database, the schema-less approach is very convenient, since developers do not have to think about schema change management at all.

Reading objects from the database

While schema-less databases make it extremely easy to write documents of different forms to the same collection, this can pose problems when reading documents back from that same collection and deserializing them. In reality, the problem of schema management is not removed, but deferred to a later point in time.

Continuing the example from the previous section, deserializing the first person that was saved on the new C# `Person` class definition will result in a null value for the city property. This can be unexpected, since the C# code guarantees that a person without a city can never be constructed. This is a clear example of the challenges that schema-less databases pose.

In this example, the issue can be circumvented by updating the `Person` class to the following:

```
public class Person
{
    [JsonConstructor]
    private Person() {}

    public Person(string name, string city) {
        Name = name ?? throw new ArgumentNullException();
        City = city ?? throw new ArgumentNullException();
    }

    [JsonProperty]
    public string Name { get; private set; }

    [JsonIgnore]
    private string _city;

    [JsonProperty]
    public string City {
        get { return _city; }
        private set { _city = value ?? _city = string.Empty}
    }
}
```

Next to this scenario, where a property was added, there are many other scenarios that will require the C# class to be adapted in order to handle deserialization scenarios. Some examples are as follows:

- Adding a property of a primitive type
- Adding a complex property, another object, or an array
- Renaming a property

- Replacing a property of a primitive type with a complex property
- Making nullable properties non-nullable

Adding code to objects to handle these situations increases the size and complexity of the code base, and pollutes the primary code base with the capabilities for coping with past situations. Especially when this happens often, this can lead to unwanted complications in a code base. To prevent this, a possible solution is to go through the following process whenever the schema of an object changes:

1. Change the schema of the object, ensuring that there are only properties added. Even when the goal is to remove a property, at this stage, only a property with the new name is added.
2. Implement logic on the object to cope with the deserialization of old versions of the object.
3. Deploy the new version of the object.
4. Start a background process that loads all objects of the type from the database one by one, and saves them back to the database.
5. Once the background process has processed all existing entities, remove the code that is responsible for coping with the schema change during deserialization from the code base, along with any properties that are no longer used.

Using this approach, all changes are propagated to all stored versions of the object over a period of time. The downside to this approach is that the change to the object's structure is spread over two changes that must be deployed separately. Also, deployment of the second change must wait until all objects in the database have been converted.

Other approaches and concerns

Besides the more common approaches that were discussed previously, the following tips and approaches might help with reducing the amount of work in dealing with databases, or help reduce the risk associated with making database changes.

Minimizing the influence of databases

A first step in dealing with databases can be to reduce the chance that a database change has to be made. In many databases, it is possible to write stored procedures—or some other code or script—that executes within the database engine. While stored procedures come with some benefits, changing them can also count as a database schema change, or at the least result in changes that can be difficult to test.

One simple approach for this is to just replace stored procedures with application code that allows for easier side-by-side changes using feature toggles.

Full side-by-side deployment

When working in a high-risk environment, or with a fragile database, there is also another approach to database schema changes that can be taken. This approach is based on applying feature toggles and the blue–green deployment pattern, and goes as follows:

1. Change the application code in such a way that it writes any update to not just one, but to two databases.
2. In the production environment, create a complete, full copy of the existing database and configure the application code to write all changes to both databases. These databases will be called *old* and *new*, from now on.
3. Introduce the required changes to the new database schema and the application code *only* in the path that writes to the new database.
4. Introduce the necessary changes in all code paths that read data in such a way that all queries run against both databases.
5. Update the application code to detect differences in the query results between the new and the old databases, and log an error when it finds any discrepancy.
6. If the changes run without any issues, remove the old database, and the old read and write access paths, from the application code.
7. If the changes run with errors, fix the issue. Next, restart by restoring the backup of the intended new database, and resume at step five.

The advantage of this approach is that it is very lightweight. The downside is that it is very involved, takes a lot of work, and is more expensive. Also, the extra database costs and duration of backup and restore operations should be taken into account.

Testing database changes

Just as with application code, insights into the quality of database schema changes can be gathered through testing. Links to performing tests on database schemas can be found at the end of this chapter.

In most cases, in order to fully cover the risks introduced by database changes, system tests are needed that execute against a fully deployed stack of the application. This type of test can cover most of the risks that come from faulty schemas, invalid stored procedures, and database and application code mismatches.

Summary

In this chapter, you have learned how to manage your database schema and schema changes using source control. You know about both the migration-based and end state based storing of changes, and how to apply them to your production database in a safe manner.

Additionally, you have learned how schema-less databases can remove the burden of traditional schema management. However, this comes at the price of having to cope with schema differences when reading older versions of an object back from the database.

In the next chapter, you will learn about continuous testing. You will not only learn about testing techniques, but also about which to apply at what point, and how testing is a crucial part of DevOps and a critical enabler of a continuous flow of value to end users.

Questions

As we conclude, here is a list of questions for you to test your knowledge regarding this chapter's material. You will find the answers in the *Assessments* section of the Appendix:

1. True or false: When working with Entity Framework, schema management is built in using migrations-based support.
2. True or false: When working with a migrations-based approach for schema management, you do not need extra tracking tables in your database schema.
3. True or false: When working with an end state-based approach for schema management, you do not need extra tracking tables in your database schema.
4. What are the benefits of a full side-by-side approach to database schema changes? (Choose multiple answers):
    1. The risks are reduced to almost zero.
    2. You can measure the actual performance impact of changes in a production-like environment.
    3. Side-by-side migrations reduce cycle time.
5. True or false: Schema-less databases remove the need for thinking about schema changes completely.
6. What is a possible technology choice that you can make to limit the impact of changes on your database schema?

Further reading

- More information about Entity Framework and Entity Framework Migrations can be found at `https://docs.microsoft.com/nl-nl/ef/` and `https://docs.microsoft.com/en-us/ef/ef6/modeling/code-first/migrations/`.
- More information about Redgate and its database tooling can be found at `https://www.red-gate.com/`.
- More information on SQL Server Data Tools can be found at `https://docs.microsoft.com/en-us/sql/ssdt/sql-server-data-tools?view=sql-server-2017`.
- The Azure Pipelines extension for deploying Entity Framework Core migrations from a DLL can be found at `https://marketplace.visualstudio.com/items?itemName=bendayconsulting.build-task`.

8
Continuous Testing

In the previous chapters, you learned about the different types of techniques that are used to help to increase the rate at which you deliver changes to your production environment. If you are already using these techniques in your daily work, you will quickly notice that this is only possible if your work is of sufficient quality. If the quality of your work is not high enough, you will face many outages or issues and your end users will not be happy. To be successful, increasing the rate of change and increasing the quality of your work must go hand in hand. To recognize the quality of your work and to increase it, you first need to know what is meant by quality. This is where testing comes in. Testing is the discipline of reporting about the quality of software.

To introduce the topic of testing, this chapter will start by looking at how the quality of software development can be measured. Next, the topic of functional testing will be explored. First, the testing cone and pyramid will be introduced. These are models that can be used to determine which types of tests are needed and how many of each should be used. After this, the different types of tests will be discussed one by one. You will learn about how they work, what they test, and the benefits and downsides of the different types of tests. Finally, the last section will focus on how all metrics and test results, once generated and collected by your pipelines, can continuously report on the quality of the work of your team and even prevent changes of insufficient quality propagating to your users. All of this will help you to maintain the high quality of your software and enable you to confidently deliver that software quickly and frequently.

The following topics will be covered in this chapter:

- Defining quality
- Understanding test types
- Executing functional tests
- Executing nonfunctional tests
- Maintaining quality

Technical requirements

To experiment with the techniques described in this chapter, you might need one or more of the following:

- An Azure DevOps project with access to build and release pipelines and dashboards
- Visual Studio 2019
- A Basic + Test Plans license for Azure DevOps
- A SonarCloud subscription

All of these are available for free or can be obtained for free for a limited trial period.

Defining quality

One of the primary goals of the DevOps mindset discussed in Chapter 1, *Introduction to DevOps*, is increasing the flow of value to end users. To do this, software must be deployed frequently, maybe even multiple times per day. To make frequent deployments possible, two things are important: automation and quality. Automation has been discussed extensively in the previous chapters, and so now it is time to move on to the topic of quality.

Once an automated build and release pipeline is in place and changes are starting to flow to production at an increasing speed, it is time to start measuring the quality of these changes. Even more importantly, this allows us to abort changes that are not of sufficient quality. What actually makes quality *sufficient* can differ from project to project. When creating games, a few bugs might be annoying for the user but nothing more. When creating software for airplanes or medical use, a single bug may cost lives. In software, higher quality is more expensive and/or takes more time. So, there is a trade-off between the number of features we can deliver and the quality that can be guaranteed. For every project, there is a different optimal trade-off between these.

Before quality can be measured, it is important that you first establish how to measure the quality of software. A common approach to monitoring the quality of software is to gather one or more metrics. For example, it could be decided to collect a set of five measurements every week. Graphing these metrics over time provides insight into how the quality of the software is evolving. An example of this might look something like the graph shown here:

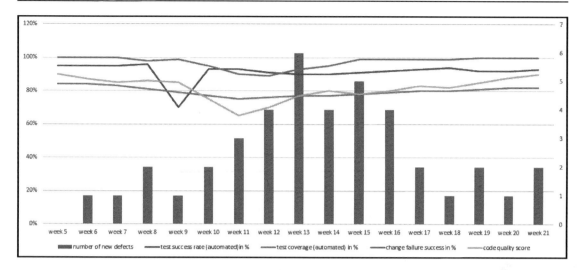

The next sections discuss several examples of metrics.

Metrics for quality

Metrics are a means of capturing something that is measured as a number. In software development, metrics are often used to represent a particular quality aspect that can be hard to quantify in itself. For example, the quality of a piece of software can be very hard to describe by itself. This holds even more for how quality changes. For this reason, we often capture numbers that, taken together, say something about the quality of software.

It is important to realize that metrics are a great tool, but should always be used with caution. For one thing, there might be more factors influencing the (perceived) quality of software than the metrics that are being measured. Also, once people know that a specific metric is recorded, they can optimize their work to increase or decrease the metric. While this might show the desired numbers in reports, this might not necessarily mean software quality is really improving. To combat this, often, more than one metric is recorded.

A well-known example is that of story point velocity in agile work environments. Recording the sprint velocity for a team to see whether it is becoming more efficient over time sounds effective; however, if the team size varies from sprint to sprint, then the metric might be useless since attendance is influencing velocity as well. Also, the metric can be easily falsified by a team agreeing on multiplying all estimations by a random number every sprint. While this would increase the numbers every sprint, this would not relate to an increase in team throughput anymore.

Moving on to metrics for measuring the quality of software, it can be difficult to objectively measure the quality of written code. Developers often have many opinions as to what constitutes *good code*, and the more the topic is discussed, the harder it can be to find consent in a team; however, when shifting attention to the results that come from using that code, it becomes easier to identify metrics that can help to provide insights into the quality of the code.

Some examples of this are as follows:

- **The percentage of integration builds that fails**: If code does not compile or pass automated tests, then this is an indication that it is of insufficient quality. Since tests can be executed automatically by build pipelines whenever a new change is pushed, they are an excellent tool for determining the quality of code. Also, since they can be run and their results gathered before we deploy a change to production, the results can be used to cancel a change before deploying it to the next stage of a release pipeline. This way, only changes of sufficient quality propagate to the next stage.
- **The percentage of code covered by automated tests**: If a larger part of the code is being tested by unit tests, this increases the quality of the software.
- **The change failure rate**: This is the percentage of deployments of new versions of the code that lead to issues. An example of this is a situation where the web server runs out of memory after the deployment of a new version of the application.
- **The amount of unplanned work**: The amount of unplanned work that has to be performed in any period of time can be a great metric of quality. If the team is creating a SaaS offering that it is also operating, there will be time spent on operational duties. This is often referred to as unplanned work. The amount of unplanned work can be an indicator of the quality of the planned work. If the amount of unplanned work increases, then this may be because the quality has gone down. Examples of unplanned work can be live site incidents, following up on alerts, hotfixes, and patches.
- **The number of defects that are being reported by users**: If the number of bugs reported by users increases, this can be a sign that quality has been declining. Often, this is a lagging indicator, so once this number starts increasing, quality might have been going down for a while already. Of course, there can be many other reasons for this number increasing: new operating systems, an increase in the number of users, or changing expectations from users.

- **The number of known issues**: Even if there are very few new defects being found or reported, if defects are never fixed and the number of known issues keeps increasing slowly, then the quality of the software will slowly decline over time.
- **The amount of technical debt**: Technical debt is a term used to describe the consequences of sacrificing code quality for short-term gains, such as the quick delivery of code. Technical debt is discussed in detail in the next section.

Testing is an activity that is performed to find and report on the quality of software. Test results (insights into quality) can be used to allow or cancel a change progressing to the next release stage.

In the next section, another dimension of quality is explored: the amount of technical debt in a code base.

Technical debt

Technical debt is a term that describes the future costs of sacrificing code quality for something else. For example, to expedite the delivery of a new feature, a developer may choose to quickly expand an existing class with a few new methods to realize this feature. If the resulting class does not adhere to the principles of object-oriented design or grows to be too large, this can make for a class that is difficult to understand and maintain or change later. The term "debt" implies that something (time, quality, attention, or work) is owed to the solution. So long as this debt is not paid off, you have to pay interest in the form of all other work being slowed down a little bit.

Technical debt can take many forms, but some examples are as follows:

- Code that is not covered by any unit test where changes to the implementation of said code cannot be verified using the original tests that were used to create it
- Code that is not written in a self-explanatory fashion using meaningful variable and method names
- Code that does not adhere to coding principles, such as KISS, YAGNI, DRY, and/or SOLID
- Classes that are too complex because they have too many variables and methods
- Methods that are too complex because they have too many statements (flow-control statements specifically)
- Classes or namespaces that have circular dependencies through different parts of the application
- Classes that do not adhere to the architectural design for the application

There are many forms of technical debt, and it can be daunting to oversee all of them. For this reason, there are many tools available that can measure the technical debt in a code base automatically and report on that. Tools for doing this will be discussed in the *Maintaining quality* section.

While technical debt is often considered a bad thing, there might be good reasons for creating technical debt on purpose. Just as with a regular debt, it is important to manage the height of the debt and to ensure that interest can be paid and the debt itself can be paid off.

Companies often take on technical debt during the start-up phase, where it is often a conscious decision to quickly create a working solution. While this first version is used to validate the business proposition and attract funds, developers can pay off this debt by reimplementing or refactoring (parts of) the application.

Another reason might be a market opportunity or an important business event that has been planned months in advance. Taking on some technical debt to make deadlines and deliver on time can be worth the cost.

However, never paying the debt and only taking on more debt over time will also increase the metaphorical interest to be paid every time a developer needs to make a change. The result will be that any change will take longer than the previous one. If this starts happening, it is unavoidable that at some point no change will be worthwhile anymore, since the cost always outweighs the benefits. At this point, a project or product has failed.

When talking about tests, it is important to understand which types of tests exist. The next section will go into this subject.

Understanding test types

In traditional software development, tests were often executed when *development was complete*, the *application was declared dev-done*, the *feature set was frozen*, or a similar statement. After declaring the development done, testing was performed, and often, a long period of going back and forth between testing and bug fixing started. The result was often that many bugs were still found after going live.

Shifting left is a testing principle that states that automated testing should be done earlier in the development process. If all activities involved with software development are drawn on a line from inception to release, then shifting left means moving automated testing activities closer to inception.

To do this, a wide selection of different types of tests are recognized—for example, unit tests, integration tests, and system tests. Different sources can suggest different types of tests, but these are some of the more well-known types. No matter the specific name of a type of test, when looking at tests with a high level of abstraction, they are often divided into the following two categories:

- **Functional tests**: Functional tests are in place to test whether the desired functionality is actually realized by the application.
- **Non-functional tests**: Non-functional tests are used to verify whether the other desired properties of an application are realized and whether undesirable properties are not present.

These types are further broken down into smaller subcategories, as shown in the following diagram:

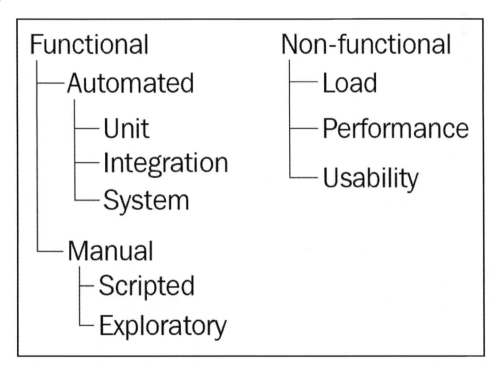

The following three sections contain brief recaps of the different types of functional and non-functional tests. This is to facilitate later discussions on which type of test to choose in which situation and how much of each type of test your project might need.

Types of automated functional tests

When talking about automated functional tests, the three most-used types are unit tests, integration tests, and system tests. These types of test can be compared along several axes: the time it takes to create a test, the time it takes to execute a test, and the scope that they test:

- **Unit tests**: Unit tests are the quickest to write, and they execute very quickly, often in less than a millisecond. They test the smallest possible scope in an application, often a single class or method. This means that, once written, it should virtually never be necessary to change a unit test. For many systems, it is more likely that a test will be deleted rather than changed.
- **Integration tests**: Integration tests take more time to write since they concern themselves with multiple units that have to be set up to work together. The execution of these tests should still be fast, averaging from below a second up to tens of seconds. Integration tests have a larger test scope, which means that, in return for this, they will cover a larger part of the code and are more likely to detect defects that are introduced with a change.
- **System tests**: System tests test a fully assembled and running application. Depending on the type of application, these are often API tests or automated UI tests. These tests take a lot of time to create since they rely on a deployed system to run and often require the setting up of an initial state in a database or another persistent store. The tests take a long time to execute, sometimes minutes per test. They are also less reliable and much more fragile than unit and integration tests. Even a minor change in an interface can cause a whole series of tests to fail. On the other hand, system tests can detect errors that both unit and integration tests cannot, since they actually test the running system.

Please note that having a large test scope in a test has both an upside and a downside. The upside is that it can detect many errors. The downside is that a failing test with a very large test scope provides only a limited insight into what has gone wrong. Such a test failure will often require more investigation than a failing test with a smaller test scope.

The following sections explore each type of test in more detail.

Unit tests

Unit tests are used to test a single unit in isolation. When working in an object-oriented programming language, this will come down to having one test class for every class in an application. For full test coverage, the test class will then have one or more tests for every public method of the corresponding application class.

Unit tests should run extremely fast—on average, in a few milliseconds or less. To make this possible, each class is instantiated without its dependencies. This is enabled by the use of interfaces, where classes depend on interfaces instead of directly on other classes. For tests, the dependencies are then replaced with mock classes, as shown in the following diagram. On the left, the runtime configuration is shown; on the right, the configuration during tests is shown:

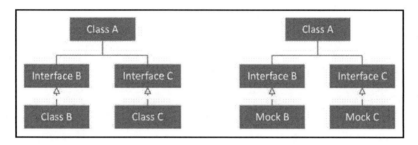

A mock class implements the same interface but has no behavior associated by default. Specific behavior can be set up on a per-test basis. Mocks can also be used to verify that certain operations or functions on a dependency are called. As an example, take the following C# class:

```
public class WorkDivider
{
    private readonly IMessageSender _messageSender;

    public WorkDivider(IMessageSender messageSender)
    {
        _messageSender = messageSender;
    }

    public void DivideWork(IEnumerable<WorkOrder> workOrders)
    {
        foreach(var workOrder in workOrders)
        {
            _messageSender.SendMessage(workOrder.GetMessage());
        }
    }
}
```

To instantiate this class in an automated test, an implementation of the `IMessageSender` interface is needed. To work around this dependency, a mocking framework such as Moq can be used to test `WorkDivider`, as follows. In these examples, `NUnit` is used as the testing framework:

```
[TestFixture]
public class WorkDividerTest
{
    private Mock<IMessageSender> _messageSender;
    private WorkDivider _subject;

    [SetUp]
    public void SetUp()
    {
        _messageSender = new Mock<IMessageSender>();
        _subject = new WorkDivider(_messageSender.Object);
    }

    [Test]
    public void
WhenSendingAnEnumerableOfWorkingOrders_EverOrderIsSendToTheMessageSender()
    {
        var workOrder = new WorkOrder();

        _subject.DivideWork(new[] { workOrder });

        _messageSender.Verify(x => x.SendMessage(workOrder), Times.Once);
    }
}
```

This means that it is not possible to write unit tests for classes that interact with other systems, such as databases, caches, or service buses. To ensure that this does not make it impossible to cover large parts of the application with tests, it is common practice to isolate the integration with other systems in separate classes. These classes contain the interaction with a remote system, but no business logic and as little code as possible. It is then accepted that these classes are not covered by unit tests. The typical design patterns that are used to do this are the facade, adapter, and repository patterns.

 Links to a more detailed guide on writing unit tests and how to mock classes are included at the end of this chapter.

Unit tests should be ready to run at the computer of every developer that clones the code base of an application. They should not require any special configuration or setup on the local computer and should be ready to go. This way, everyone who works with the code base can run the unit tests on their local computer. It is, therefore, a good practice for developers to run all unit tests on their own computers before pushing changes to the central repository.

Next to this local verification step, unit tests should also be a part of the continuous integration build. You will learn how to do this in the *Executing tests in a pipeline* section later on. As long as there are failing unit tests in a pull request, it is better not to merge the changes to the master branch. This can even be made impossible using Git repo branch policies, which were discussed in `Chapter 2`, *Everything Starts with Source Control*.

In the next section, the discussion of automated functional tests continues with integration tests.

Integration tests

Integration tests are used to test whether a group of components works together correctly. These tests are used for two purposes:

- Increasing the test coverage for those parts of an application that are not covered by unit tests—for example, classes that interact with other systems
- Addressing risks that are not addressed in unit tests and deal with classes interacting

It can be hard to understand what integration risks are since it might seem clear that the whole will work as expected, as soon as all parts are working as expected. To understand this risk better, imagine that two components working together are responsible for climate control. One is written measuring the temperature in degrees Celsius and the other is acting on that temperature, expecting its input in degrees Fahrenheit. It will quickly become clear that, while both components are working as intended, exchanging numbers and taking action based on those numbers, the combination will not produce the desired outcomes.

Integration tests, especially those that interact with other systems, will not only take longer to run than unit tests but often require more setup or configuration to run as well. This may even include secrets such as usernames, passwords, or certificates. To handle configuration such as this, a settings file can be created next to the tests from which settings are loaded before the tests are executed. Every developer can then create their own copy of that file and run the tests using their own configuration.

Continuing the example from the previous section, let's assume that the `MessageSender` class that implements the `IMessageSender` interface needs a connection string to do its work. A test class for `MessageSender` might then look as follows:

```
[TestFixture]
public class MessageSenderTest
{
    private MessageSender _messageSender;

    [SetUp]
    public void SetUp()
    {
        var connectionString =
TestContext.Parameters["MessageSenderConnectionString"];
        _messageSender = new MessageSender(connectionString);
    }
}
```

`connectionString` needed for constructing the `MessageSender` class is received from the `Parameters` object on `TestContext`. This is the `NUnit` approach for making settings from a `.runsettings` file available. The exact approach can vary per test framework. An example `.runsettings` file would look as follows:

```
<?xml version="1.0" encoding="utf-8"?>
<RunSettings>
 <TestRunParameters>
 <Parameter name="MessageSenderConnectionString" value="secret-value" />
 </TestRunParameters>
</RunSettings>
```

Moving the settings out to a separate file ensures that secrets are not checked into source control. In the *Executing tests in a pipeline* section, you will learn how to build a `.runsettings` file for running tests in a pipeline.

This is because integration tests should also be part of the continuous integration build if possible. However, there is a risk that this will make a continuous integration build too slow. To counter this, one of the following solutions can be implemented:

- Integration tests are executed in a separate build that is triggered in parallel to the continuous integration build. This way, the duration of the continuous integration build stays low while the integration tests are still continuously executed, and developers get fast feedback on their work.
- Integration tests are executed later in the pipeline, closer to the release of the software—for example, before or after the deployment to a test environment.

The downside of the first approach is that executing integration tests this way will mean that the tests will no longer work as a quality gate before code is merged to the master. They will, of course, continue working as a quality-reporting mechanism. This means that, while errors might be merged, they will be detected and reported by the build.

The second approach does not have this risk since executing the tests is still part of the pipeline from source control to production; however, in this approach, the execution of the tests might be deferred to a later moment in time if not every build enters at least part of the release pipeline. This means that defects might become visible later on, extending the time between detecting and fixing an issue.

In either approach, failing integration tests will no longer block merging changes and you hence have to find another way to ensure that developers will take responsibility for fixing the defect that caused the tests to fail.

These trade-offs become even more evident with system tests, which often take so long that it is not possible to make them part of the continuous integration build.

System tests

The third and final type of automated functional tests is system tests. These tests are meant to run against a fully assembled and running application. System tests come in two flavors, depending on the type of application: an API test or a UI test. System tests can take a long time to execute, and it is not uncommon for long tests with an elaborate setup of test data to take well over a minute.

 You might come across something called coded UI tests. This is a now-deprecated Microsoft solution for writing UI tests. These tests could be executed from Azure Pipelines. Luckily, there are many alternatives, as referenced in Microsoft's deprecation message at `https://devblogs.microsoft.com/devops/changes-to-coded-ui-test-in-visual-studio-2019`.

System tests execute against a running application, which means that they will need configuration and setup before they can be run. The application needs to be running in a controlled environment and all of the integrations with data stores need to be fully operational. Integrations with other systems need to be either up and running or swapped out with a replacement mock to ensure that all operations that integrate with those systems will function properly.

These conditions make it less likely that developers will execute these tests on their local machines as they are making changes to the application. It is only when they are creating a new test or changing a test that they might do so. However, even then they may be executing these tests not against a locally run version of the application, but against a version that is already deployed to a test environment. This is not necessarily a good thing, but often just the reality in most teams.

 An introduction to creating API or UI tests is unfortunately beyond the scope of this book. There are many products available on the market and which one is the best to use will differ from project to project.

When executing system tests as part of the pipeline, they are often run after the code has been deployed to at least one environment. This will often be the test environment. This implies that the system tests are on the critical path from a source code change to the deployment to production. If this path becomes too long, they can also be taken out of the pipeline. They are then run on a schedule—for example, every night. Just as with integration tests, this speeds up the pipeline, but it removes the opportunity to use system tests as a quality gate.

System tests, and UI tests in particular, are often fragile and can stop working unexpectedly after minor changes. For this reason, it is advised that you keep their number as low as possible; however, keep in mind that these are the tests that can catch particular errors, such as misconfiguration or other runtime errors, database-application mismatches, or series of operations that create error states.

Besides automated function tests, there are also manual functional tests that have value in many DevOps projects. These are discussed next.

Types of manual functional tests

While automated tests are a great tool for receiving feedback on development work quickly and often, there are still things that will be tested manually. While automating repetitive tests is the best way to continuously monitor quality, some things will require the human eye.

Manual testing is the tipping point for shifting left. Whenever any type of test or validation is shifted left, this means that it is executed before manual tests are performed. The benefit of this is that all of these automated activities add to the amount of confidence that we might have in the version of the application that is being tested, increasing the chances that the version will also pass manual testing. In other words, when manual testing starts, it should be very unlikely that any new issues will be uncovered.

There are two types of manual tests:

- Scripted tests
- Exploratory tests

Both types of tests will be discussed in the following sections.

Scripted testing

Scripted testing is a technique that is used to minimize the amount of time spent on the test execution while still ensuring full coverage of all relevant test cases. This is done by splitting the testing into two distinct phases: test preparation and test execution. Test preparation is done in parallel to the development of the feature that is to be tested or even before development starts. During test preparation, the feature is analyzed and formal test cases are identified.

Once the test cases that must be executed are identified, manual test scripts are written that describe every step that is to be taken during the test execution phase later. These scripts are engineered in such a way that they are easy to follow and leave no room for questions or doubts. They are also written in such a way that the number of steps to execute is as low as possible. While this may cost more time to prepare, all of it is done to ensure that as little time as possible is spent during the test execution.

A deeper discussion of test analysis and how to identify test cases is beyond the scope of this book. While you are responsible for test case creation, Azure DevOps supports you in this. Using the Test Plans service, you can create test plans and record the test cases within them for quick execution later on.

To create a new test plan, perform the following steps:

1. Open the Azure **Test Plans** menu:

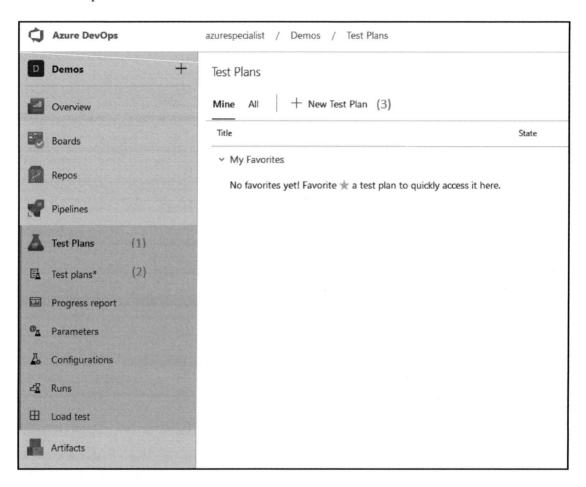

2. In this menu, click on **Test Plans**. Here, you will be presented with an overview of all of the test plans you currently have.
3. Click the **New Test Plan** button to start creating a new test plan. This will open a new dialog, as shown in the following screenshot:

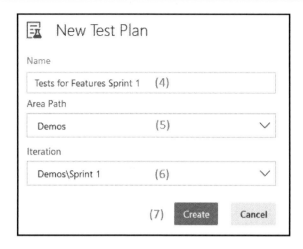

4. Give a meaningful name to the test plan, for example, a name that illustrates what the test plan is for.
5. Link the test plan to the correct product area path.
6. Select the correct iteration, or sprint, that this test relates to.
7. Press **Create** to finalize creating the test plan. This will automatically open this test plan, as shown here:

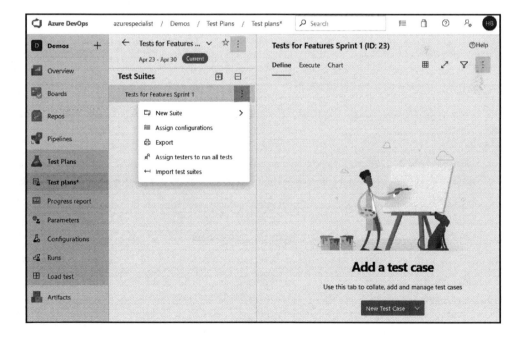

A test plan can be split into multiple test suites, which in turn can be split into test suites again. In essence, test suites are for tests what folders are for files. Suites can be managed by pressing the ellipsis button that appears when hovering over the test suite. This is shown in the preceding screenshot.

After creating a test plan, it is time to add one or more test cases to the plan. To do this, ensure that the **Define** tab is open for a test suite and click the **New Test Case** button. A new popup will open:

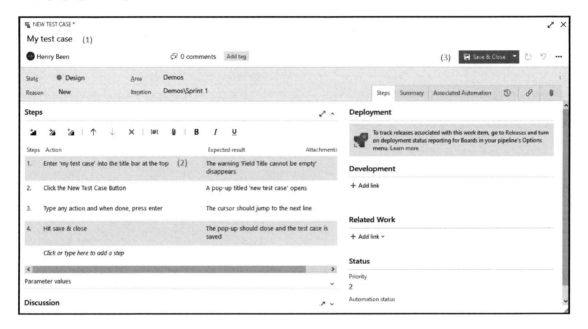

Here, the test steps and expected outcomes can be defined. To define a new test case, perform the following steps:

1. Enter a title for the test case.
2. In the dialog, enter one or more actions and expected results that describe the test case in detail.
3. Once the test case is completely described, press the **Save & Close** button to save the test case and return to the previous screen where you can manage the test suites.

Once the preparation is done and a feature is ready to be tested, all tests are executed. Since all tests are scripted in detail, this can be done quickly and effectively. There might even be developers, business analysts, or people from other parts of the company helping with the test execution. This means that the test execution itself will be really quick.

To start the execution of a test suite or plan, perform the following steps:

1. Navigate to the **Execute** tab:

2. Select one or more test cases.
3. Select one of the run options at the top-right.

When choosing to run the tests against a web application, a new browser window with a *test runner* will open. This test runner can be used to go through all of the test cases and for every test case, through all of the steps, and keep track of all successes and errors as shown here:

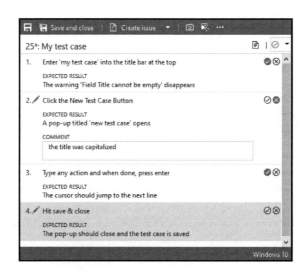

The tick or cross after every test step can be used to keep track of the outcomes for individual steps. If a step is marked as incorrect, a comment with the defect can be added. To mark a test case as passed or marked, the blue drop-down menu at the top-right can be used for marking the outcome. Once a test outcome is selected, the runner automatically progresses to the next test. Once all tests are performed, the results can be saved using the **Save and close** button on the top-left.

To view the outcome of a test run, navigate to **Test Plans** and then **Runs** to get the following dashboard:

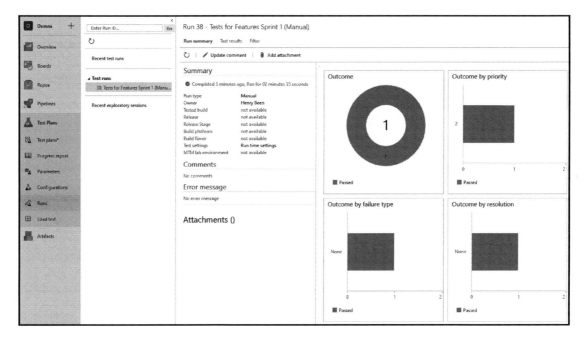

Here, you can select the run for which you want to see the outcomes to get a quick overview of the test outcomes. On the second tab, **Test results**, it is possible to view a list of all test cases and whether they passed or not.

A major benefit of having detailed scripts is that the same tests can be performed more than once, reducing the cost per execution. If a test plan is executed multiple times, all run history is maintained and can be accessed using the view shown in the preceding screenshot. This is useful if manual tests are used as part of a regression test; however, once this becomes the case, it is often even more beneficial to automate the tests using system tests, if possible.

It is possible to execute the same test multiple times, but for different *configurations*. When developing web applications, this is often done to test using different browsers. For desktop applications, this might be used to test for different operating systems. Working with configurations is detailed in the Microsoft documentation at `https://docs.microsoft.com/en-us/azure/devops/test/mtm/test-configurations-specifying-test-platforms?view=azure-devops`

The next section will discuss a final form of functional testing, namely, exploratory testing.

Exploratory testing

Writing and executing detailed test scripts can take a lot of time from both the test engineer and test executioner, so often these tests are automated. Once they are automated, they will fall into the category of system tests and automated UI tests in particular.

This does not necessarily mean that manual tests provide no value or no good return on investment at all. There are just some things that the human eye will catch that a computer will not, such as interfaces that are just not user friendly, misaligned interface elements, and text lines or images that are not fully displayed but get hidden behind other elements.

To catch these errors while not spending large amounts of time on detailed test scripting, exploratory testing might be a solution. In this approach, a tester opens the application and starts investigating those parts of the application that they feel contain the most risks with regard to the upcoming release. While exploring the application, the tester keeps track of which parts of the application they have visited and which test cases they have performed. Meanwhile, the tester also keeps track of new risks they identify or test cases they have not performed yet. In doing so, they are creating a list of covered and uncovered test cases while they are working. It also allows the tester to keep focusing on the most important risk and test cases all of the time. Once the exploratory test run is over, the tester can report on which application areas and test cases have been covered, which have not, and which risks are still not explored at all. This report can be valuable input for a product manager who must decide whether to move forward with a release or not.

A common misconception is that exploratory testing means that a tester is just clicking around to see whether the application is working okay. This is not the case, and the previous paragraphs have shown that exploratory testing is a highly structured activity that requires practice. If performed well, test preparation and test execution are interwoven during an exploratory testing session.

Exploratory testing is a great tool for when there is limited time or the amount of time available for testing is not known upfront. Exploratory testing may yield findings that need to be recorded as defects. How to do this is up next.

Reporting manual test results

One of the activities that is also part of testing is the reporting of any defects or other issues found. This is often tedious and time-consuming work. You must try and reproduce the issue one more time, trying to remember how the issue manifested itself again, and write down all of these steps. Then, both the desired and undesired outcomes must be described, screenshots must be taken, and everything has to be inserted into a bug tracker or work management tool, such as Azure DevOps.

To make this easier, there is a **Test & Feedback** extension for Azure DevOps available. The extension simply provides buttons for recording screenshots or videos and annotating them with text or drawings. Once an issue is found and documented by a recording or screenshot, it can be automatically submitted to Azure DevOps boards.

This extension is freely available from the Azure DevOps marketplace and runs in both Firefox and Chrome. Support for Edge is being worked on at the time of writing. A link to the extension is included at the end of this chapter.

 The Test & Feedback extension can be used when both executing scripted tests and when performing exploratory tests.

This concludes the discussion of different types of functional tests. The next section will help you to decide which type of test to use in your projects.

Strategies for deciding which types of functional tests you need

With so many different types of tests, which type of test is the best for your project? Given the wide range of types of tests and their different properties, the answer is as you might expect: a mix of all of them, as they all have different properties.

The following diagram shows the relation between the time the different types of tests take to execute and the confidence in the quality of the software they provide. It shows that while manual tests that complete successfully have the highest likelihood of identifying any defects, they also take the longest to execute. For automated tests, the time taken for tens of thousands of unit tests can often be kept to a few minutes, while ten to a hundred system tests can take over 30 minutes:

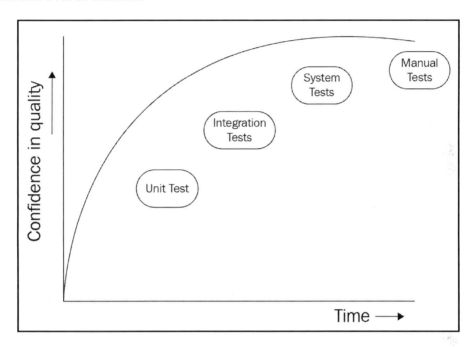

Looking at this trade-off, it often makes sense to prefer unit tests over integration tests, integration tests over system tests, and any type of manual test over automated tests.

If the quality of unit and integration tests increases, then this line will climb even more to the top-left. High-quality software architecture will also help to reduce the need for system and integration tests and increase the guarantees that unit tests bring. Both of these can make the positive effects of automated tests that run fast and often even stronger.

The understanding of this trade-off also helps to understand two models that can be used on deciding on your testing strategy: the testing pyramid and the testing trophy, which are discussed in the following two sections.

The testing pyramid

In many older projects, there are not too many automated functional tests. Often, many of these tests are slow to run, have a large test scope, are hard to maintain, and fail regular without a clear cause. The value that these tests provide is often very limited. To counter the lack of good automated tests, there are then many manual tests that are used to do a full regression test of the application before a new version is deployed. These automated tests are very time consuming and rarely executed. There is no fast feedback to developers and defects are often detected late. It is hard to practice DevOps in such a situation since the focus in DevOps is on creating new versions often and at a high rate.

Such a group of tests for an application is often called an ice-cream cone of tests: many manual tests and few automated tests, of which only a few are unit tests. The ice-cream cone of tests is an anti-pattern, yet often found in older and/or long-running projects:

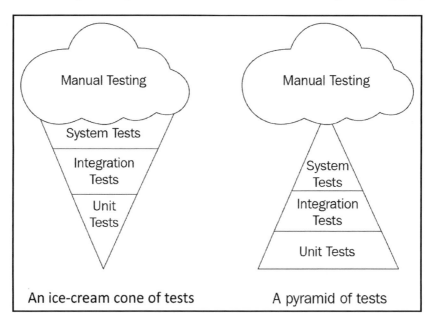

To battle this, another, opposing, model was introduced: the test pyramid. This model advocates having many unit tests that give feedback on the quality of the application within minutes, quickly pointing out most of the errors. On top of this, other types of slower tests are layered to catch only those errors that previous layers cannot catch. Using this approach, there is a good trade-off between test coverage and test duration.

Please note that the test pyramid does NOT advocate a layered approach. Do not first build a layer of unit tests and only proceed to integration tests when all unit tests are done. Instead, it advocates proportions: you should have a healthy ratio between unit tests, integration tests, and system tests.

General advice on the best ratio between different types of tests is very hard to give. But in most projects, a ratio of 1:5-15 for each step in the pyramid can be reasonable.

The testing trophy

While the testing pyramid is a well-known and often-used approach for classifying tests and deciding on which types of tests to create, this approach has been criticized as well. While moving away from manual and system tests is widely accepted to be needed in DevOps teams, the focus on unit tests is not universally accepted. Some object to the fact that the testing pyramid hints at creating many more unit tests than integration tests.

These reasons for this objection are as follows:

- **Unit tests tend to be closely tied to the implementation that they test.** Looking back at the test of `WorkDivider` in the section on unit tests, it can be seen that it relies on knowing how the `DivideWork` method is implemented. The test actually verifies the actual implementation: the call to `SendMessage()`. Many unit tests have this characteristic and, as a result, adding many unit tests increases the effort needed to change the implementation of the class-level design of a solution.
- **Unit tests tend to have a higher rate of change than integration tests.** Unit test classes are closely tied to the class they test. That means that if the class they test is replaced, the unit tests for this class also lose all value. For this reason, it is argued that integration tests might have a higher return on investment.
- **Real value comes from integrating components, not from individual components.** Even when all units are working in isolation, there might not be any value delivered by a system. The real value of software only comes once it is integrated and ready to run. Since testing should confirm value delivery, it is argued that the focus should be on writing integration tests over unit tests.

To deal with these objections, the testing trophy was introduced by *Kent C. Dodds*. This model adopts the testing pyramid in the sense that it advocates as few manual and system tests as possible but differs in the fact that it does not emphasize unit tests over integration tests, but the other way around. The name testing trophy comes from the fact that if this was drawn, this would result in a figure that would resemble a trophy.

Unfortunately, there is no silver bullet and the best advice is to know about all three models and the reasoning behind them and apply the appropriate lines of reasoning to your current situation. When it comes to testing, there is no single best solution for all.

Types of non-functional tests

Functional tests are mostly concerned with verifying whether the behavior displayed by an application is the behavior that is expected; however, there are more risks when it comes to application development: whether an application performs actions quickly enough, whether this performance degrades if more users use the system concurrently, and whether the system is easy for end users to use. Tests that verify these properties of a system under test are called non-functional tests.

There are many types of non-functional tests, but three of them that are important in DevOps scenarios are as follows:

- Performance testing
- Load testing
- Usability testing

Let's go over them one by one.

Performance testing

Performance tests are executed to establish how quickly an application can perform an action, given a set of resources. Performance tests are often executed using specialized tools and run against a fully assembled system. If the tools used for automated API or UI tests record the duration of a test, the duration of these tests can be used as performance results as well.

To compare results over multiple test runs, it is important to ensure that all factors influencing performance are kept the same between tests. The setup of virtual machines for both test subjects and test runners should stay the same. The application configuration should remain constant and integration points should be in the same state as much as possible—for example, instead of reusing the same database, the same database should be restored from a backup before every performance test. This ensures that the results are comparable.

While performance and load tests are often mixed up, they are two different types of tests.

Load testing

Load tests are performed to measure how much load the system can take before it breaks. These types of tests are sometimes also called stress tests. Unlike in a performance test, there are many requests executed in parallel. What is measured is the average performance of all requests, while slowly increasing the number of requests to the system. In most cases, this will identify a breaking point, a specific number of requests per second at which the performance will suddenly decrease. This is the number of requests per second that the system can maximally serve. When executing a load test, gathering the average performance while increasing the maximum number of requests will often result in a graph like the following:

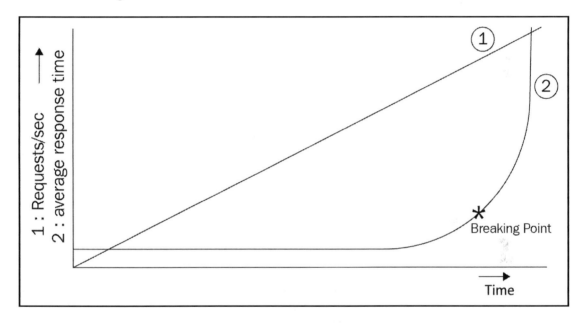

This graph shows why it is important to know the breaking point of an application: too much load might crumble a system unexpectedly because of the sudden nature of the change in response times. Knowing where this point is allows operators to act before this point is reached in a production environment.

At the end of this chapter is a link to an online Microsoft lab for developers to practice load testing.

Usability testing

Another important type of testing is usability testing. While other types of tests focus on verifying whether the implementation has the behavior desired by the product team, usability tests focus on verifying whether the expectations of the user are actually met. This means that the test scope is even larger and these tests can identify user interfaces that are clumsy and help to find unclear text or user requests that were misinterpreted.

Usability tests are run by letting the user work with the final application on one or more tasks and observing or asking about how they interacted with the application. Results are often much more verbose than "passed" or "not passed," and results are often given back to a product owner to write new user stories or change requirements.

A great technique for enabling usability testing is the use of feature flags. Feature flags enable us to gradually expose a new feature to more users. This capability can also be used to at first only expose a new feature to a select, limited set of users that are part of a usability study. This allows researchers or product owners to closely observe these users using the new feature, while other users cannot access it yet.

 Feature flags were discussed in Chapter 4, *Continuous Deployment*, as a strategy for progressive exposure. Progressive exposure of new features is in itself a form of usability or user acceptance testing.

This approach can be extended to execute A/B tests. In these types of tests, half of the users are exposed to a new feature while the other half are not. Metrics are then gathered about all of the users to see whether the new feature brings users the benefits that were predicted for it—for example, if users use the application for more hours per day or not. This topic will be expanded upon in Chapter 11, *Gathering User Feedback*, which looks at how to gather user feedback.

Doing this shifts usability testing closer to the right in the release process. It can also be shifted to the left by performing usability tests not with the final application, but with mockups.

This concludes the discussion of the different types of tests. In the next section, metrics and tests will be used to automatically measure quality and implement quality gates.

Executing tests in a pipeline

Developers should execute tests on their local machine before opening a merge request for their code. That way, they can be confident that any of the changes they made did not break any of the previous behaviors of their code. In theory, this provides the guarantee that all code merged to the master branch compiles and has all tests passing. In practice, there are many reasons why this is not the case. Some can be as follows:

- Some tests might not be able to be run locally. They depend on confidential configuration values or are configured to run against a fully configured system. One or both of these are often the case for system tests. There are many situations where it is impossible to run system tests from the local system. Not all of these situations are necessarily desirable or insurmountable—but still, this is often the case.
- Developers are only humans. They might forget to run the tests on their local machines after that one final tweak or are convinced that their changes did not break any existing behavior. Especially when delivering a bug fix under pressure, it can be tempting to skip running tests for the sake of speed.

To prevent these situations from allowing code that is not fully tested to propagate through the pipeline, it is recommended to have all tests also execute from within the pipeline. The following sections will show how to do this for unit tests and integration tests and for tests that are being run using other systems. First up are unit tests.

Running unit tests

For many languages, support for running unit tests from the pipeline is built into Azure DevOps. Unit tests can be executed for C#, TypeScript, Python, Maven, C++, Go, and many more.

For some of these languages, a single ready-made task is available. One example of this are tests written in C#. During the execution of .NET tests—for example, in C#—test results are automatically stored in an XML format that is understood by the build agent.

This allows the pipeline agent to interpret the test results and visualize them in the build results, as shown here:

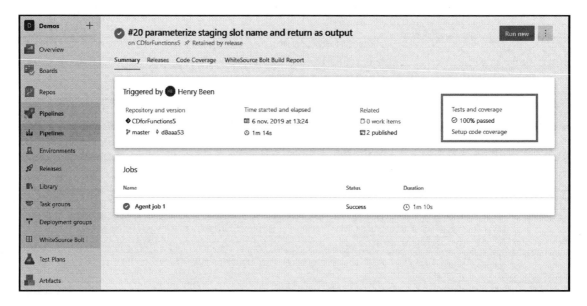

For some languages, more than one task has to be executed. For example, tests written in TypeScript are often executed via an NPM command. The following YAML can be used to do this:

```
- task: Npm@0
  displayName: 'Run unit tests - npm run tests'
  inputs:
    cwd: src
    command: run
    arguments: test
```

This will execute a custom NPM command as specified in `package.json`. Unfortunately, this will not store the test results in a format that the pipeline agent understands. To translate the outcomes into the correct format, another task is needed:

```
- task: PublishTestResults@2
  displayName: 'Publish Test Results'
  inputs:
    testResultsFiles: '**\reportTests\TEST-*.xml'
    mergeTestResults: true
  condition: succeededOrFailed()
```

Whether test results are available directly or have to be translated varies from programming language to programming language. Besides publishing test results, it is also recommended to gather test coverage results.

Recording unit test code coverage

It is a best practice to not only run all unit tests during the build but to also determine the percentage of the code base that was executed during any of these tests. This is called *unit test code coverage* and is an indication of how thorough the tests are. The build can also be configured to publish the code coverage achieved by unit tests.

To configure the build to publish test coverage for .NET Core unit tests, the following steps must be performed:

1. Install the NuGet package, `coverlet.msbuild`, into the unit test project.
2. Use the .NET Core task to execute the test and add two parameters to also generate coverage reports, `/p:CollectCoverage=true` and `/p:CoverletOutputFormat=cobertura`:

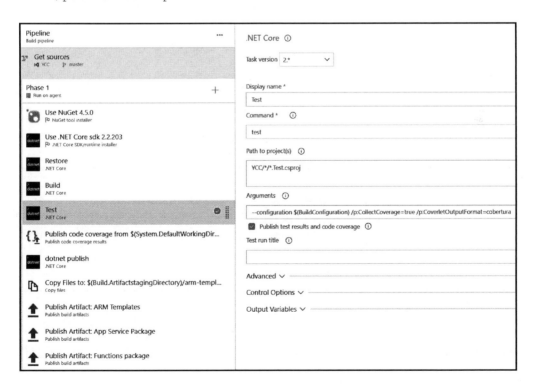

3. Add the **Publish code coverage** task:
   1. Set the code coverage tool to `cobertura`.
   2. Configure
      `$(System.DefaultWorkingDirectory)/**/coverage.cobertura`
      `.xml` as the summary file:

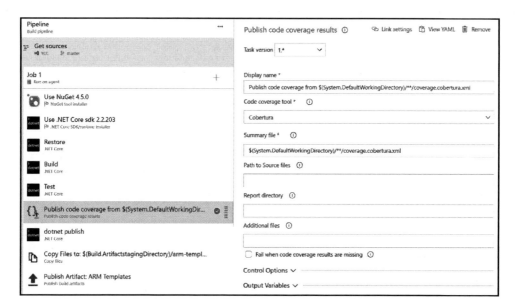

4. The build's run details will now contain code coverage reports.

This is all of the configuration needed to generate detailed code coverage reports. The generated reports contain the number of covered and uncovered code blocks and the calculated coverage percentage. These reports are part of the build results page.

Next to unit tests, integration tests can also be run as part of the pipeline and they often come with the challenge of dealing with managing configuration settings.

Running integration tests

Integration tests are often written in the same framework as unit tests. Still, they come with a unique challenge of their own. Often, they require one or more settings that specify how to integrate with one or more other components that are part of the test. Looking back at the integration test of the `MessageSender` class discussed before, this is an example of this problem.

Remember that this test had a `.runsettings` file that should specify `connectionString` to the queue that it should use? This `connectionString` setting cannot be checked into source control. Instead, a placeholder can be checked into source control, which is then replaced with the actual secret during pipeline execution.

In this case, this would mean that the following `pipeline.runsettings` file would be checked into source control:

```xml
<?xml version="1.0" encoding="utf-8"?>
<RunSettings>
    <TestRunParameters>
        <Parameter name="MessageSenderConnectionString"
value="#{MessageSenderConnectionString}#" />
 </TestRunParameters>
</RunSettings>
```

Before starting the actual test execution, another task is run to replace the placeholders with the actual values. These values can be securely retrieved from a variable group, key vault, or pipeline variable as discussed in Chapter 3, *Moving to Continuous Integration*. There are multiple extensions for Azure DevOps available that can be used for replacing placeholders with actual values. The following YAML is an example of how to do this:

```yaml
  - task: qetza.replacetokens.replacetokens-task.replacetokens@3
    displayName: 'Replace tokens in pipeline.runsettings'
    inputs:
      targetFiles: $(System.DefaultWorkingDirectory)/integrationtests-
location/pipeline.runsettings
```

After the execution of the replace tokens task, the test runner can be invoked just as with unit tests.

Running external tests

Besides unit and integration tests, you will probably want to execute tests using other systems. For example, Azure DevOps has no built-in support for executing load tests or automated UI tests. For these types of tests, it is necessary to invoke other systems from the pipeline. Many systems can be integrated in this way.

How to do this differs from system to system, but most of the time, the following steps will apply:

1. Configure the tests in the external system.
2. Install an extension for Azure DevOps that makes new tasks available for calling into that external system from the pipeline.

3. Create a service connection to the external system.
4. Add the task to the pipeline.

For details on configuring integrations, a good starting point is often the website of the vendor of the third-party product.

Maintaining quality

The previous sections detailed various types of tests and metrics that can be used for describing the quality of an application. With these in mind, it is time to start thinking about the tools that can be used for maintaining high quality or even increasing quality.

Code reviews

One of the most powerful tools for guarding code quality is the code review. When working with Git, a pull request needs to be performed to merge the changes of a developer back into the mainline. A pull request allows one or more other developers to review all changes and comment on them. The developer that opened the pull request can review the comments and make changes accordingly, increasing the quality of the changes while they keep working.

For code reviews to work at their best, it is important not to see them as a gate that you must get your changes through with as little effort as possible. It is much more fruitful to have an open attitude based on the assumption that everyone is trying to create high-quality code, and see the code review as a starter of a discussion on code quality. It is important to change perspectives, from seeing the code review as an annoying ritual in software development where others will complain about your code to an opportunity for welcoming others to give their input about your code and helping you to write code of higher quality.

Once such an attitude is in place, code reviews will become a source of learning. They will result in discussions between peers about the best way forward for tackling an issue: the best way not just for now, but for the future as well, taking no technical debt and having enough unit and integration tests along with the code that is to be merged. Code reviews are also a great tool for mentoring junior developers, allowing them to receive feedback on their own work. It can even be more valuable to have junior developers review the code of senior developers. This way, they can ask questions about things they do not yet know, and it will often lead to them pointing out overly complex solutions that might become technical debt over time.

Automatically gathering quality metrics

Next to manual reviews, there are also many tools available for automatically determining the quality of a code base. Some are built into Azure Pipelines, but more elaborate functionality comes from separate code-scanning tools. There are different mathematical approaches to measuring technical debt, and using a tool to do so provides great insights into not only the quality of an application but also the changes over time.

One possible tool for measuring the quality of an application is SonarCloud. SonarCloud is the SaaS offering based on SonarCube. This tool can automatically scan a code base for possible bugs, security risks, technical debt, and other metrics for quality. This is a paid, separate offering that integrates with the Azure DevOps pipelines. To work with SonarCloud, you have to create an account and retrieve a project key to invoke a SonarCloud scan from Azure DevOps.

For invoking SonarCloud, a set of three tasks is used that are part of an extension for Azure DevOps. After installing the extension and configuring a SonarCloud service connection, three tasks are added to the pipeline to set up the analysis, execute it, and (optionally) fail the build if the quality degrades. The first task is the only one that takes configuration, which is shown in the following screenshot:

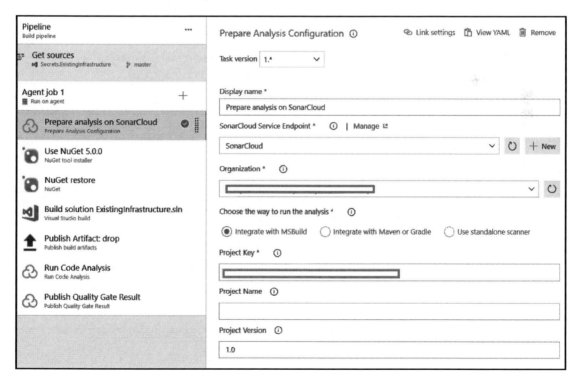

Every build that is now executed will automatically have its code scanned by SonarCloud, where extensive reports about the quality will be available. On top of these reports, a dashboard is generated that provides a quick overview of some key quality metrics:

Here is another glimpse of the dashboard showing quality metrics:

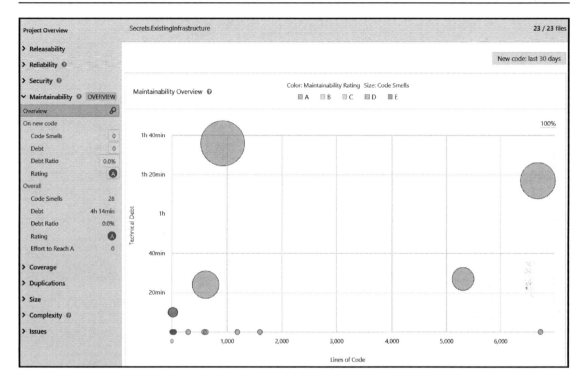

Code-scanning tools can be used for reporting the quality of the code, but can also act as a quality gate that will stop the merge of changes or deployment to a specific environment if insufficient quality is detected.

Visualizing quality

Measuring the quality of an application continuously has no value unless it is acted upon. Dashboards can be a powerful tool for gaining continuous insight into the current level of quality and how quality has changed over time.

Most code quality tools have built-in reporting options, and they can be valuable for quality assurance engineers. They provide detailed insight into which parts of the application are of higher quality and which types of issues recently occurred more frequently.

The downside of this type of dashboard is that they can be hard to read and that they are not in the tool where developers perform most of their work. For this reason, it can be beneficial to also create dashboards in Azure DevOps to report on quality. An example of such a dashboard is shown in the following screenshot:

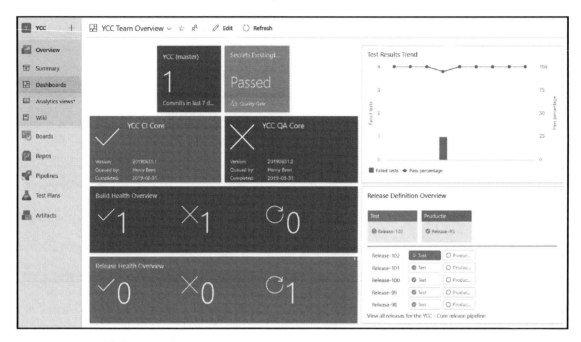

This dashboard shows an overview of the current quality and application code, as well as some recent history. Here, you can find the following information:

- The number of recent changes is shown on the top, along with the result of the most recent SonarCloud **Quality Gate** outcome, which currently reads **Passed**.
- The results of the two different builds in this project are shown in row two.
- Rows three and four show aggregations all of the builds and releases within the project. Symbols are used to denote the status of the builds and releases: successful, failed, or still running.
- On the right, two widgets are used to show the percentage of failed tests and the corresponding number of failed tests over the last 10 builds.
- The results of the latest release runs per environment are shown below this.

Dashboards such as these can be created per team or per project using built-in widgets or extensions. There are many extensions available in the Azure DevOps marketplace. For example, in the preceding dashboard, the **Team Project Health** extension is used.

Azure DevOps dashboards can be configured to automatically refresh every five minutes, making them usable as wallboards as well.

Quality gates

Measuring, reporting, and even visualizing quality is important and valuable; however, if no one is acting upon all of these metrics, it has no value to the development team. To prevent this, automatic quality gates or checks can be introduced.

One way to implement quality gates is by failing the continuous integration build whenever a test fails, the test coverage falls too low, or the thresholds that were set for the code-scanning tool are no longer being met. These are all things that have been discussed before. Another option to enforce standards is by adding gates or checks to pipelines. This way, certain conditions have to be met before the pipeline can continue.

How to do this differs between classic releases and YAML multi-stage pipelines.

Classic releases

One other option is the use of *gates* on Azure release pipelines. Here, it is possible to specify one or more conditions that have to be met before a release is allowed to be deployed to a specific environment. Gates can also be part of an extension, such as the SonarCloud extension that has been discussed before.

Gates can be added by selecting any stage in a release pipeline and editing the pre-deployment conditions. After enabling gates, one or more gates can be added. The following screenshot of a release pipeline shows how to disallow the deployment of any build of insufficient quality to an environment:

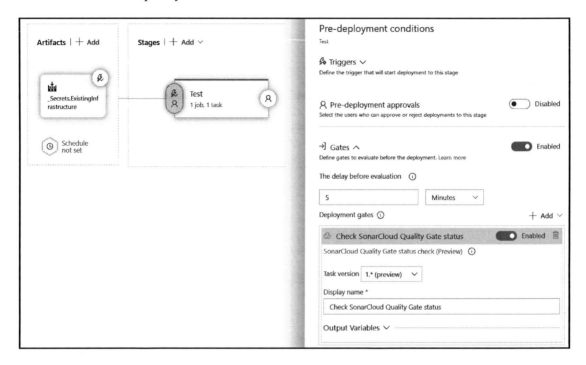

The use of deployment approves and gates are not mutually exclusive, so a mix of both can be used.

Multi-stage pipelines

Gates, as they are available for classic releases, are present in multi-stage YAML pipelines. In YAML pipelines, another mechanism is available: checks. Checks are configured to automatically validate if one or more conditions are met before allowing a pipeline to continue. Checks can be added to resources that are used in a stage. If one or more checks are found on one or more resources in a stage, all of the checks have to be passed before the pipeline continues to that stage. Checks can be added to environments and service connections.

To add a check to an environment, navigate to that environment:

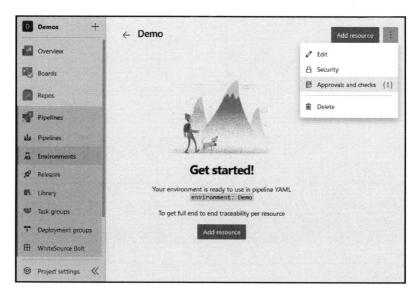

Now perform the following steps:

1. At the top-right, expand the menu and choose **Approvals and checks**:
2. In the new view that opens, choose **See all** to see all of the different types of checks that are available. Choose **Invoke Azure Function**:

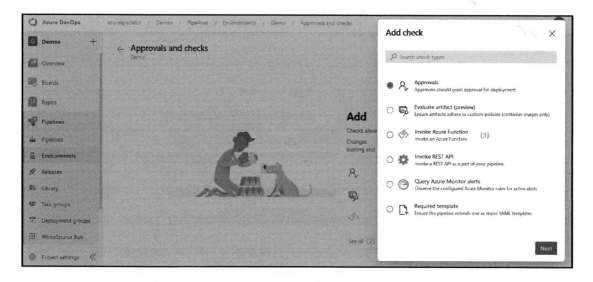

4. In the popup that opens, configure the Azure function to be called. At a minimum, the function URL and key have to be provided.

5. Choose **Create**.

Once the check is created, every deployment job (see `Chapter 4`, *Continuous Deployment*) that targets the environment has to pass this check. The check is passed when the function that is called returns a successful response code.

The following types of checks are supported:

- **Evaluate artifact**: Validate that an artifact of the type container image passes a custom policy. These policies are defined in a language called *Rego*.
- **Invoke REST API**: Post details about the pipeline to an Azure function to execute custom logic. If the API returns a successful HTTP status code, the pipeline is allowed to continue.
- **Invoke Azure Function**: The same as the **Invoke REST API** check, but with some defaults for Azure Functions.
- **Query Azure Monitor alerts**: Only continue if the specified alerts are not in an active state.
- **Required template**: Only allow the pipeline to continue if the current YAML pipeline extends one or more configured base YAML pipelines.

Checks can be a powerful mechanism for guaranteeing that one or more conditions are met before allowing a pipeline to continue.

Summary

In this chapter, you learned about how to measure and assert the quality of software development processes. Releasing quickly and often requires the software that is written to be of high quality. Testing is needed to ensure that you write software of high quality with little technical debt in it. You learned about the different types of tests and the pros and cons of the different types of automated and manual tests. Finally, you learned how code reviews and tools can help to maintain high quality in your project by reporting on quality and by serving as a quality gate.

With this knowledge, you are now able to discuss the tests and test types to help you to decide which tests are needed for your applications, which risks you can address using which types of tests, and whether you need many of them or can omit them. You are now also capable of setting up and configuring code-scanning tools to ensure that changes of insufficient quality are not merged to the mainline.

In the next chapter, you will learn about security and compliance, two topics that remain equally important when practicing DevOps.

Questions

As we conclude, here is a list of questions for you to test your knowledge regarding this chapter's material. You will find the answers in the *Assessments* section of the Appendix:

1. True or false: A unit test verifies the working of a single unit in isolation.
2. True or false: An integration test verifies the working of a fully assembled system.
3. Which of the following statements is correct, regarding the principles of the testing pyramid?
    1. Have many integration tests, fewer unit tests, and even fewer system tests.
    2. Have many unit tests, fewer integration tests, and even fewer system tests.
    3. Have many system tests, fewer integration tests, and many unit tests.

4. Which of the following is not a non-functional type of test?
    1. Load testing
    2. Usability testing
    3. Applicability testing
    4. Performance testing

5. Testing is about gaining insights into the quality of work. Which techniques can be employed to prevent work of insufficient quality propagating through to production?

Further reading

- More information about the testing trophy model can be found at `https://testingjavascript.com/` and `https://kentcdodds.com/blog/write-tests/`.
- More information about writing tests using C# can be found at `https://docs.microsoft.com/en-us/visualstudio/test/walkthrough-creating-and-running-unit-tests-for-managed-code?view=vs-2019` and `https://docs.microsoft.com/en-us/dotnet/core/testing/unit-testing-best-practices.`

- More information about the Test & Feedback extension can be found at `https://marketplace.visualstudio.com/items?itemName=ms.vss-exploratorytesting-web`.
- Practical labs to practice with load testing can be found at `https://docs.microsoft.com/en-us/learn/modules/load-test-web-app-azure-devops/` and `https://docs.microsoft.com/en-us/learn/modules/run-non-functional-tests-azure-pipelines/index`.
- Practical labs to practice with automating UI tests can be found at `https://docs.microsoft.com/en-us/learn/modules/run-functional-tests-azure-pipelines/index`.
- More information about SonarCloud can be found at `https://sonarcloud.io`.
- The team project health extension can be found at `https://marketplace.visualstudio.com/items?itemName=ms-devlabs.TeamProjectHealth`.
- More information about Rego can be found at `https://www.openpolicyagent.org/docs/latest/policy-language/`.

Security and Compliance

9

As important as it is to ensure that your application performs the functions it needs to, you also need to ensure it doesn't do things that it shouldn't. In the previous chapter, you learned about quality and testing in order to continuously measure whether your application is doing what it is supposed to do. In this chapter, you will learn how to prevent any unwanted behavior. This is the subject of security and compliance. While increasing the flow of value to your end users—by deploying faster and shortening delivery cycles—you will still want to make sure that you are delivering secure and compliant software. In this chapter, you will learn how to address these concerns in your DevOps processes.

To do this, this chapter will start by discussing the perceived trade-off between speed and security, and it will explain how security is not decreased but might even be increased when embracing DevOps. Next, a specific dimension of security is addressed: how to handle secrets such as keys and passwords that your pipeline and application need securely. Following this, code scanning tools for automatically identifying possible security risks in your application code and in your dependencies are discussed. The chapter concludes by discussing how to keep your infrastructure and configuration deployments compliant, and how to detect runtime security risks and threats using Azure Policy and Security Center.

The following topics will be covered in this chapter:

- Applying DevOps principles to security and compliance
- Working with secrets
- Detecting application code vulnerabilities
- Working with dependencies
- Ensuring infrastructure compliance
- Monitoring and detecting runtime security risks and threats
- Other tools you can use

Technical requirements

To experiment with the techniques described in this chapter, you will need one or more of the following:

- An Azure DevOps project with access to build and release pipelines and the right to install extensions
- An Azure subscription. (To sign up for Azure, you can go to `https://portal.azure.com` and follow the guide there if you do not have an account yet)
- PowerShell with the PowerShell Azure module installed. (Instructions on how to install the PowerShell Azure module can be found at `https://docs.microsoft.com/en-us/powershell/azure/install-az-ps?view=azps-4.1.0`)
- Optionally, subscriptions for WhiteSource Bolt, SonarCloud, or similar products

The preceding are all available, for free or as a trial, for learning or evaluation purposes.

Applying DevOps principles to security and compliance

Concerns about security and compliance can be a reason for companies to be reluctant to accept a full DevOps mindset, in order to ship software often and quickly. In the past, they used to have fewer releases that were all handed off for a security or pen test before being deployed to production. This gave them the confidence that they were not shipping software that contained security vulnerabilities.

This practice of fewer releases and having a big final security test before the final release conflicts with a DevOps mindset, and this is where some companies struggle. They are looking for ways to ensure that they are shipping business value to their users but are not willing to compromise on security to do so. The question is whether this is a fair trade-off. Wouldn't it be possible to have both speed and security? Might it not actually be the case that releasing faster and more often, in combination with rigorous automation, can help to increase the level of security in software development? To answer this question, it is good to first explore how security is often practiced in non-DevOps environments and how this needs to be changed when adopting DevOps.

Bringing developers and security engineers together

In many companies, security engineers are part of a different department compared to developers. The thought behind this separation is that it is beneficial to have some distance between those who are writing the code (that is, the developers) and those who are checking it.

In the past, the same separation often existed between software developers and software testers. However, recent insights have shown that putting developers and testers closer together does not result in unwanted behaviors such as group thinking, only testing what is already known to be working, or trying to cheat the tests by developing only for known test cases. Both experience and research show that the opposite is true. Putting developers and testers together results in products of higher quality. It is for this reason that movements such as Agile recommend development teams to incorporate, among other things, the discipline of testing.

It is by this same reasoning that the call for integrating security engineering into DevOps development teams is becoming louder. This movement is often called "DevSecOps" or "rugged DevOps." Both movements advocate that using DevOps principles such as shifting left and automating as much as possible can help to increase security. They advocate that pen tests or vulnerability reviews of applications are no longer done manually, but that they are fully automated as part of the delivery pipeline. This enables automation, faster feedback loops, and continuous delivery and deployment practices.

It is also advocated that shipping software more often can also help to increase security further, for the following reasons:

- When a reliable mechanism for shipping software automatically is available, any change that addresses a security risk can be deployed within minutes or days. Being able to react quickly to a new finding is a great security improvement.
- Speed itself can be a security measure. If the working of a system changes multiple times a day, it is significantly harder to figure out what its inner workings are at any given time and to misuse them.
- Applying the principle of immutable deployments and using infrastructure as code ensures that the infrastructure that is running an application is refreshed pretty often. This is a good mitigation of advanced persistent threats.

One of the things this chapter will explore is how to configure delivery pipelines to add security scanning. Please note that running these tools from a pipeline is a different discipline, which ensures that these tools are properly configured and apply the correct policies and requirements. For these activities, a security background and a close collaboration with security engineers are still essential. This is just another area where close collaboration can make a difference. Particularly on the subject of security, collaboration with other disciplines will be necessary; not to introduce manual checks, but to automate them together.

Security concerns

The rest of this chapter will introduce a number of security concerns, but it is helpful to realize that some of the previous chapters have also introduced security concerns already. As you already know from software development, security is not just something that you add in one place. Security should be applied everywhere. The following diagram shows different activities surrounding the creation and delivery of software. Next to each activity, the applicable security concerns are shown:

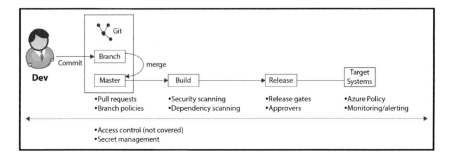

Let's walk through a quick recap of the security concerns at each of these stages:

- **Branch-master merge**: At this stage, the four-eyes principle is applied using pull requests. Pull requests allow another engineer to review the changes before they are merged into the master branch. Branch policies are used to make the use of pull requests mandatory, to ensure that the code compiles and that the unit tests run. This was discussed in `Chapter 2`, *Everything Starts with Source Control*, and `Chapter 3`, *Moving to Continuous Integration*.
- **Build**: During this stage, a security scan of all source code and third-party dependencies is executed by adding additional tasks to the build pipeline. This prevents security risks from propagating unchecked. We discuss how to do this in this chapter, in the *Working with secrets* section.

- **Release**: During the release, approvers can be configured. An approver is a user who has to give their approval before the deployment to a specific stage can continue. Additionally, automated release gates are used to ensure (and further enforce) that certain criteria are met before a release can continue. We discuss how to do this in `Chapter 4`, *Continuous Deployment.*

- **Deployment environment (target systems)**: All applications will run on a target environment. This can be on-premises; however, in this book, the focus is on Azure. For runtime security and compliance concerns, this chapter will introduce Azure Policy and Azure Security Center.

- **Cross-cutting**: All of the preceding points are only useful if there is sufficient access control within the Azure DevOps environment. While this is not in the scope of this book, it is an important angle to cover. Users should have enough rights to do their work, but they should not be able to make unauthorized changes to policies, builds, and deployment processes. Additionally, proper secret management is needed to keep secrets such as certificates, keys, and passwords secure during all phases of the delivery process. How we can do this is also covered in this chapter.

Now, with an understanding of how software and security engineers can come together to work on an application, it is time to address the different aspects of this work in the following sections. The next section will discuss how to handle secrets.

Working with secrets

An important security element is the handling of secrets. When deploying an application, there are always secrets involved. Especially when deploying to the cloud, that is, over the internet, handling these access keys in a secure way is very important. Besides the secrets that are necessary for deployment, there are also secrets that need to be inserted into the runtime configuration of an application. A common example is for accessing the database.

In `Chapter 6`, *Infrastructure and Configuration as Code,* multiple mechanisms for delivering application configurations were discussed, including **Azure Resource Manager (ARM)** templates. However, templates require the input of external secrets, since they cannot be stored in parameter files in source control.

Secrets should not be stored in source control.

If secrets cannot be stored in source control, then where should they be stored instead? Common options include storing secrets in service connections or in variable groups.

Storing secrets in service connections

The first group of secrets that are needed for the deployment of any application is those secrets that are required for connecting to the target system. No individual person should have access to these secrets as they are only used during deployments. This is why Azure Pipelines allows you to store them securely in service connections.

A service connection is the abstraction of another system that can be connected to from Azure DevOps. Service connections have a specific type, that is, to specify the family of systems they can be used to connect to. There are out of the service connection types for connecting to Azure, GitHub, Jira, NPM, NuGet, and over a dozen more systems. New service connection types can also be added through the Azure DevOps extension mechanism.

Service connections can contain a reference to the location of another system—often, a URL. Next to the location, they can contain an authorization token, a username, and/or a password, depending on the type of service connection. Secrets that are stored inside a service connection can never be retrieved again, not even by administrators. Also, whenever any details of the service connection are changed, the secret must be re-entered as well. This is to prevent a previously entered secret from being misused to access another location. These details indicate how service connections are designed to provide a secure location for storing connection credentials.

Service connections can be managed in a central location for each Azure DevOps project. You can create new connections, edit existing ones, alter user permissions, and much more. Practice this by following these steps:

1. To open this view, navigate to **Project Settings**. A vertical list of various setting options will open.
2. From the list, click on **Service connections**. You will be able to view the various connections, as shown in the following screenshot:

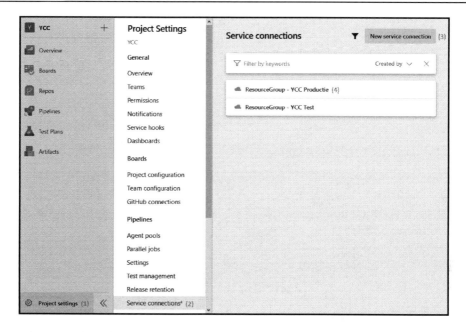

3. Now, click on the **New service connection** button in the top-right of the screen if you wish to create new service connections.

4. To modify an existing entry, simply click on it. This will take you to a screen that is similar to the following screenshot:

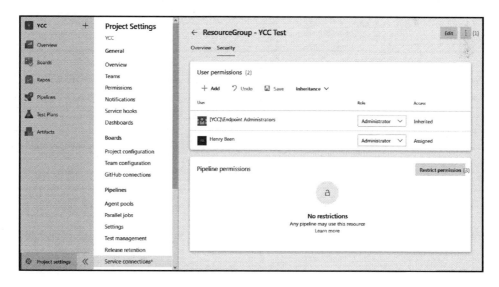

From this view, you can now carry out these actions:

1. Edit the service connection details.
2. Alter user permissions.
3. Restrict permissions.
4. Add more users or groups, and specify, for each, whether they can use or administer the endpoint.
5. Specify which pipelines can use this service connection.

In the current view, every pipeline in the project can use the service connection. This is not recommended and can be secured using the **Restrict permissions** button (3). After securing the pipeline, each pipeline that wants to use the service connection must be authorized by a service connection administrator first.

Storing secrets in variable groups

There are more secrets involved in application development than those that are required to connect to other systems. Examples include license keys, which are required during application compilation, or database usernames and passwords, which need to be passed on to the application after deployment or as part of an ARM template deployment.

These secrets can be stored in pipeline variables or variable groups, which we covered in Chapter 3, in the *Creating a build definition in Azure DevOps* section. Microsoft will store all variables that are marked as secrets securely and make them non-retrievable through the user interface.

However, there might be reasons for not wanting to store secrets in Azure DevOps but in a specialized key store such as Azure Key Vault instead. Doing so will provide the extra guarantees that come with Key Vault and the ability to further control access policies using **Azure role-based access control (Azure RBAC)** and Key Vault access policies.

When storing secrets in an Azure key vault, they can still be used as a variable group as well, by connecting an empty variable group to the key vault through a service connection, as shown in the following screenshot:

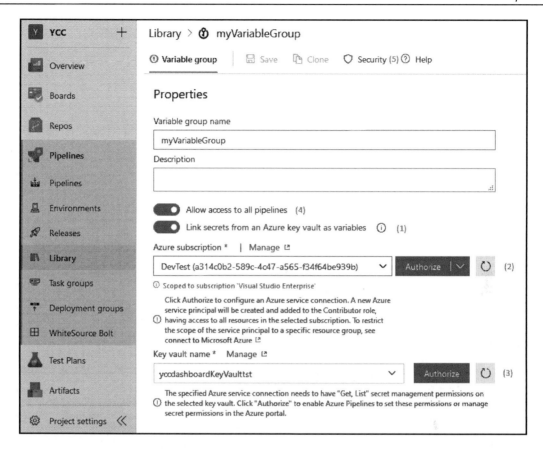

To use a key vault as the storage for a variable group, perform the following actions:

1. Enable the second slider to load the secrets from the key vault.
2. Select an already existing ARM service connection from the drop-down menu, or create a service connection with a new managed identity for Azure on the fly by selecting an Azure subscription from the list.
3. Type in the name of the key vault that the secrets should be loaded into. You can also select one from the drop-down menu. In that case, only key vaults that are accessible by the selected service connection are shown.
4. It is recommended that you disable the slider that allows access to all pipelines. In general, open authorizations are considered a risk, but, in particular, variable groups that hold secrets should only be available to explicitly authorized users.
5. Access for specific users can be configured using the **Security** tab.

The proper authorizations for the service connection to Azure and the key vault can also be automatically created. Please note that both operations will make changes to the Azure security setup, so ensure that these are (still) correct.

Detecting unsecured secrets

As mentioned previously, secrets should not be stored in source control, which is why the capabilities discussed earlier are available. Still, a developer can, by accident or for local testing, write down secrets in the application source code.

To ensure that these secrets do not end up in source control, a local plugin can be used to detect secrets and emit a warning to alert the developer to this risk. One tool that can do this for Visual Studio is the **Continuous Delivery Tools for Visual Studio** extension. This extension scans any open file for secrets and emits a compiler warning when it detects a possible secret. A link to this extension is added to the references at the end of this chapter. After running the installer, any secret it detects in Visual Studio will result in a compiler warning. Unfortunately, at the time of writing, the extension does not yet support Visual Studio 2019.

In addition to this, it is advised that you run a similar tool as part of the delivery pipelines to identify any secrets that have accidentally been checked in. Even though it will be too late to keep the secret secure, it does provide a clear signal that the secret is compromised and needs to be changed. One tool that can do this is **CredScan**. CredScan is a build task that is part of the **Microsoft Security Code Analysis Extension** build task.

 The Microsoft Security Code Analysis Extension comes with more capabilities than just CredScan. It also includes other security tools offered by Microsoft.

A link to the details of this extension is available at the end of this chapter; it also includes all of the installation details. Please note that the extension is only available under certain conditions and is not free.

Once the extension has been installed, CredScan can be added to your pipeline, as shown here:

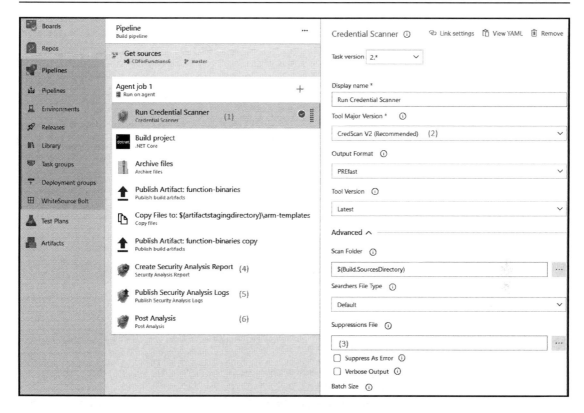

Perform these steps while referring to the annotations in the screenshot:

1. Add the **Run Credential Scanner** task to the pipeline.
2. Update the **Tool Major Version** to V2. For all of the other options, the default settings are good enough for a first scan.
3. If there have been previous scans that result in one or more false positives, they can be removed from the results by pointing to a suppressions file.
4. Add the **Create Security Analysis Report** task to the pipeline.
5. Add the **Publish Security Analysis Logs** task to the pipeline.
6. Add the **Post Analysis** task to the pipeline.
7. Save and queue the build definition.

While some tasks fail and cancel the build when an error is detected, the CredScan task does not. It will always complete successfully, even if passwords are detected. Only the **Post Analysis** task at the end of the build will act on discovered problems and fail the build if there are any issues found. The advantage of this is that all issues are identified, not only the first one. It also allows any other tasks you want to run to be completed.

The security analysis reporting task (*step 4*) is used to gather the logs of the different scanning tools that are part of the suite and combine the output into CSV and HTML files. The publishing task (*step 5*) publishes all of the generated files as a build artifact. If a possible password is detected, the following HTML will be generated and published as a build artifact:

Microsoft Security Analysis Report

Build Summary

View	File Path	Line	Error Id	Name	Description
View	SimpleFunction\SimpleFunction.Function\local.settings.json	9		SecretinFile	{{Searcher}}CSCAN-GENERAL0060 {{Code}}See local.settings.json line 9 for the code resulting in match {{Info}}Found General Password. {{Suggest}}Validate file contains secrets, remove, roll credential, and use approved store. For additional information on secret remediation see https://aka.ms/credscan

This concludes our discussion of secrets and how to keep them secure in a DevOps pipeline. The next section covers the detection of application vulnerabilities.

Detecting application code vulnerabilities

The security assessments that are often conducted at regular intervals in the pre-DevOps era cannot be just left out when moving to a DevOps culture. This means that, instead of leaving them out, they must be conducted in some other way. There are two approaches for doing this.

The first approach is to keep doing pen tests, security reviews, and other security inspections at regular intervals just as before. However, instead of waiting for an OK from the tests before moving to production, the code is deployed to production separate from the security assessment(s). This implies that there is an accepted risk that there might be vulnerabilities shipped to production that are found only during the next security scan and will be addressed in the next release. Using this approach, it is possible to achieve speed, but then it also needs to be accepted that some vulnerabilities might exist for a while.

The second approach relies on making application security scanning part of the regular workflow for committing code to the source code repository. For example, security code reviews do not have to be done per increment or every two months. They can also be done per pull request—before the code gets merged. Now, all of a sudden, you are no longer detecting vulnerabilities but are instead preventing them. The same can be done with security vulnerability scans. They can become part of the delivery pipeline, or a full nightly QA build that reports back on the quality of development every morning.

Of course, it is often not as black and white, and many companies use a combination of these approaches. They use automated feedback mechanisms to detect whatever they can, make security code reviews part of the pull request workflow, and then combine this with manual pen testing at regular intervals. In this way, the speed of delivery is increased, while there is no increase or even a decrease in security risks, the last being the consequence of the speed at which vulnerabilities can be mitigated.

OWASP Top 10

When it comes to the security of web applications, there are several types of security issues that are both common and responsible for the vast majority of all security issues. These types of issues are known as the OWASP Top 10. This is a list of the 10 most common types of security issues, published by the **Open Web Application Security Platform (OWASP)**. The list is reviewed every few years but has remained quite stable over the last couple of years.

Most of the errors in the OWASP Top 10 can be prevented by implementing automated security tests; either by using static code analysis for security vulnerabilities or with dynamic testing using the **OWASP Zed Attack Proxy (OWASP ZAP)**.

Implementing automated vulnerability scanning

In the previous chapter, in which continuous testing was discussed, SonarCloud was already introduced as a code scanner for technical debt and code quality. Besides assessing the quality of application code, SonarCloud can also be used to scan for security vulnerabilities. In `Chapter 8`, *Continuous Testing*, you learned how to add a SonarCloud scan to your pipeline. There are other, more specialized tools available as well, which we will discuss in the last section of this chapter.

These tools assess the application based on static tests. They scan the code to identify any risky code. This is called a white-box approach because they can see, inspect, and scan all of the code. In other words, everything is visible. This is the opposite of a black-box approach, where the running is application is treated as a closed whole and is only tested by invoking it and observing the responses. One tool that can do this is the OWASP ZAP.

OWASP Zed Attack Proxy

The OWASP ZAP is a tool that can perform the automated pen test of an application. This tool can run in two modes:

- **A baseline scan**: The baseline scan takes only a few minutes, and it is optimized to iterate over as many security risks as possible within those few minutes. This makes the baseline scan quick enough to be run early on in the deployment pipeline. It is even possible to run the security scan after every deployment to the first test environment, resulting in fast feedback to developers.
- **A full active scan**: The full active scan takes more time. In this type of scan, the proxy will examine every response from the application to identify other URLs that are part of the application, scanning them as well. In this way, the full application is discovered on the fly, using a spidering approach. This type of scan is more complete, but it also takes more time. For this reason, full scans are often run at intervals, for example, every night.

The OWASP ZAP proxy tries to identify any possible security risks. Some of the most notable risks are SQL injections, JavaScript reflections, and path traversals.

The OWASP ZAP is an application that can be installed on any virtual machine. The disadvantage of this is that the virtual machine is always running, even when there is no scan running. This is more costly, and, of course, the virtual machine itself needs to be patched and secured too. More recently, a containerized version of the proxy was also made available. This container can be run in Azure Container Instances, spinning up the proxy only when needed and tearing it down right after execution.

This completes our introduction to code scanning tools and their implementation. With the help of these tools, you can detect vulnerabilities in your application and prevent any security issues. The next section will examine how you can scan application dependencies.

Working with dependencies

Next to the security risks that the application code developed in-house pose, there is also a risk associated with components that are reused. Between 50% and 80% of modern application code is not developed in-house, but is taken from other parties in the form of packages or dependencies. Some of these might be open source, but this is not necessarily the case. There can also be components that are bought from other development companies or binaries taken from galleries such as NuGet.

Dependencies not only pose security risks, but also licensing risks. What happens if a team starts using a component that is published under the GPL license for a closed source component? If anyone ever finds out, they can be forced to open source their product, or at least suffer public shame for not using the work of others according to the license.

To mitigate these risks, a number of tools can be used to detect and scan all of the dependencies that are used when building an application. One of the tools available to do this is WhiteSource Bolt, which is available as an extension from the Azure DevOps marketplace.

Working with WhiteSource Bolt

To start executing scans with WhiteSource Bolt, perform the following actions:

1. Install the WhiteSource Bolt extension from the Azure DevOps marketplace.
2. Navigate to the **WhiteSource Bolt** menu under **Pipelines**.
3. Sign up and accept the license terms.
4. Add the **WhiteSource Bolt** scanning task to build or release definitions, as shown in the following screenshot:

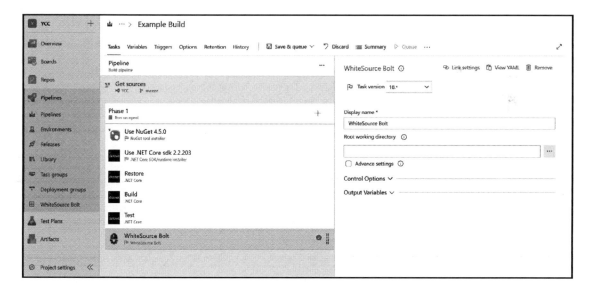

5. Once a pipeline with the WhiteSource Bolt task installed has run, the page with the build results will contain an extra tab called **WhiteSource Bolt Build Report** that shows the results, as shown in the following screenshot:

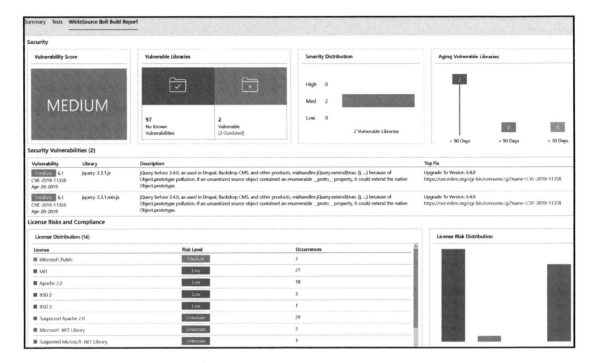

This report provides a number of insights about the overall security and licensing risks of the scanned application build:

- The top row, with four widgets, provides an overview of the vulnerability score and three different breakdowns into how that score was calculated.
- Below this, all of the vulnerable packages are listed by name, with a reference to the dependency and a recommended mitigation.
- The section at the bottom provides a list of all licenses used by the dependencies. This list is sorted from high risk to low risk.
- Below this overview, WhiteSource Bolt also generates a list of dependencies for which a newer version is available (this is not visible in the preceding screenshot).

The results shown in this report can also be accessed from the **WhiteSource Bolt** menu, under the **Pipelines** menu. In this view, all of the reports for all of the builds can be accessed. This view is great for those who are responsible for accessing security or licensing standards across a project or organization.

This completes our discussion on dependency scanning. As mentioned earlier, you can use these tools to your advantage to detect and scan all the dependencies that are used when building an application. In the next section, infrastructure compliance is introduced.

Ensuring infrastructure compliance

Another important topic is that of compliance. In many countries or markets, there are sets of rules and policies that must be implemented or adhered to when creating software. A fair share of these policies relates to the infrastructure that the applications are running on. If this infrastructure is deployed and managed on the Azure platform, Azure Policy can be a powerful tool for ensuring that the infrastructure complies with regulations.

In Chapter 6, *Infrastructure and Configuration as Code*, the topic of ARM templates was discussed. ARM templates can be viewed as a technique for describing a complete Azure environment as a JSON array with many objects, each describing one resource in an application's infrastructure.

Azure Policy allows you to write policies that query this document and the changes that are being made through any of the APIs or ARM templates. Whenever a resource is found that matches the query, it is prevented from being created or the match can be added to a list of audit results.

Next to writing custom policies, there are many policies readily available for all Azure users. These policies can be used to audit resources that do not comply with best practices or general advice. There are also groups of policies available, called initiatives, that describe the applicable parts of market standards.

Assigning an Azure Policy or initiative

Policies can be assigned at different levels within Azure, either at the resource group level, subscription level, or management group level. This can be done through the portal, ARM templates or blueprints, or PowerShell.

To use PowerShell, the following series of commands can be used:

1. To retrieve a reference to the resource group and policy, use the following command:

```
$rg = Get-AzResourceGroup -Name myResourceGroupName
$definition = Get-AzPolicyDefinition | Where-Object {
$_.Properties.DisplayName -eq 'Audit VMs that do not use
managed disks' }
```

The policy that is chosen here is a built-in policy that will audit all virtual machines that do not use managed disks but have custom disks in storage accounts. This policy definition will be used in the command in the following assignment.

2. To assign the policy to the resource group, use the following command:

```
New-AzPolicyAssignment -Name 'audit-vm-manageddisks' -
DisplayName 'Audit VMs without managed disks Assignment' -Scope
$rg.ResourceId -PolicyDefinition $definition
```

Within 30 minutes of this assignment, the new policy will become active. At this point, a policy evaluation cycle is started, and all of the resources within the assignment scope will be evaluated against the policy. At the time of writing, there is no published SLA regarding how long such an evaluation cycle can take. Experience shows that this can be anything between 15 minutes and multiple hours—depending on the size of the assignment scope.

Writing an Azure Policy

While there are many built-in policies available, there are many use cases in which the creation of custom policies is needed. Just like any other Azure resource, a policy is written as a JSON document. The appropriate ARM resource type is called `policyDefinitions` and has the following structure:

```
{
    "name": "string",
    "type": "Microsoft.Authorization/policyDefinitions",
    "apiVersion": "2019-01-01",
     "properties": {
       "parameters": {
         "location": { ...}
       },
         "displayName": "...",
         "description": "...",
         "policyRule": {
```

```
          "if": {
            "field": "location",
            "equals": "[parameters('location')]",
          },
          "then": {
              "effect": "<audit|deny >"
          }
        }
      }
    }
```

The `parameters` object can be used to specify one or more parameters that need to be specified when assigning the policy later on. These parameters follow the same syntax and work the same as the parameters of an ARM template.

The `displayName` and `description` properties can be used to give the policy definition a meaningful name and description for later reference.

The body of the definition contains two elements, as follows:

- **The `if` statement** is used to specify a query that selects the Azure resources that this policy should apply to. There is a specific syntax for writing complex queries in JSON that is detailed in the ARM template reference that is linked at the end of this chapter.

- **The `then` statement** is used to describe the action that needs to be taken for any resource that matches the condition. This can be *deny*, that is, to automatically deny the creation of any non-compliant resource. Another approach is not to deny non-compliant deployments but rather to audit them. While denying non-compliant deployments is very straightforward in theory, there is good cause for temporarily allowing non-compliant deployments. In such cases, an audit policy can help to keep tabs on these resources. All non-compliant deployments get audit records in their Azure Activity log and can be viewed in the Azure portal, under **Azure Policy** in the **Compliance** tab. This is as follows:

After writing the policy definition, we need to create it within an Azure subscription for it to be usable. This can either be done through an ARM template or manually within the portal. From a DevOps perspective, writing policies in source control and delivering them through a pipeline as part of an ARM template is the recommended approach. In this way, Azure policies are written in the same way as the application and can be reviewed and automatically deployed to Azure as part of a DevOps pipeline.

Initiatives

When working with Azure Policy, many companies find that they need to create many policies to define all the rules that they want their software developers to adhere to. For this reason, it might be beneficial to group policies. Such a grouping is called an "initiative" and these are defined in JSON as well:

```
{
  "name": "string",
  "type": "Microsoft.Authorization/policySetDefinitions",
  "apiVersion": "2019-01-01",
  "properties": {
    "displayName": "string",
    "description": "string",
    "parameters": { ... },
    "policyDefinitions": [
      {
        "policyDefinitionId": "string",
        "parameters": {}
      }
    ]
  }
}
```

The body of an initiative is an array of objects. Each object must contain a `policyDefinitionId` property and, optionally, an object with `parameters` for the policy. The `policyDefinitionId` property must reference a valid `policyDefintions` through its Azure resource ID. The `parameters` array should specify all of the parameters that the policy requires. Often, this is implemented by having the initiative specify the combined set of all parameters of all policies as an initiative parameter. The parameters for the individual policies are then specified with a reference to the initiative parameters.

Fetching audit results

After assigning a policy with the audit effect, the policy will automatically evaluate all of the resources within the scope of the assignment once it is active. There is no guarantee of how long this can take. For new resources, the results of policy evaluation are visible within 15 minutes, but, often, this is faster.

Once the results are in, the compliance status for each policy or initiative can be viewed in the portal, resulting in an overview, as shown in the following screenshot:

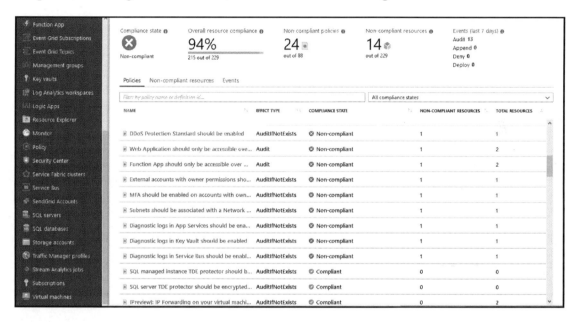

The difference between this report and other reports, which are the result of a manual audit, is that this overview is constantly updated to reflect the actual, current state of compliance—it is not a snapshot of compliance at a specific point in time.

An important benefit of this type of compliance is that the rules or policies are applied continuously to all the existing resources and any incoming change. This means that it is possible to ensure that the application environment is always compliant and always adheres to any rules and policies that apply.

Contrast this with the often-used approach of having security and compliance audits only every so many months. Often, this results in environments that are only compliant just before the audit and with its compliancy slowly decaying afterward. That is, until it is time for another audit, of course, at which point it rises close to 100% again. At many companies, this results in a compliance graph as follows:

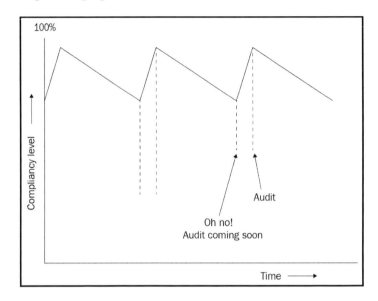

With this, we've discussed another example of how DevOps practices can help increase security and compliance—by ensuring infrastructure compliance. In the next section, several alternative tools for those mentioned in this chapter will be discussed.

Monitoring and detecting runtime security risks and threats

All of the security tools that have been discussed up to this point have focused on preventing shipping vulnerable code to production environments. However, the complete, deployed software solution, including all its support infrastructure is made out of so much more than just the code. On top of that, there are many interactions with a solution that may be unexpected or unplanned. Monitoring all of this continuously in production is necessary, not just to prevent security concerns but to also detect any security concerns coming up. In Azure, one of the tools available for doing just that is Azure Security Center. Azure Security Center is offered via the Azure portal and can be selected as any other service using the menu on the left or by searching for it in the top bar.

After opening Security Center, something similar to the following screenshot will open:

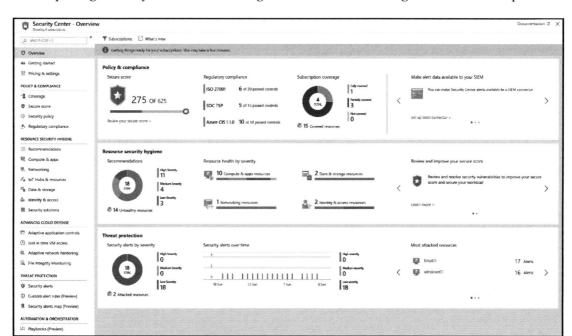

This dashboard delivers insight into three main categories:

- **Policy and compliance**: This part gives an overview of how compliant all of the selected Azure subscriptions are with regard to the security policies you have configured.
- **Resource security hygiene**: Azure has many security controls that can be turned on or off, along with many security configuration settings. Just as anywhere else, it is up to the user to balance cost and security with risk and ease of use. This dashboard will show recommendations for turning the security up for your resources. Users can decide for each recommendation whether they want to follow it.

- **Threat protection**: This section shows how many threats or attacks have been automatically detected and reported:

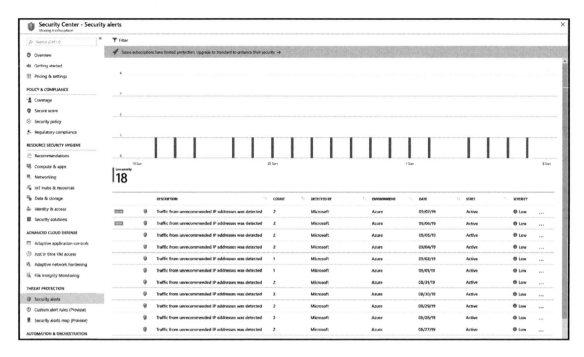

All of these overviews and categories can be drilled down further. The preceding example shows the results of opening the **THREAT PROTECTION** overview. Here, it lists all of the possible security threats it has identified. In this case, it lists different access attempts to virtual machines that are hosted within the subscription.

There are many more capabilities within Azure Security Center and more are being added on an ongoing basis. When deploying in Azure, this is the place to identify and manage security risks.

This concludes our discussion of the various techniques for monitoring runtime environments for security risks. The next section looks at several alternative tools for performing some of the scanning tasks that were mentioned in earlier sections.

Other tools you can use

There are many tools available on the market for performing security scans of application code and dependencies. Some examples include WhiteSource, Black Duck, Veracode, and Checkmarx.

WhiteSource is the paid version of WhiteSource Bolt. It offers the same services and more. For example, it doesn't only report risks at the time of the dependency scan; it also gives you alerts when new risks become available for dependencies that were present in the last scan of an application.

Black Duck is a product that helps teams to manage the risks associated with using open source software. The services it offers are comparable to WhiteSource.

Veracode and **Checkmarx** are code scanning tools that are used to identify vulnerable code. Whereas SonarQube checks both the code quality and security risks, these two products focus solely on security risks. In general, they are better at security scanning, with the downside being that they are more expensive.

Summary

In this chapter, you have learned that DevOps and security are not two conflicting goals, but that DevOps practices can help you to reinforce security. First, you learned how to handle passwords and other secrets when working with continuous deployment pipelines. Next, you learned how to enhance your pipelines with code and dependency scanning tools, applying the shift-left principle to security as well. Finally, you learned how to use Azure Policy to define constraints and rules for your infrastructure and how you can have these automatically applied or have non-compliant deployments audited or automatically denied.

With the knowledge you have gained, you are now able to have a conversation within your company about how to address security concerns within your DevOps teams. You can cooperate with security engineers to configure the tools you work with and receive automated feedback on the security implications of your work.

In the next chapter, you will learn about application monitoring. Additionally, you will learn how to monitor whether your application is running smoothly and how to gather runtime metrics.

Questions

Here is a list of questions for you to test your knowledge regarding this chapter's material. You will find the answers in the *Assessments* section of the *Appendix*:

1. True or False: Securing the delivery of software is just a single step in a deployment pipeline.
2. Which tool can be used for security testing, where a proxy is used to identify valid application URLs and then perform different attacks, such as injections on an application?
3. True or False: In most modern applications, over 50% of the code base comes from open source libraries.
4. What are the secure locations for storing the secrets needed during deployment or for running an application? (You can choose more than one answer.)
    1. Azure Pipelines variables that are marked as secret
    2. Azure Key Vault
    3. Azure DevOps Key Vault
    4. Azure Variable Groups
    5. Azure DevOps Secure Variables
    6. Azure DevOps Service Connection
5. Which two Azure offerings can be used to detect security risks at runtime?

Further reading

- The OWASP Top 10 and the details of every type of risk can be found at `https://www.owasp.org/index.php/Top_10-2017_Top_10`.
- WhiteSource Bolt can be found on the Azure DevOps marketplace at `https://marketplace.visualstudio.com/items?itemName=whitesource.ws-bolt`.
- A detailed walk-through on using the OWASP ZAP can be found at `https://devblogs.microsoft.com/premier-developer/azure-devops-pipelines-leveraging-owasp-zap-in-the-release-pipeline/`.

- More information about the Azure Policy resource types and JSON specifications can be found as part of the ARM reference at `https://docs.microsoft.com/en-us/azure/templates/microsoft.authorization/allversions`.
- More information about the continuous delivery tools for Visual Studio can be found at `https://marketplace.visualstudio.com/items?itemName=VSIDEDevOpsMSFT.ContinuousDeliveryToolsforVisualStudio`.
- More information about the Microsoft Security Code Analysis Extension can be found at `https://secdevtools.azurewebsites.net/helpcredscan.html`.
- More information about WhiteSource Bolt and WhiteSource can be found at `https://bolt.whitesourcesoftware.com/` and `https://www.whitesourcesoftware.com/`.
- More information about Black Duck can be found at `https://www.blackducksoftware.com/`.
- More information about Veracode can be found at `https://www.veracode.com/`.
- More information about Checkmarx can be found at `https://info.checkmarx.com`.

Section 3: Closing the Loop 3

In this section, you will learn that DevOps is not only about shipping code to production faster and faster and delivering more iterations per week. Another important aspect is to observe and measure the software that has been delivered, to shape the direction of future iterations. This part of the book will cover both monitoring applications and user feedback.

This section comprises the following chapters:

- Chapter 10, *Application Monitoring*
- Chapter 11, *Gathering User Feedback*

10
Application Monitoring

In the previous chapters, you learned about applying DevOps principles to software delivery. You learned how to create a pipeline from source control all the way to production. You also learned how to ensure that your delivery is compliant and secure, without sacrificing speed or a focus on the delivery of business value. In this chapter, you will learn how to start transforming this pipeline into a DevOps loop, a continuous process of delivering new software, and then measure how your application performs. This is a continuous journey, as you evaluate how your application fares in production and learn how to proceed next.

To do this, this chapter starts by introducing a means for gathering application crashes. Almost every application will, at some point, throw an unhandled exception and crash. Ensuring that application crashes are gathered and reported will enable you to investigate the causes and to address them. Next, attention shifts to instrumenting applications. Instrumentation is the practice of gathering logs and metrics that help you understand how your application performs in production. You can use them to get alerts when things go wrong or, hopefully, before they go wrong. The chapter concludes by exploring several options for integrating with other tools.

The following topics are covered in this chapter:

- Investigating application crashes
- Instrumenting web applications
- Integrating with other tools

Technical requirements

To experiment with the techniques described in this chapter, you will need one or more of the following:

- An App Center account for gathering mobile application crashes
- A Raygun subscription for gathering desktop application crashes
- An Azure subscription for instrumenting web applications

Free-trial options are available for all of these.

Investigating application crashes

No matter how well an application is engineered, at some point, it will crash due to an unexpected condition. To learn from these crashes and to try and prevent them in the future, it helps to add code to applications to gather crash reports and send them to a central location. Here, they can be analyzed and grouped to identify application improvements. How to do this differs depending on the type of application.

The following sections discuss how this process for mobile and desktop applications works. Regarding web applications, gathering crash reports can be done using the same tool as for instrumentation; we will discuss this in the *Instrumenting web applications* section later on.

Gathering crash reports for mobile applications

One of the many tools available for gathering crash reports and errors from mobile applications is Visual Studio App Center. Besides distributing mobile applications, App Center also allows applications to submit their crashes and errors for analysis.

To get started with crash reporting using App Center, the application first needs to be defined. This is called an app definition and how to work with it was discussed in `Chapter 4`, *Continuous Deployment*. With this app definition, an app secret is created, which is needed to configure the application to send out crash reports. To start sending crash reports, the following steps need to be performed:

1. Install the `Microsoft.AppCenter.Crashes` NuGet package on the project.
2. Add the following code to the application initialization:

```
AppCenter.Start("ios={appSecret};android={appSecret
};uwp={appSecret}", typeof(Crashes));
```

Besides crashes, it is also possible to track other errors that are of interest to developers. This can be done using the following code:

```
Crashes.TrackError(ex);
```

Now, all the unhandled exceptions are automatically caught and sent back to App Center. Here, they become available for analysis, as in the following screenshot:

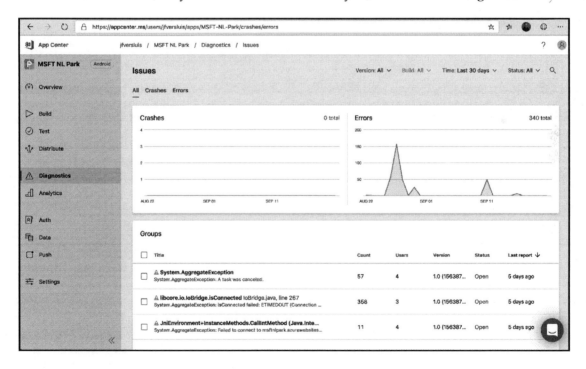

3. Click on any of the reported errors or crashes to open a detailed view, as shown:

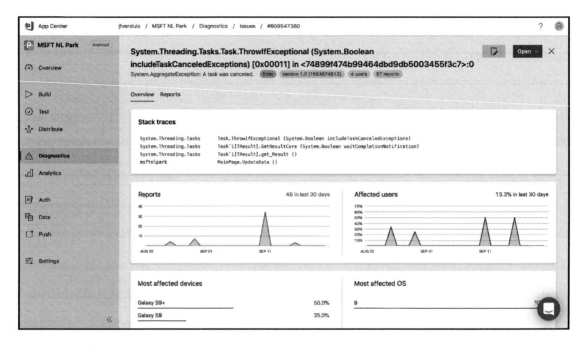

A dashboard with the most important information is shown for each crash or error. This includes the number of reports and the number of affected users. Also, the impacted device types and operating systems are shown. At the top of the page, the stack traces are shown, which can be used by developers to investigate and, hopefully, fix the issue.

This covers gathering crash reports and errors from mobile applications. The next section introduces the same concepts for desktop applications.

Gathering crash reports for desktop applications

Crash reporting is also available for desktop applications. There are, again, many solutions available for desktop applications and most of them work in roughly the same way. One of these solutions is Raygun. Raygun is a commercial offering available for .NET applications, but works for many other languages and platforms as well.

To gather crashes using Raygun, follow these three steps:

1. Sign up for a Raygun account.
2. Install the `Mindscape.Raygun4Net` NuGet package on the solution.
3. Catch unhandled exceptions and forward them to Raygun.

The following example shows you how to catch and forward unhandled exceptions to Raygun:

```
class Program
    {
        private static readonly RaygunClient _raygunClient = new
RaygunClient("myKey");

        static void Main(string[] args)
        {
            AppDomain.CurrentDomain.UnhandledException += HandleEx;
            throw new Exception("Boom!");
        }

        private static void HandleEx(object sender,
UnhandledExceptionEventArgs e)
        {
            _raygunClient.Send(e.ExceptionObject as Exception);
        }
    }
```

Once this is done, all the exceptions can be explored in the Raygun web interface. Here, exceptions are automatically grouped if stack traces are sufficiently similar. They can also be grouped and browsed individually, but in most cases, it makes sense to only focus on the larger groups of exceptions.

The following screenshot shows how these groups can be browsed in Raygun:

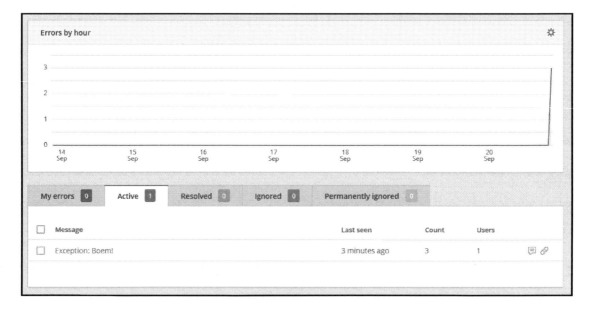

Clicking on the exception message in this interface shows the complete stack trace and all the shared properties of any instance of the exception that has occurred.

This completes our look into gathering crash reports from mobile and desktop applications. Doing so allows you to find and investigate issues that customers face in production. In the following section, instrumentation for web applications is introduced to further enhance our insight into how applications behave in production.

Instrumenting web applications

Web applications are different from mobile and desktop applications in many ways—for instance, the fact that large parts of the application do not run on a client, but on a server. This allows developers to collect information on how the application is run for web applications more easily than for other types of applications. Doing so is called instrumenting an application.

Logs are text messages that are saved by the system to describe the execution path that the server follows. This helps developers go back in time and explore what has happened by examining the logging output. Structured logging is quickly becoming the standard for trace logging. Structured logging is a technique where logs are no longer only text messages. Instead, logs are parameterized text messages with a set of values for each parameter. This has two advantages—logs can be better compressed and they can be searched more quickly.

Metrics are values that are recorded for an application. They take the form of a timestamp, metric name, and value. One example is recording the percentage of CPU in use every second.

When instrumenting an application, it is easy to focus on many server-level types of logs and metrics. For example, many operators will, by default, start collecting metrics such as CPU usage, memory pressure, and I/O operations. While there is nothing wrong with these metrics, they are not always indicative of an application's performance from a user's point of view. Other metrics, such as response times or queue message processing delays, might yield better insights into the user experience. While there is nothing wrong with measuring system metrics (they are often great indicators of future issues), you should also try to gather user-centric metrics.

Azure offers the Application Insights service for instrumenting applications, with a focus on web applications. An Application Insights workspace can be created using the Azure portal, which opens up a workspace as in the following screenshot. One of the important things here is **Instrumentation Key**, which will be used in later sections. Even though this field is plainly shown, it is recommended that you treat this as an application secret:

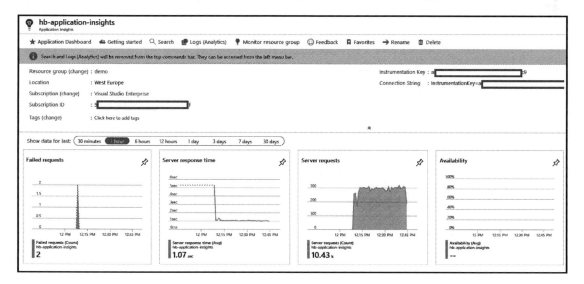

If you want to experiment with Application Insights and Azure Monitor using a ready-made application, there is a link to an example at the end of this chapter in the *Further reading* section. The example is a simple URL shortning application that uses multiple application components and has logging and monitoring built-in and can be used to start experimenting with the concepts introduced in this section within minutes.

The following subsections will go into detail about logging, metrics, and investigating individual requests.

Logging

One of the most basic types of instrumentation is adding logging statements to application code. In the past, these logs were saved to the disk of the server that ran the application. Retrieving and investigating these logs then took a lot of time and effort.

In modern hosting environments, logs are no longer saved on the local filesystem but instead stored remotely. With transient infrastructure and servers added or removed on the fly, it is no longer possible to store logs on the server and be sure that they can be retrieved later. For this reason, they are transmitted over HTTP to specialized log stores, such as Application Insights.

Emitting logs

To write log entries to a log store, such as Application Insights, from an ASP.NET application, two things must be done:

1. Log entries need to be emitted from application code, where applicable, using the `ILogger` interface. This interface is available from the `Microsoft.Extensions.Logging.Abstractions` NuGet package.
2. The Application Insights NuGet package (`Microsoft.ApplicationInsights.AspNetCore`) needs to be installed and Application Insights needs to be registered as `LoggingProvider`. This way, all logs sent to the preceding interface are forwarded to the Application Insights code. In turn, this code forwards all the logs to the Application Insights service.

The following example code shows you how to use the `ILogger` interface from a class to emit a structured log entry:

```
public class Example
{
    private readonly ILogger<Example> _logger;
```

```
public Example(ILogger<Example> logger)
{
    _logger = logger;
}

public void DoSomething(User user)
{
  _logger.LogWarning(
     "Doing something for user with id '{userId}' and username
'{username}'",
       user.Id,
       user.Username);
}
}
```

 There should be no dollar sign ($) at the start of the log entry. There is no string interpolation used here, but two placeholders are inserted into the text message. The structured logging entry will recognize these and when showing the entry, insert the provided values.

With log entries emitted, a logging provider should be registered to capture these logs. This is done using the .NET Core built-in dependency injection.

After installing the Application Insights NuGet package, the following code needs to be added to the `CreateWebHostBuilder` method:

```
public static IWebHostBuilder CreateWebHostBuilder(string[] args)
{
  return WebHost.CreateDefaultBuilder(args)
    .UseStartup<Startup>()
    .ConfigureLogging(builder => {
       builder.AddApplicationInsights("myKey");
    }
}
```

When using version 2.7.0-beta3 (or later) of the Application Insights NuGet package and using Application Insights for metrics, the preceding configuration is no longer needed.

After starting the application, all log entries of level warning and higher are automatically forwarded to Application Insights. To change which entries are forwarded and which aren't, filters can be configured. A link to more details on configuring Application Insights in detail is provided at the end of this chapter.

Searching logs

Within a few minutes of emitting a log entry to Application Insights, it becomes available on the interface for querying. To do this, open the Application Insights instance and navigate to **Logs (Analytics)** on the left-hand side menu (1). This opens the view shown in the following screenshot:

Here, it is possible to write queries (2) that search the recorded logs in **Kusto Query Language** (**KQL**). Application Insights is optimized for handling large amounts of data and most queries return results within a second or less, even when searching millions of log entries.

Alerting on logs

Gathering and searching logs is useful when troubleshooting specific situations or bugs in response to a user complaint. However, there are situations where it is better to be notified automatically when a certain condition arises. This is called alerting.

Within Azure, it is possible to create alert rules that notify developers whenever a certain condition is met. Alerting functionality is provided by the Azure Monitor offering that is integrated with many Azure services, including Application Insights.

To create a new alert rule, follow these steps:

1. Navigate to Azure Monitor using the portal.
2. Now, choose **Alerts**. This opens the view shown in the following screenshot:

If there are any alerts that need attention, they are shown here.

3. To add new alert rules, use the button at the top-left hand side of the screen. Doing so opens another view, as in the following screenshot. Here, the alerting conditions can be configured:

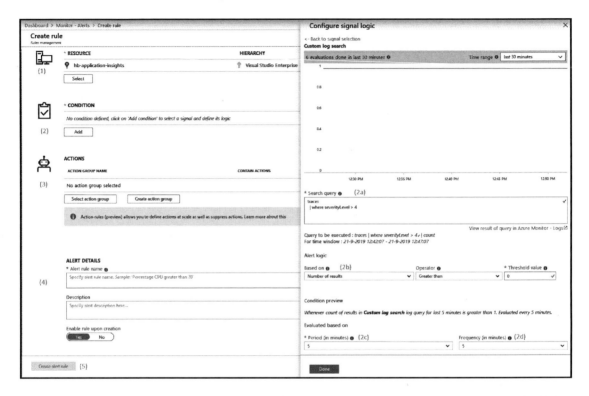

In the preceding screenshot, the view that opens for configuring alerts is shown on the left. Here, it is necessary to make several selections to create an alert:

1. This is the resource that is the subject for the alert. This can be any type of resource and, in this instance, the alert will be on an Application Insights workspace.

2. These are the conditions to alert under. To select these, the popup on the right opens. Here, a choice can be made between different types of alerts. Pick the **Log Search** alert type to open the detailed view shown here. Here, the following selections must be made:
   - **A query on the trace logs** (refer to **2a** in the previous screenshot): In this example, the trace log is queried for entries that have a severity of 4 or up, which means that they are emitted using the `LogWarning` or `LogCritical` methods.

- **A condition and operator for triggering the alert (2b):** In this case, the alert is triggered whenever there is one or more matches.
- **The interval to evaluate the alert condition over (2c):** When specifying a query that matches a specific number, this determines the interval in which this amount must be met.
- **How often to evaluate the alert condition (2d):** Evaluating an alert condition too frequently can result in too many alerts opening and closing in a fast series. Evaluating an alert condition too infrequently can result in alerts coming in too late. Experimentation will help you understand how to configure this.

2. This is the action to execute when the alert condition is met. Since there might be a lot of alerts that have to invoke the same group of actions, actions can be grouped, and these action groups can be referenced here. Some examples of actions are calling a webhook or sending an SMS message or email.
3. The alert configuration is completed by putting in a name and description.
4. Finally, the alert can be saved.

After the alert is created and activated, which is done automatically, within a few minutes, the alert is ready to inspect application logs and signal whenever the alert condition is met.

Logging is a great method of gaining deep knowledge about what happened with a request and how an error came to be. Another technique for learning more about an application's behavior is by using metrics.

Metrics

Besides logs, an application can also emit one or more metrics. A metric is a series of values over time that describes one or more aspects of a system. Some examples of metrics are as follows:

- The number of users currently logged in
- The number of products viewed by users
- The number of database transactions

Gathering metrics such as these can provide insight into how a system is used and how it currently operates. Metrics are often used for creating dashboards and alerts.

Emitting metrics

To start working with metrics, they first have to be emitted by an application and stored in a centralized location. Besides logging, Application Insights can be used for metrics as well.

To use Application Insights for metrics, the following steps need to be taken:

1. Metrics need to be emitted from application code where applicable, using the `TelemetryClient` class. This interface is available from the `Microsoft.Extensions.Logging.Abstractions` NuGet package.

2. Install the `Microsoft.ApplicationInsights.AspNetCore` Application Insights NuGet package.

3. Register `TelemetryClient` with the `Dependency` container. Do this by using the extension method on the container builder, as in the following code snippet:

```
builder.RegisterType<TelemetryClient>().SingleInstance();
```

4. Once this is done, the application is ready to start emitting metrics. This is done using the `TelemetryClient` class:

```
public class Example
{
 private readonly TelemetryClient _telemetryClient;

 public Example(TelemetryClient telemetryClient)
 {
     _telemetryClient = telemetryClient;
 }

 public void DoSomething()
 {
_telemetryClient.GetMetric("doSomethingCalledCounter").TrackVal
ue(1.0);
 }
}
```

Emitting a metric involves two steps. First, a reference to the metric is retrieved using the `GetMetric()` method. Next, a value is submitted using the `TrackValue` method. Submitted values should be doubles or allow an implicit conversion to a double.

Once the metrics are emitted, they can be used to create graphs and metrics. However, before moving on to these topics, first, another type of metric is discussed—namely, Azure platform metrics.

Besides, the metrics that an application emits, there are also numerous metrics that can be recorded from the Azure platform that the system is running on. Some examples are as follows:

- The percentage of CPU used
- The number of messages on a service bus
- The number of database transactions per second
- The amount of free disk space

These metrics are often closely related to how an application performs and may even be leading indicators. For example, when the amount of free disk space reaches 0, most web servers stop working.

In Azure, each service emits a series of metrics by default. These are called platform metrics. Which metrics are emitted differs from service to service and cannot be influenced by the user. Azure Monitor gathers these metrics automatically as well, and these metrics can be used in the same way for graphing and alerting as metrics are emitted by an application. The first one—graphing—is explored in the next section.

Platform metrics are built-in and free of charge and are retained for 93 days.

Graphing metrics

All metrics that are gathered, either in Application Insights or in Azure Monitor, can be used to build graphs and dashboards that visualize the metric. Graphs can be created using the **Metrics** tab that is available on every Azure resource. Graphs can also be created using the Azure Monitor offering. This way, graphs for multiple resources can be combined on a single canvas. To do this, do the following:

1. Open Azure Monitor, which is available from the menu on the left.
2. Navigate to the **Metrics** menu. This opens the view shown in the following screenshot:

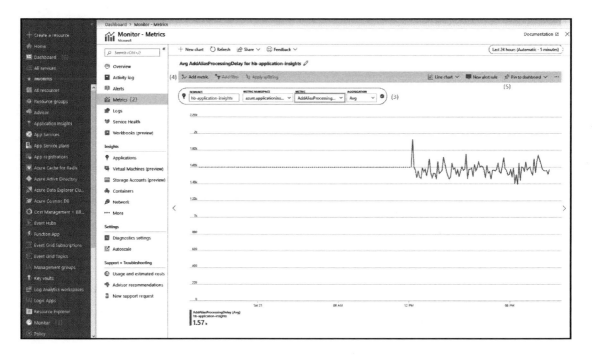

3. Once the canvas opens, one or more graphs can be added to it. A graph is built using the graph builder at the top. Four selections have to be made here:

- The resource that a graph needs to be drawn for.
- The metrics namespace belonging to that resource that a graph needs to be drawn for: For every Azure resource type, there is only a single namespace. The only exception is Application Insights, for which there are two—one with default metrics and one with application metrics that are emitted using `TelemetryClient`.
- The metric to draw: For custom metrics, this refers back to the name chosen in the `GetMetric()` method from the previous section.
- The mathematical operation to combine multiple measurements into a single point on the graph: This can be the minimum, maximum, average, or sum count.
- To add multiple graph lines to the same graph, choose **Add Metric** at the top. Repeat the preceding four selections to configure the new graph.

4. To make this graph part of a dashboard for easy reuse, click the **Pin to dashboard** button at the top.
5. Dashboards can then be accessed directly using the menu on the right.

Having a graph of a metric, or even multiple graphs in a dashboard, is great for investigating issues. However, no one likes to continuously watch dashboards to see how things are going. For that reason, it is also possible to configure alerts on metrics.

Alerting on metrics

Just as with log entries, it is possible to be alerted by Azure Monitor when a metric goes above or below a certain threshold. Log entries that require a follow up could be related to only a single user or customer that is having trouble. Metrics, on the other hand, are useful for detecting situations where all users are impacted by an issue, or situations where infrastructure no longer works or will stop working soon.

Creating alerts for metrics works in a way that is very similar to creating alerts from logs. To create a new alert rule, navigate to Azure Monitor using the portal and then choose **Alerts**. Next, click on the **New Alert Rule** button to open the view shown in the following screenshot:

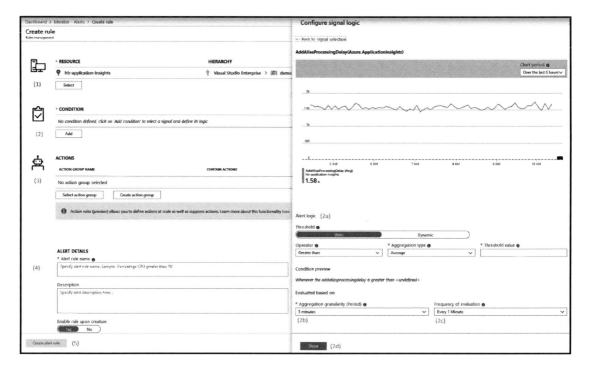

In this screenshot, the following selections have to be made to create an alert on a metric:

1. Select the resource that is the subject for the alert. This can be any type of resource that outputs metrics—in this instance, an Application Insights workspace has been selected.

2. Configure the condition to raise the alert under. For this, a new window opens on the right. To get to the view in the preceding screenshot, select a **Metric** alert type and from the list that populates, choose the correct alert. Next, the view changes to what is shown in the preceding screenshot. Here, the following selections must be made:

    - Select the threshold for the alert to raise (refer to **2a** in the previous screenshot). Static thresholds are the default and require the configuration of an operator, aggregation type, and value.
    - Pick the granularity interval that the alert should be evaluated over (**2b**).

- Pick the frequency of evaluation (**2c**). The more often an alert is evaluated, the shorter the delay between an occurrence and the alert that is sent out.
- Save the alert condition (**2d**).

2. Select one or more action groups that need to be triggered when the alert condition has been met.
3. Configure an alert rule name and description.
4. Save the alert.

The alert becomes active within minutes after saving. Now, whenever an alert condition is met, the developers are notified using the methods configured in the alert group.

Investigating requests

When using Application Insights for logging and metrics, there are many more built-in capabilities of Application Insights that you can use. One of these capabilities is the possibility to execute search queries against all types of data collected by Application Insights from one view, called **Search**.

Here, it is possible to search all the information collected by Application Insights, including the following:

- Logs emitted by the application code, which includes NuGet packages and the .NET framework.
- All dependency calls: These are calls to databases and other systems that are automatically detected by Application Insights. Application Insights records the target system and duration.
- All exceptions: All exceptions that occur in an application are recorded by Application Insights, even if properly handled by the application code.
- Requests: Every user request that comes in over HTTP is logged. Important properties, such as the URL, duration, and HTTP verb, are also included.

To open the search view, navigate to the correct Application Insights instance and navigate to the **Search** tab (1) to get the view shown in the following screenshot:

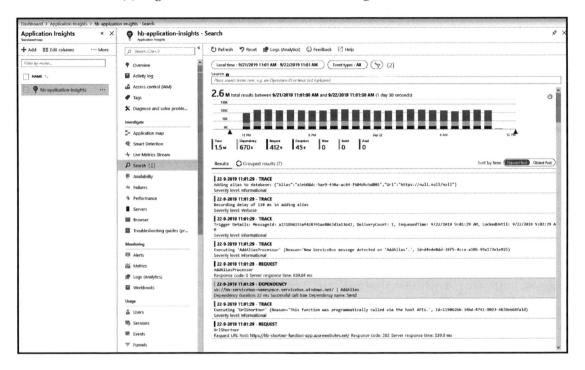

In the **Search** view, several search parameters can be configured (2):

- An interval to search within: This defaults to the last 24 hours.
- The types of events to search in: This can be requests, log entries, page views, exceptions, dependency calls, and more.
- Any text to search for.

Within seconds, all matching results are shown in a bar chart. Each bar stands for a time period and shows how many matches there are within that time frame. Below this chart, all the individual matches are shown. These are a mix of all of the types of events available.

Clicking on any of the results opens a new view that shows the selected record in relation to all the other types, grouped per request. This allows you to quickly navigate to all the logs, dependency calls, and exceptions that are gathered by Application Insights during the execution of a single user request. The results can be displayed as a list and as a timeline. This allows you to very quickly see what the server was doing when performing the user request:

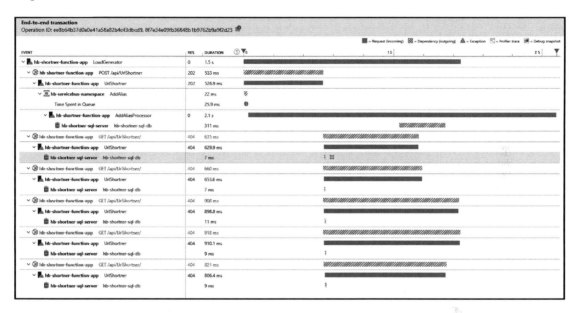

With all of these means to investigate applications and be notified regarding events, it is important to decide which alerts to create and which not to, not only in order to create a healthy working environment, but also to balance monitoring with new work. This is the topic of the next section.

Optimizing alerting

Once teams start instrumenting their applications and adding alerts to metrics that they find important, it will not be long before the first alerts start coming in. At this point, it is important to not only respond to the alerts, but also to investigate them and then close the alert. Alerts should also be evaluated and viewed as an opportunity for learning.

Optimizing alerts

An important thing to do after creating a series of alerts is to re-evaluate them on a regular basis. Two things that might come out of an evaluation such as this are as follows:

- **Changes in the alerting threshold**: Evaluating alerts regularly involves taking a look at the metric over time and seeing where the alerting threshold is at now. This might lead to the conclusion that the threshold is too low or too high.
- **Removing duplicates**: Looking at alerts that have been raised over the month(s), it is very likely to identify one or more groups of alerts that are always raised at the same time. For example, a set of alerts set on a specific web server can be so related that they are always raised at the same time. A common example is the CPU usage and the average response time for an HTTP request; these two often rise at the same time. If this is the case, it is worth considering either removing one of them or downgrading one of them to be a warning only. Duplicate alerts increase the number of items that need an immediate reaction, leading to increased pressure on the team without a clear benefit.

Constantly optimizing the set of alerts not only helps to reduce waste, but also prevents so-called alert fatigue.

Alert fatigue

If alert rules are not constantly reviewed and updated, they could negatively influence a team, especially when alert rules trigger too easily or too frequently as people will no longer respond to them properly. If there are too many alerts, it will wear people out and they will become numb to the effect of an alert. It does not even matter whether these are false alerts or real alerts; just the number of alerts can be enough to get people into a state where they do not care anymore.

If a situation such as this is observed within a team, it is time to drastically change the way alerts are generated and responded to. If this does not happen, team members might fall ill or leave the company altogether.

One of the ways to prevent this situation is by implementing a healthy on-call schedule.

Which metrics to capture

One question that comes up frequently when talking about metrics is about what metrics to emit and monitor. There are many possible metrics and even more opinions on this subject. As a good starting point, the following metrics are often gathered for web applications:

- Requests per minute, transactions per minute, or something similar: This is a metric that is intended to capture the current load or throughput on a web application.
- The average response time: This metric captures the response time for all requests within a time window.
- The error rate: This metric captures the percentage of all requests that result in an error. As a guideline for an error, often, all HTTP response codes of 400 and up are taken.

When these three metrics are captured and graphed together in one graph, they provide the first step toward understanding the behavior of an application. Let's explore a few examples:

- When the average response time goes up but the throughput (requests per minute) stays the same, this might be an indication that the infrastructure that hosts the application is having issues.
- When both the throughput and the average response times go up, this might be an indication that traffic is increasing and that the current infrastructure is not capable of sustaining that throughput at the same response times.
- When the error rate goes up but the other metrics stay the same, this might be an indication that a deployment has gone wrong or that a specific code path is starting to generate (more) errors.

Of course, these are just examples and there are many more possible scenarios. Other metrics can help to rule out a specific scenario or try to avoid them. For example, also starting to monitor the database load as a percentage can help detect a specific instance of the second scenario. If the database load gets close to 100%, it might be time to scale the database up to a higher performance tier to help to sustain the higher throughput at the same response times as before.

To conclude this section, there is one final recommendation—when starting with monitoring, there is often a tendency to focus on the systems that host the application. As an alternative, also consider monitoring metrics that have a direct business impact or metrics that are an indication of user satisfaction in terms of the usability of an application. This comes much closer to measuring business value than when only you watch systems.

Some examples of this are as follows:

- In an online shop, the number of books sold per minute can be a very valuable business metric. Just imagine the impact it can have on a business if this metric is available in near real time using Azure Monitor and custom metrics from the application code.
- For an online reading platform, the number of virtual page turns can be a valuable metric that signals whether users are happily working with the service. As soon as this number sees a sharp drop or rapidly increases, this might be an indication that something is going wrong.

To find out which metrics make sense in a given scenario, it might help to talk to the business or subject matter experts.

Having an on-call schedule

Once alerts are configured and start to be raised, it does not make sense to configure them to not trigger before 8 AM and after 5 PM. In other words, it is necessary to make sure that alerts of a certain severity are followed up even outside of business hours.

In many companies where having alerts is new, there is some form of implicit expectation that some people will be available outside of office hours (alongside their regular duties) to handle these alerts. Sometimes, when an alert is raised only once or twice a year, and there are no agreements about response times, this might not even be a problem at all.

However, in many organizations—especially over time—there is an expectation that these alerts are responded to within a certain period of time. Besides that, the number of alerts may increase as systems become larger and more complex or the number of systems grows.

The way to cope with this is by creating an on-call schedule and formal agreements on what is expected of engineers and how the organization will reward them for their efforts. This allows them to set clear expectations and allows engineers to guard their free time based on these agreements. Having enough downtime helps the engineers relax between periods of higher stress. This allows them to stay alert when they are on call, ready to react when this is expected of them.

There is much material available on what constitutes a healthy on-call schedule and what doesn't, and the keyword here is *healthy*. Some general pointers are as follows:

- Those who are on call during non-business hours should not be on call during business hours as well.
- Provide engineers who are on call with reasonable compensation for being close to a phone, not under the influence, and so on. What is reasonable differs from situation to situation, but the more demanding being on call is, the higher the compensation should be.
- Provide the proper tools for being on call. For example, when a response time of 30 minutes or less is expected, provide those on call with a backpack with a laptop, phone, and means to connect to the internet.
- Ensure that every employee is not on call at least 75% of the time.
- Allow employees to take time off in lieu, so they can be late for work if they had to respond to an alert overnight.

After every disturbance of the normal operation of a system, whether this is during business hours or after, a live site incident review can be performed to learn what happened and how to reduce the chance of it happening again.

Live site reviews

After an alert is triggered and the team has responded and remediated the situation, it is time to evaluate what happened. This is called a live site incident review. Here, the whole team gathers to address the following:

1. What happened—to start, a timeline should be constructed from the time the incident was discovered to the point that normal operations were restored. Next, the timeline is expanded with the events that led to the situation that triggered the incident.
2. Next, the series of events is evaluated to learn what worked well in the response. If one member of the team used a new tool to quickly diagnose a problem, this can benefit other members of the team as well.
3. Only then is it time to look at the possible points of improvement and translate these points into high-priority work for the team. Possible fail-safes are identified and scheduled for implementation or new alerts are identified that send an alert before a similar problem occurs again.
4. The alert or group of alerts that triggered the initial response is evaluated to determine whether they are adequate or possibly contain duplicates.

The best time for a live site incident review is as soon after the incident itself as possible. In practice, this means giving everyone enough time to rest and recuperate and plan a meeting for the next business day.

This completes our overview of Application Insights and the Azure Monitor capabilities for instrumenting web applications. The following section describes several approaches for integrating Application Insights and Azure Monitor with other tools.

Integrating with other tools

Azure Monitor and Application Insights are excellent tools for gathering application logs and metrics, as well as storing them and making them searchable. However, there could be reasons why development teams or businesses prefer to work with other tools to visualize application performance or responding to alerts. One important driver for integration is often the primary tool used by a person or team. If a team operates mainly in ServiceNow or Grafana, it is often useful to integrate these with Azure Monitor instead of forcing these teams to work with multiple tools.

Many possible integrations exist; some examples are detailed in the following subsections.

IT service management applications

Action groups were introduced in the previous section where we looked at instrumenting web applications. Action groups are groups of actions to be performed in response to an alert.

Next to the rich built-in capabilities, it is also possible to automatically raise an alert in an existing **IT Service Management (ITSM)** solution. If there is already an ITSM solution in place within a company, it makes sense not to create a separate alerting channel using Azure Monitor. Instead, using an ITSM connector from Azure Monitor allows you to manage all the company-wide alerts from one solution.

Currently, there are integrations available with ServiceNow, Provance, System Center Service Manager, and more. These connections are created through the ITSM connector.

Azure Boards

In many development teams, Azure DevOps is the tool that developers spend most of their time with. This is also where they perform their backlog management using Azure Boards.

Meanwhile, operators (and hopefully, developers, too) perform investigative work in Application Insights to determine the cause of user errors and to drill down into the reasons for failure. This investigative work could result in new work that needs to be backlogged in Azure DevOps.

To facilitate this, integration between Application Insights and Azure DevOps can be configured from Application Insights by taking the following steps:

1. Navigate to the **Work Items** option on the left-hand side menu (**1**). This opens the view shown on the left in the following screenshot. Here, a connection to Azure Boards can be configured:

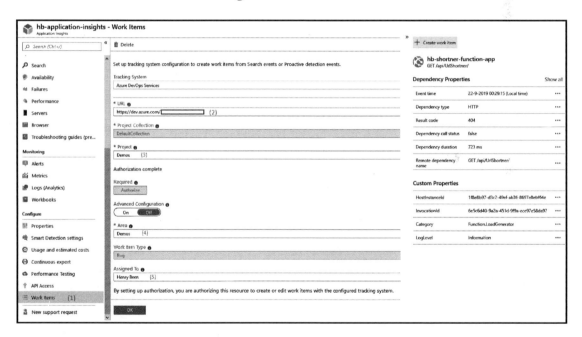

To configure the connection, the following details need to be filled out:

1. Enter the Azure DevOps link. Here, the name of the organization needs to be appended.
2. Select the Azure DevOps project to use. This can be selected from the dropdown.

3. Select a product area where new items will be created. By default, this is the same as the name of the project, unless you change it.
4. Provide the name of a user as the default owner of new work items.

After configuring this connection, a new **Create work item** button is visible on the relevant pages in Application Insights. This button allows you to create a bug with all the relevant information directly on the backlog.

Grafana

Azure Monitor allows you to build simple, easy-to-use dashboards. The advantage of using Azure Monitor dashboards is that they integrate perfectly with all the other Azure practices, such as **Role-Based Access Controls (RBAC)** and Azure Resource Manager templates.

However, teams may have already adopted other tools for visualization, such as Grafana. Grafana is a well-known platform that works well for operational dashboards. Grafana can be configured to connect using Azure Monitor and can query metrics for graphing. Grafana also has alerting capabilities. It does not, however, support querying logs.

To connect Grafana to Azure Monitor, the following steps need to be taken:

1. Create a new app registration in the Azure Active Directory account that is used by your Azure subscription. Take note of the **Tenant Id**, **Client Id**, **Subscription Id**, and **Client Secret** properties of this app registration.
2. Create a new RBAC role assignment for the app registration, with at least the **Reader** permissions set on the resources to monitor.
3. Configure a new data source in Grafana of the **Azure Monitor** type. Insert the properties collected in *step 1* for authenticating to Azure.
4. Add a new graph to the dashboard, selecting **Azure Monitor** as a data source.

By taking the preceding steps, a Grafana-to-Azure Monitor connection can be set up within a matter of minutes.

Summary

In this chapter, you learned how to start completing the DevOps loop. You also learned how to work with crash reports and gather them from all types of applications, as well as how to instrument web applications. You now know how to use Application Insights to centralize logs and metrics and to get insight into requests and dependency calls. You also learned how you can integrate Azure Monitor with other tools to further streamline your development processes.

With this knowledge, you can now start learning about how your applications operate in production. By doing so, you can not only deliver your software faster but also learn from its usage and start improving from there.

In the next chapter, you will learn about gathering user feedback to complement what you have learned from your system logs and metrics. You will also learn how to measure the end user satisfaction of your application and new features.

Questions

As we conclude, here is a list of questions for you to test your knowledge regarding this chapter's material. You will find the answers in the *Assessments* section of the Appendix:

1. True or false – it is possible to capture custom metrics from the Azure platform offerings using Application Insights.
2. How long are platform metrics retained for in Azure Monitor?
3. True or false – it is possible to capture custom metrics from your own application code using Application Insights.
4. What do you call a situation where engineers start ignoring alerts as they are worn down by too many of them?
5. True or false – it is possible to call a webhook when an alert fires in Azure.

Further reading

- More information about the App Center SDK can be found at `https://docs.microsoft.com/en-us/appcenter/sdk/`.
- More information on Raygun can be found at `https://raygun.com`.
- A complete example application that uses Application Insights and Azure Monitor is available at `https://github.com/henrybeen/MonitoringLogging.UrlShortnerDemo2`.
- More detailed information on configuring Application Insights is available at `https://docs.microsoft.com/en-us/azure/azure-monitor/app/app-insights-overview`.
- The KQL reference page can be found at `https://docs.microsoft.com/en-us/sharepoint/dev/general-development/keyword-query-language-kql-syntax-reference`.

Gathering User Feedback **11**

In the previous chapter, you learned how to measure how your applications are performing in production. You learned how to gather crash reports and logs and how to instrument an application. However, the purpose of software is not just to deliver perfectly running applications, but to create business value. Gathering user feedback is necessary to determine whether your application is also achieving this higher goal. In this chapter, you will learn techniques to measure whether your users are satisfied, which features they are using and which they are not, and how you can use this information to steer future developments.

To do this, this chapter starts by introducing the concept of continuous feedback. Next, it moves on to introduce different approaches to asking users for feedback and recording their responses. This can be both in-application or via other channels. Besides gathering feedback directly, you can also tap into other, indirect channels. Examples are reactions to your software on Twitter and the usage of features in your application. Finally, this chapter will introduce hypothesis-driven development, an approach to software development practiced by Microsoft.

The following topics will be covered in this chapter:

- Understanding continuous feedback
- Asking for feedback
- Gathering indirect feedback
- Implementing hypothesis-driven development

Technical requirements

There are no technical requirements for this chapter.

Understanding continuous feedback

As explained in `Chapter 1`, *Introduction to DevOps*, DevOps is a cultural movement that tries to bring developers and operators closer together, to help them to deliver business value faster and more reliable. Feedback loops are an important element in doing this. In the previous chapter, we saw numerous feedback loops:

- Developers can run unit tests on their local machine to verify that their changes did not break existing behaviors.
- After source code check in, all unit tests are run again and a pipeline with more tests starts running.
- Besides functional tests, security tests and dependency scans can be run.
- After releasing, logs and metrics are gathered to determine whether the application is running smoothly.

All of this provides feedback on the technical quality of the work and now it is time to add one more feedback loop—a loop intended to verify whether the application actually fulfills the needs of its users.

As obvious as this may sound, it is more often forgotten than most developers would care to admit. In many companies, there is faith in product owners or business analysts and they are trusted to be able to predict which features users need and to sort them in order of priority.

This is while we know that developing software is a complex activity where the results of a change often cannot be predicted in advance. In such situations, it is important to continuously look for feedback from the user to identify whether features are delivering the value they should.

Continuously looking for feedback will help to make decisions such as the following:

- Removing features that are not being used by most of the users; this removes the need for maintenance on them, therefore reducing cost and freeing up development time
- Expanding features that are most used by users, making them more prominent in the interface
- Increasing or decreasing testing efforts, based on the perceived quality of the application by users

Going further along this line of reasoning, we might conclude that it is impossible to predict whether a feature will actually deliver enough business value to justify its existence or not. Companies that do this often adopt the practice of hypothesis-driven development, which will be discussed later.

First, the next section will introduce different approaches for asking application users for feedback.

Asking for direct feedback

One very straightforward way to collect user feedback is by just asking for it. Over the last few years, more and more applications have been enriched with feedback mechanisms built into the application. Other approaches that are commonly used are publishing a public roadmap and engaging with customers directly.

Advantages of in-product feedback

Collecting feedback in-product is a good way to get started with direct user feedback. Examples of in-product feedback are grading a specific view or action, giving a thumbs up or down, or sending a happy or sad smiley face.

Collecting in-product feedback has the following advantages:

- It is one of the easiest ways for customers to give feedback, taking virtually none of their time.
- Due to the non-intrusiveness of this approach, a larger group of users might choose to respond.
- Recorded feedback can be context-aware.
- When recording a grade, smiley face, or thumbs up or down for feedback, an application can also record the current state and most recent user activities and send all of that along with the user feedback. This makes a single click by the user much more valuable than it seems at first sight. It allows quick insights into the most loved and most hated parts of an application.
- Finally, allowing in-product feedback makes the user feel heard and listened to.

Of course, recording data about users and how they use an application requires their consent. It needs to be fully transparent what you intend do with the information gathered about users. Also, an opt-in for explicit content is often required as well as an option to revoke a previously given consent. The precise requirements vary from country to country and are a legal consideration.

The disadvantage of this type of feedback is that it can be too much to analyze in detail. Also, since the results are often anonymized, it is not possible to follow up on feedback. This makes it hard to understand *why* a user was satisfied or dissatisfied with a screen. Sometimes this is countered by adding a checkbox under the feedback box stating something like: "I give one-time permission to be contacted about this subject".

For understanding the reasons for a user's feedback, other feedback mechanisms such as interviews or focus groups might be more appropriate.

Having a public roadmap

Another approach for gathering user feedback is by publicly sharing what is currently in the backlog and what isn't. One team that publicly shares which features they are working on is the Azure DevOps team. Naturally, this list does not contain all features the product group is planning. The reasons for this might be to keep a competitive edge or to keep some new feature secret until a big announcement. However, their backlog provides a good insight into what is currently brewing.

Adopting this practice allows the users of a product to reach out and comment on this public list. It allows them to request features to be moved up or down the list of priorities and they can share which features they are missing.

This can bring the following advantage to a company: When users engage with feedback on the list of features, they are encouraged to specify why they make a certain request. This might provide new insights into customer demand and may lead to a shift in priorities.

There are also downsides to this approach:

- Not all users will engage in and provide feedback on a public backlog. This might result in a bias toward more vocal or more demanding customers in the group that provides feedback. While not necessarily an issue, it is good to keep this in mind.
- Engaging with users over feature requests or features that they want to be moved up or down the list can be very time-consuming. Especially when comparing with in-product feedback, this approach takes more time.

As well as having a public feature roadmap, there are also other ways to give users an insight into what a company is currently working on and what they are planning. Some examples include the following:

- **UserVoice**: UserVoice is a platform that allows users to propose new features and vote on features proposed by others. It allows gathering user ideas, without opening the actual backlog to users.
- **Bugtrackers**: If customers are very vocal about reporting bugs and errors in an application, it can help to open up a bugtracker. This allows users to see which issues are already known and if and when they might be fixed.

Public backlogs and UserVoice-like platforms are more common than open backlogs. Open lists of bugs or issues are more often seen in open source development.

Using interviews or focus groups

Other forms of requesting user feedback are one-on-one interviews and focus groups. While these are even more time-intensive then open backlogs and public discussions, they also have the benefit of allowing more balanced user selection.

For example, if an application is clearly targeting four different market segments, it can be beneficial to have five focus groups—one for each market segment and an additional one with a mix of those. The first four will allow focusing on the specific needs of each group, while the fifth will incite a lot of discussion and allows getting insight into how different wishes from different groups compare.

Interviews and focus groups are also more suitable for not only getting the feedback but for understanding the reasoning of users. Sitting face to face with users allows exploring their way of reasoning and how they perceive an application.

This concludes the discussion of direct user feedback. In the next section, indirect user feedback is discussed.

Gathering indirect feedback

A well known saying in software development is that *users do not know what they want.* While this may sound harsh, there are a few reasons why direct user feedback from discussions, interviews, and focus groups does not necessarily lead to good product feedback:

- One reason for this is that everyone wants to be liked. When conducting an interview, or talking to a group of users, there is a chance that they will only say what they believe the interviewer wants to hear.
- It has a high turn-around time. Scheduling interviews and focus groups takes time and finding a time that everyone can attend can easily take days or even weeks.
- It is hard to keep asking the same group of users for feedback every few weeks. This is especially important when trying to determine whether the quality of a feature is improving with the newest updates or not.

For these reasons, it can be worthwhile to cut back on asking for feedback, but instead, measure how users are interacting with an application on a functional level and whether they are satisfied with the value they receive from an application.

One way to do this is by measuring user behavior in an application and emitting metrics based on that. In Chapter 10, *Application Monitoring*, Application Insights was introduced for gathering application-level metrics. While metrics are traditionally used for emitting metrics regarding application performance, metrics can also be used to emit metrics regarding application usage. Some examples are the following:

- How frequently is every page visited?
- How many times are specific operations performed?
- How long it takes to complete a certain view?
- How many users open a specific form, only to never complete it?

Gathering these metrics can deliver important insights into how users are interacting with an application and which parts they use or do not use.

Besides usage, another indicator of user satisfaction can be Twitter sentiment or the number of support requests.

Sentiment analysis

Besides gathering metrics in-product, there are also metrics that can be gathered outside of the product. One example source of information is Twitter. Using the Azure cloud and machine learning algorithms, it is now possible to continuously analyze all of the tweets that are directed to a Twitter handle or a hashtag and automatically detect sudden changes.

This even goes so far as that there is an Azure Pipelines extension that allows continuously measuring Twitter sentiment and canceling the progress of a release to the next stage if sentiment turns too negative. This extension is implemented as a pipeline gate and is available in the Azure DevOps Marketplace.

Support requests

Just like the Twitter sentiment, there might be other indicators of user satisfaction that can be gathered automatically. Continuously collecting the number of support calls or emails per minute and detecting a certain spike can be a clear indicator of a user issue. Using machine learning and system integrations this can be harnessed for automated responses or signaling a user to the results.

Adopting practices like this can save minutes or hours detecting production issues. Taking user feedback and making decisions based on that sentiment can go even further. This is called hypothesis-driven development, which is discussed next.

Implementing hypothesis-driven development

A risk in software development is that teams are so busy creating more and more features that they forget to reflect upon their business value while everyone knows that not every feature is a success. Some features may not be used at all or may even be disliked by users. As an industry, we have come to learn that product owners have a hard time predicting which features will be really liked by users and which will not. Even when using all of the feedback mechanisms discussed previously, predicting what users want is difficult.

Another important thing to recognize is that every feature in the product also brings a future cost. Every feature requires documentation, support, and maintenance. This means that unnecessary features are driving costs up as well. From this stance, it makes sense to not only leave non-value features but to even remove them from the product as soon as possible.

Hypothesis-driven development is a practice that starts with acknowledging that it is impossible to predict whether a feature will add value, add no value, or, even worse, decrease business value. Next, it recommends transforming features in the backlog into quick, lightweight experiments that are run in the product to determine whether a new feature adds value or not.

Such an experiment can be written in a similar shape as a user story, for example, like this: *We believe that users want a new one-field popup to quickly create an appointment, instead of the full dialog. We are convinced that this is the case when we see that over 25% of appointments are created using this new dialog and that the average approval rate of appointments goes up by 2 points or more.* The first part is called the hypothesis, and the second is the threshold for confirmation of that hypothesis.

Once this is written down, a minimal implementation of such a one-field popup is created and its usage and the usage of the original form are monitored using metrics. Depending on the measurements, one of the following can occur:

- The belief stated in the hypothesis is confirmed to be true and the new feature adds value. More stories surrounding this feature can be added to the backlog to increase the business value the product brings.
- The belief stated in the hypothesis is not confirmed and further experimentation is not expected to yield different results. The feature is dropped from the backlog and the current, minimal implementation might even be removed from the product.
- The belief stated in the hypothesis is not confirmed but experimentation continues. This can happen when there are numerous user complaints about a certain feature that the team is set on fixing. If one approach does not work, they might try another.

Using the approach outlined before, teams can increase the impact they make on business value by minimizing the time they spend on features that, after experimentation, do not add value and even remove them from the product again.

Often, hypothesis-driven development is combined with phased roll-out mechanisms such as feature flags or deployment rings. The experiment is then run on only a small percentage of the users, which makes it easier to pull the feature if it does not add enough value.

This completes the discussion of the means for gathering and using user feedback on applications and how user feedback ties into the DevOps goal of delivering business value to end users.

Summary

In this chapter, you learned how to measure the business outcomes of software development activities. First, you learned about the importance of feedback and how this helps to understand customer needs and whether those needs are actually being met. Then, numerous approaches to asking for feedback were introduced, both direct and indirect. Finally, you learned about hypothesis-driven development and how a mindset of experimentation can help to cut down waste.

With this knowledge, you can now choose and implement feedback mechanisms that allow you to learn what the user sentiment regarding your application is. You are now able to implement an experiment-based approach to creating software, focusing on value-adding features and ignoring or even removing features that do not add value.

In the next chapter, you will learn all about containers. Containers are rapidly changing the way software is delivered and are often used for applying DevOps principles to both existing and new applications.

Questions

As we conclude, here is a list of questions for you to test your knowledge regarding this chapter's material. You will find the answers in the *Assessments* section of the Appendix:

1. True or false: There are no downsides to publicly sharing a roadmap.
2. What is an important concern to keep in mind when evaluating user feedback on a public roadmap?
3. What are two indirect indicators of user satisfaction that are relatively easy to capture?
4. Which of the following is not part of a hypothesis, as used in hypothesis-driven development?
    1. A hypothesis
    2. A confirmation threshold
    3. A conclusion
5. What are two benefits of interviews or focus groups over other means of gathering feedback?

Further reading

- The list of features planned for Azure DevOps can be found at `https://docs.microsoft.com/en-us/azure/devops/release-notes/features-timeline`.
- The Twitter Sentiment extension can be found on the Azure DevOps Marketplace at `https://marketplace.visualstudio.com/items?itemName=ms-devlabs.vss-services-twittersentimentanalysis`.

Section 4: Advanced Topics

4

In this section, you will learn about containers and designing your Azure DevOps organization.

Containers have changed, and will continue changing, the way that software is created and delivered. Also, you have to give thought into how you will create your own Azure DevOps organization. How you organize your projects and teams determines how people can work together.

Finally, the last chapter will help you prepare for taking the AZ-400 exam and test your readiness.

This section comprises the following chapters:

- Chapter 12, *Containers*
- Chapter 13, *Planning your Azure DevOps Organization*
- Chapter 14, *AZ-400 Mock Exam*

12
Containers

Over the last couple of years, containers have become a hot topic. They allow you to package any application, any tool, written in any language, and deploy it on a basic host or cluster. When implementing DevOps, containers can be of tremendous value. That is why DevOps and containers are often mentioned in the same breath. However, they are not the same thing. While DevOps is more of a cultural thing, containers are a type of technology, an alternative way of hosting your applications.

In this chapter, you will learn more about containers and how they work. This is achieved by exercises wherein custom container images are created and run on different hosting platforms, such as Azure Container Instances and Kubernetes.

The following topics will be covered in this chapter:

- An introduction to containers
- Building a container image
- Building images in Azure DevOps and running them in Azure
- An introduction to Kubernetes
- Kubernetes in action
- Upgrading containers
- Scaling containers and Kubernetes
- Deploying to Kubernetes with Azure DevOps

Technical requirements

To experiment with the techniques described in this chapter, you need one or more of the following:

- Docker Desktop
- Visual Studio 2019
- An Azure subscription
- The Azure CLI

All these are available for free or can be obtained for a limited period for free for evaluation purposes.

An introduction to containers

Containers are the evolution of virtualization. With virtualization, the resources of physical machines are shared among several virtual machines. Sharing those resources also means that all virtual machines have their own operating system. This is different when using containers. With containers, not only are the resources shared, but also the operating system kernel, making it very small in comparison with a virtual machine image.

Since the operating system kernel is shared, containers are also very portable. Images can be deployed on any type of host environment that supports running containers. This works because all the application's binaries and configurations are stored inside the container. As a result, environment variables outside the container do not impact the application. Naturally, there are a number of caveats, however: a container shares the operating system kernel; Linux containers can only run on a Linux operating system, and the same applies to Windows containers.

Containers provide the ability to virtualize an operating system in order to run multiple workloads on a single operating system. This is visualized in the following diagram, where you can see the difference between regular hosting, virtual machine hosting, and containers:

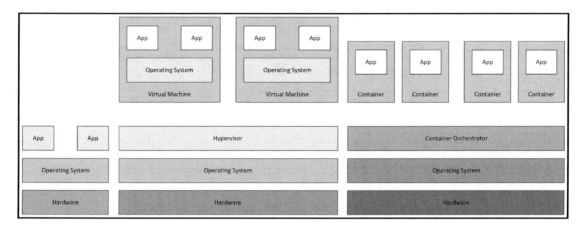

If you have ever heard of containers, you almost certainly have also heard of Docker. This is because Docker is one of the most well-known container engines that can be used for running containers. The next section will delve into DevOps and containers, while the remainder of the chapter will go into more technical detail regarding containers.

DevOps and containers

As mentioned in the introduction, DevOps and containers are not the same thing. Containers are the technology that makes DevOps easier. This is because containers have benefits that make them *the* perfect tool for DevOps:

- **Consistent**: Because you build the container images, the hurdle of "*it works on my machine*" is eliminated.
- **Separation of concerns**: When using containers, your application will be distributed between separate containers, which makes it easier to maintain and separate the processes.
- **Platform**: The solution can be run on different platforms. It does not matter whether this is in Azure, on Amazon Web Services, or in an on-premises environment.

That aside, DevOps is more cultural than technical and, as mentioned in `Chapter 1`, *Introduction to DevOps*, technical components are used to support DevOps. In the remainder of this chapter, we will focus on the technical side of things.

Hosting options

As mentioned previously, one of the benefits of containers is that they are extremely portable. This also means that containers can be hosted on numerous platforms and technologies.

To run the containers, there are a lot of options that will vary according to your use case. Some of these options are as follows:

- Azure App Services
- Azure Service Fabric
- Docker Swarm
- Docker Desktop
- Kubernetes

Depending on the demands of the application/container, it could run on all the options mentioned in the preceding list.

The images used to run containers (container images) also need to be hosted. These images are hosted in a so-called container registry. In a container registry, they are published privately or publicly. The two most well-know registries are the Docker Registry and the Azure Container Registry within the Azure platform.

Now that we have gone through some of the background information regarding containers, we are ready to go more deeply into the techniques behind containers and find out what is needed to create a custom container image.

Building a container image

This section will take you through the process of building a container image and executing it on your local system. To do this, we will first have to create an application and then add Docker support to it before we create an image and finally test it. So let's begin!

Creating an application

To be able to test and check what is running on the container, an application is required. For this, a new application can be created or you can use an existing application.

When creating a new application, the easiest option is to use the default ASP.NET Core website template within Visual Studio 2019. Container support can be added in a few clicks. This is simply done by checking the **Enable Docker Support** box when creating the project:

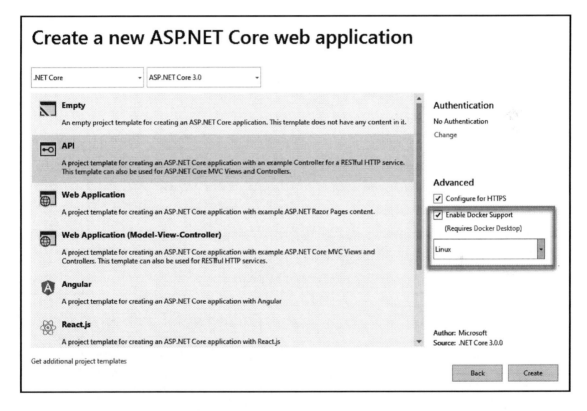

Keep the new application open or open your existing application. In the next section, we will investigate how Docker support can be added to an existing application.

Adding Docker support to an existing application

Adding Docker support to an existing application requires a couple of simple steps:

1. Open the project/solution in Visual Studio 2019 and right-click on the project.
2. Choose **Add** and select **Docker Support**:

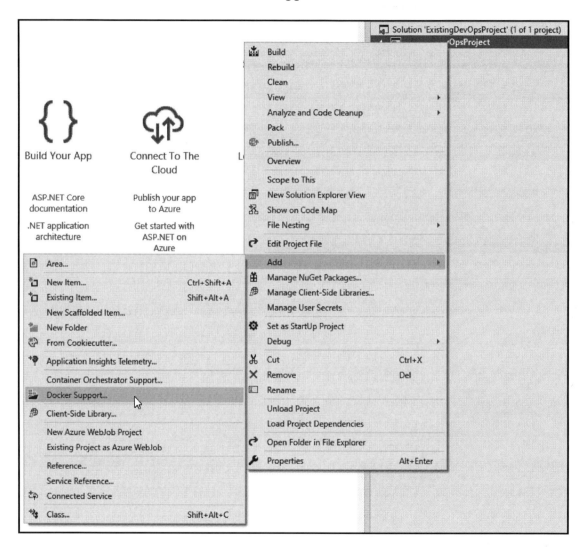

Depending on your client tools and Visual Studio configuration, there may also be a **Container Orchestrator Support** option. With this option, the cloud orchestrator of your choice can be chosen. In this sample, we used Docker because this format is supported by the major container orchestrators. Other cloud orchestrator options do exist, however:

- Docker Swarm
- Kubernetes
- Mesos Marathon

Depending on the cloud orchestrator used, a file is added to the project in the specific format for that orchestrator.

By adding Docker support, a new file is added to the project named `Docker`. The Dockerfile is the specification of a container image. This file can be read by Docker, which sees it as instructions. The file is a text document that contains separate commands that can also be called within a command-line tool to assemble an image:

```
FROM mcr.microsoft.com/dotnet/core/aspnet:3.0-buster-slim AS base
WORKDIR /app
EXPOSE 80
EXPOSE 443
EXPOSE 555
FROM mcr.microsoft.com/dotnet/core/sdk:3.0-buster AS build
WORKDIR /src
COPY ["ExistingDevOpsProject/ExistingDevOpsProject.csproj",
"ExistingDevOpsProject/"]
RUN dotnet restore "ExistingDevOpsProject/ExistingDevOpsProject.csproj"
COPY . .
WORKDIR "/src/ExistingDevOpsProject"
RUN dotnet build "ExistingDevOpsProject.csproj" -c Release -o
/app/build
FROM build AS publish
RUN dotnet publish "ExistingDevOpsProject.csproj" -c Release -o
/app/publish
FROM base AS final
WORKDIR /app
COPY --from=publish /app/publish .
ENTRYPOINT ["dotnet", "ExistingDevOpsProject.dll"]
```

The example uses a technique called a multi-stage build file. This is because the file uses multiple `FROM` statements where there is a reference to a specific image.

Prior to multi-stage build, it wasn't possible to use multiple `FROM` statements. During this time, it was hard to build efficient container images. Each statement in the file represented an additional layer on the image that resulted in it becoming larger and larger.

During this build process, it was also necessary to remove any components that were required during this process. For this reason, it was very common to have separate Dockerfiles for development and production.

As mentioned, the Dockerfile comprises instructions and the most commonly used instructions are as follows:

- **FROM**: The `FROM` command is used to specify on which operating system or base image the image will be based. In the example, the `mcr.microsoft.com/dotnet/core/aspnet:3.0-buster-slim` image is used for the production version of the application, and the `mcr.microsoft.com/dotnet/core/sdk:3.0-buster` image is used to build the image.
- **RUN**: The `RUN` command is used to install components or perform operations during the build process of the container image.
- **ENTRYPOINT**: The `ENTRYPOINT` command specifies what the entry point for a container image needs to be. In the example, the entry point is specified as a `.NET` application that references the library that was built during the compilation process.

So far, we've created our application and added Docker support. Next, we'll see how to create an image with the application.

Creating an image with the application

To be able to create a Docker image, Docker Desktop needs to be installed, as Visual Studio uses this to construct the image. With a complete Dockerfile, the image can be built using the following steps:

1. Right-click the Dockerfile in Visual Studio and select **Build Docker Image**:

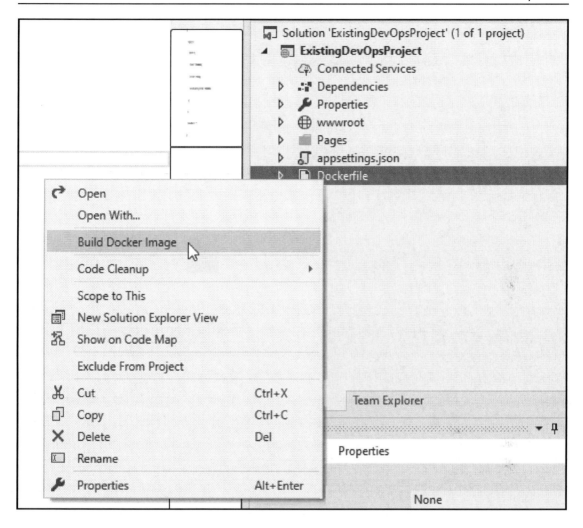

2. During the compilation and building of the image, take a look at the output window. Looking at it will provide more insights into the layered approach of container images. This layered approach is visible via the steps shown in the output window:

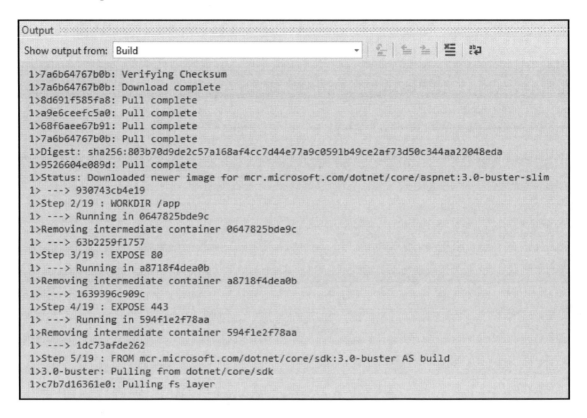

3. Docker Desktop also makes it possible to run and store images locally. After building the image, open a Terminal and run the following command:

```
docker images
```

The command displays all images currently on the machine. In this list, the base images that are downloaded during the creation of images are also listed.

Running the container image

The container image can be started locally by running it within Docker. As we now have a container image, a container can be created:

1. Run the following `docker container run` command:

   ```
   docker container run --publish 8123:80 --detach --name
   [container name] [image name]
   ```

   The preceding command will start the container image specified at the end of the command. In addition, different arguments are specified:

   - **Publish**: The `publish` argument opens a port from the host to the container. As mentioned in the example, this will open port `8123` and will route traffic to port `80` within the container.
   - **Detach**: The `detach` argument will run the container in the background and print out its specific ID.
   - **Name**: The name for the container within Docker.

2. To list all running containers, use the `docker ps` command within the Terminal.
3. With the container running, open a browser and navigate to `http://localhost:8123`. If everything works fine, this should show a default ASP.NET Core web page:

Since building stuff locally and running it on your machine is not really the DevOps way of thinking, we will move to a different hosting platform in the upcoming sections.

Building images in Azure DevOps and running them in Azure

To support continuous integration and continuous delivery, the source files need to be shared in a repository. So, let's share the resources in Azure Repos and try to build our container by using Azure Pipelines. After building the container image, a place to store the images and run the container are also required. Within the Azure platform, there are two perfect services for this scenario:

- **Azure Container Registry**: This service is a managed private Docker registry based on the open source Docker Registry. Here, you can maintain and register container images.
- **Azure Container Instance**: The Azure Container Instance, also referred to as ACI, is a solution for running isolated containers without a lot of management.

 For the simplicity of this guide, the files are already added to the repository and the Azure resource is already created.

Creating a service endpoint

As already discussed within the book, connections within Azure DevOps with external services such as Azure and container registries are configured within a service endpoint. Because the image needs to be available in order for Azure Container Instances to retrieve it, it needs to be published to a container registry. The connection from Azure DevOps to the registry is configured within a service connection.

Perform the following steps to configure the service connection:

1. In the Azure DevOps project, open the project settings.
2. Within the project settings, click on **Service connections.**
3. In the service connection overview, click on **Create service connection** and choose **Docker Registry**.
4. In the fly-out that appears, fill in the correct information and save the connection:

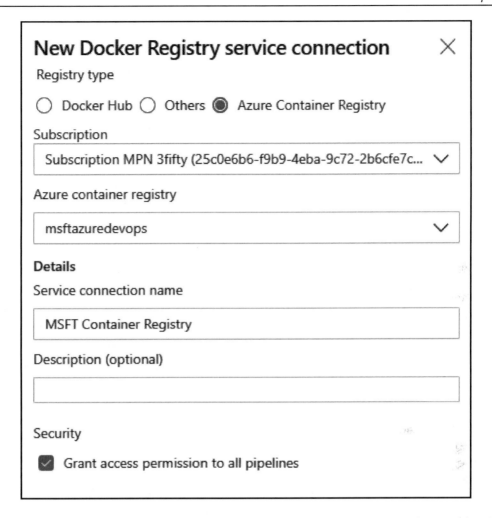

New Docker Registry service connection ✕

Registry type

○ Docker Hub ○ Others ◉ Azure Container Registry

Subscription

Subscription MPN 3fifty (25c0e6b6-f9b9-4eba-9c72-2b6cfe7c... ∨

Azure container registry

msftazuredevops ∨

Details

Service connection name

MSFT Container Registry

Description (optional)

Security

☑ Grant access permission to all pipelines

Saving the connection will add a service connection to the project that can be used by the pipelines we will create, or that you will create in the future.

Creating a new pipeline

To be able to start building the container image and publish it to the registry, we will create a new pipeline. For this example, we will make use of the YAML pipeline experience.

Perform the following steps to get started with the pipeline:

1. Open you Azure DevOps project and click on **Pipelines**.
2. In the pipelines overview, click on **New Pipeline**.
3. Select **Azure Repos Git**, choose the correct repository, and then choose the **Starter pipeline**:

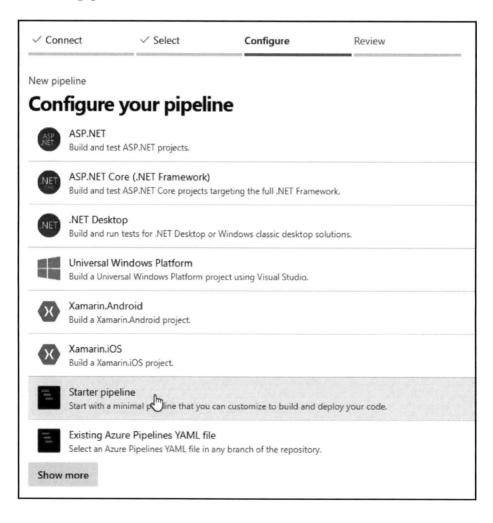

4. From the starter pipeline, remove the two dummy script tasks and open the assistant.

5. In the assistant, search for the `Docker` tasks and add the tasks to the pipeline.

6. Choose the service connection created for the container registry and keep the other information as the defaults.

 Make sure to change the `buildContext` property of the tasks to point to the correct directory. This is required for Docker to be able to reference the correct paths when building your image.

When added, the YAML should look like this:

```
- task: Docker@2
  inputs:
    containerRegistry: 'MSFT Container Registry'
    repository: 'azuredevops'
    command: 'buildAndPush'
    Dockerfile:'**/Dockerfile'
    buildContext:
'$(System.DefaultWorkingDirectory)/ExistingDevOpsProject'
```

7. Save and run the pipeline. After the first run, the container image is created and published to the container registry.

The images in the container registry can be retrieved by using a predefined URL. This URL comprises a few specific components:

- `[container registry]/[repository]:[tag]:`
  - **Container registry**: The base URL of the container registry.
  - **Repository**: The repository as specified during the process of publishing the image.
  - **Tag**: The tag for the specific version of the image. By default, the Docker tag used is `BuildId`.

8. Now that we have a reference to the container image, Azure Container Instances should be able to retrieve the container and run it. The only thing needed for this is an Azure CLI command:

```
az container create --resource-group [resource group] --name
[ACI name] -location westeurope -image [Image reference] --dns-
name-label [dns reference] -ports 80 --registry-username
[username of the registry] --registry-password [password of the
registry]
```

Since the reference to the image is different for each build (BuildId for the tag value), BuildId is retrieved in the Azure CLI command via the $(Build.BuildId) variable:

```
az container create --resource-group aci-rg-devops --name aci-
demo-app -location westeurope -image
msftazuredevops.azurecr.io/azuredevops:$(Build.BuildId) --dns-
name-label aci-msft-demo -ports 80 --registry-username
$(username) --registry-password $(password)
```

To execute the preceding script, the Azure CLI task is added to the pipeline. In this task, we configure the correct subscription via the service endpoint and set the inline script.

The script will create a container instance in the aci-rg-devops resource group with the name aci-demo-app and retrieve the azuredevops container image from the msftazuredevops.azurecr.io repository.

The complete YAML for this task looks like this:

```
- task: AzureCLI@2
  inputs:
  azureSubscription: 'Subscription MPN'
  scriptType: 'bash'
  scriptLocation: 'inlineScript'
  inlineScript: 'az container create --resource-group aci-rg-
devops -
name aci-demo-app --location westeurope --image
msftazuredevops.azurecr.io/azuredevops:$(Build.BuildId) --dns-
name-label aci-msft-demo --ports 80 --registry-username
$(username) --registry-password $(password)'
```

Running this pipeline will result in an Azure Container Instance in Azure. That container will be running the exact same application that was running locally:

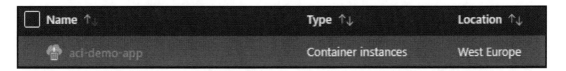

When opening the Azure Container Instance in the Azure portal, you will see that it is a running instance and that there is an FQDN attached to the Azure Container Instance based on the value supplied, `dns-name-label`, within the Azure CLI command, `aci-msft-demo.westeurope.azurecontainer.io`. Open the URL in your browser and see the application we have pushed to the container:

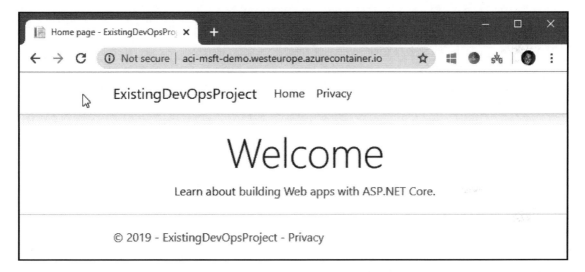

It shows the same content as the container that was started locally. This is because, in both places, the same container image was started.

In this section, we started the container on Azure Container Instances, but how will we manage running containers and restart them when there are problems? This is where Kubernetes comes in.

An introduction to Kubernetes

Kubernetes is another service for running your containers. Kubernetes is a cluster orchestration technology first developed by Google. It is now an open source platform for automating deployment, scaling, and operations of application containers across clusters of hosts, thereby providing a container-centric infrastructure.

Functionalities of Kubernetes

As mentioned earlier, containers offer you a great way to package your applications. When running the applications, you need to make sure that applications keep running and this is where Kubernetes comes in as it has the following core functionalities:

- **Service discovery and load balancing**: How a container is exposed is controlled within Kubernetes and, in addition, it is also capable of balancing the traffic within the orchestration.
- **Storage orchestration**: The ability to mount different kinds of storage providers to the platform.
- **Rollouts and rollbacks**: Kubernetes can automatically create and restart containers for the specified deployment.
- **Self-healing**: Kubernetes can heal containers when they are failing.
- **Secret and configuration management**: Kubernetes has a built-in functionality to manage secrets such as tokens, passwords, and keys.

In order to provide these functionalities, Kubernetes consists of a number of components.

Kubernetes core components and services

Kubernetes consists of a few core components that make it run. These components together make a great and stable product for running and managing containers. The next few subsections will go over each of these components individually.

Master node

One of the important components within Kubernetes is the master node. The node manages the cluster. It contains all the Kubernetes core components in order to manage the cluster:

- `kube-apiserver`: A component for exposing the Kubernetes API. This API is used by management tools of Kubernetes, such as `kubectl`, and the Kubernetes dashboard.
- `etcd`: Used to maintain the state of the Kubernetes cluster.
- `kube-scheduler`: A component that selects nodes for the pods to run on.
- `kube-controller-manager`: The controller manager oversees a number of smaller controllers that perform actions such as replicating pods and managing node operations.

By using these components, the master node can maintain the desired state for the cluster. It is good to know that when you are interacting with Kubernetes, you are communicating with the master node. The master node itself will then communicate with the other components within the cluster.

Regular nodes

These nodes are the nodes that will run the containers. These can be virtual machines or even physical machines. On these machines, the so called `kubelet` is installed. `kubelet` is the agent that's used to run pods/containers within the nodes.

As you may have noticed in the preceding sections, there are also other core services within Kubernetes and we will discuss these next.

Pod

Within Kubernetes, pods are used to run the applications. Within the pods, it is specified which resources are required to run the application. The scheduler (`kube-schedular`) within Kubernetes checks where to run the application depending on the demands and the nodes coupled to the cluster.

Pods themselves have a limited lifespan and are removed when new versions are deployed or, for example, when a node fails, pods can be replaced by pods on the same or another node.

Service

The service is sometimes also referred to as the load balancer and is used to provide a logical grouping of pods and furnish them with connectivity (a way to connect).

Three major services are as follows:

- **Cluster IP**: Adding an internal IP to a cluster of pods.
- **Node port**: Port mapping to the underlying node directory to connect to the application/pod with the IP address of the node.
- **Load balancer**: This service adds a load balancer resource and configures an external IP address on the load balancer. On the external side, the load balancer will route traffic to the specific nodes based on the rules configured in the load balancer and internally to the correct pod.

With these services, the internal and external connections for pods are arranged. The services and pods are all specified within a deployment.

Deployment

A deployment describes the desired state of an application. It describes the number of replicas, but also the update strategy. Kubernetes will track the health of the pods and will remove or add pods when needed to comply with the desired state that is described in the deployment.

These deployments are specified in a YAML file. For example, when running a container in Kubernetes, you must specify a replica set. A replica set ensures that a specified number of pod replicas are running at any given time.

Operation of Kubernetes

When you are new to containers, and especially to Kubernetes, it is hard to figure things out immediately. However, to aid your understanding of the concept, take a look at the following diagram:

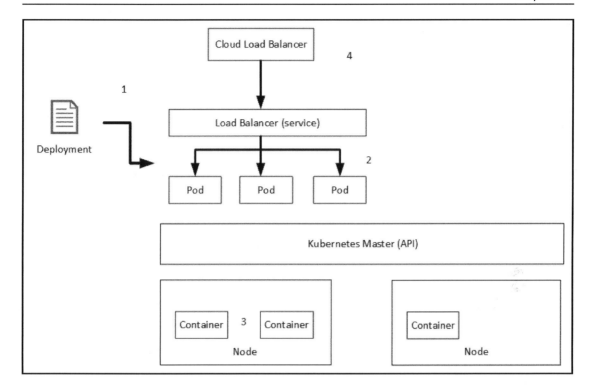

Deployments of containers to a Kubernetes cluster are defined in the so-called deployment file (**1**). In these deployment files, the desired state of the application is described. This desired state is described as a YAML file.

In this example, the desired state is a load balancer service and three pods (**2**). These pods are divided by the Kubernetes API on the nodes that run the containers (**3**). The service defined in the deployments file ensures that the traffic is routed to the specific pods. The deployment can be changed by updating it.

The scheduler can also change deployments when, for example, automatic scaling is configured for the application. In that kind of scenario, a fourth pod could be added to the cluster. In the service, there can also be an external load balancer to route traffic to the internal load balancer of Kubernetes (**4**).

Azure Kubernetes Service

Azure Kubernetes Service, or **AKS**, is the Microsoft implementation of Kubernetes. Setting up a regular Kubernetes cluster is a lot of work, but with AKS, it has been made easier. This is because Kubernetes is a managed platform and the reason why almost all operational tasks are handled by the platform itself.

Some key functionalities of AKS are as follows:

- Azure manages critical tasks, such as health monitoring and maintenance, including Kubernetes version upgrades and patching.
- Azure performs simple cluster scaling.
- The master node of Kubernetes is fully managed.
- Master nodes are free, and you only pay for running agent nodes.

By using the AKS, a Kubernetes cluster can be operational within minutes. Besides that, the focus will be on the application as the master node is fully managed. Now, let's try to run a Kubernetes cluster with custom images.

Kubernetes in action

In the first few sections of this chapter, we created a container and deployed it to an Azure Container Instance. Let's now deploy this container to a Kubernetes cluster.

Creating a cluster can be done via the Azure CLI or an ARM template. For ease of demonstration, the Azure CLI is used.

First, a new resource group needs to be created to host the Azure Kubernetes cluster:

```
az group create --name mpn-rg-kubernetes --location westeurope
```

Now, we can create our Kubernetes cluster.

Creating a Kubernetes cluster

When the resource group is created, a new Kubernetes cluster can be added to the group:

```
az aks create --resource-group mpn-rg-kubernetes --name mykubernetescluster
--node-count 1 --enable-addons monitoring --generate-ssh-keys
```

This command creates a new Kubernetes cluster with the name
`mykubernetescluster` and with a single node. This means that there will be one virtual
machine created in the Azure portal that is configured as a node for the Kubernetes cluster.
In addition, the monitoring add-ons will be enabled on the cluster.

The creation of this cluster will take a couple of minutes. In Azure, the
`mykubernetescluster` service will be created in the specified resource group. Alongside
this resource group, another group will be created by the Azure platform itself.

Kubernetes infrastructure

In this resource group, all virtualized infrastructure that is needed to run the cluster is
created. This also means that in the future, new components can be added to this resource
group depending on the demands of the application:

In the resource group created, you will find all the resources as mentioned to run the
cluster:

With the Kubernetes infrastructure now up and running, the management and deployment
of resources can begin.

Managing Kubernetes

To manage Kubernetes, the `kubectl` command line is used and installed locally (or used in the Azure cloud shell). This is command-line interface tooling that will communicate with the Kubernetes API. Let's see how to work with Kubernetes with this command line:

1. If you do not already have it installed, run the following command to install the Azure CLI on your machine:

   ```
   az aks install-cli
   ```

2. To connect to the cluster, the credentials need to be retrieved and saved to the local system. This can be done by using the `az aks get-credentials` command and specifying the resource group and cluster name:

   ```
   az aks get-credentials --resource-group mpn-rg-kubernetes --name mykubernetescluster
   ```

3. With all the prerequisites configured, a lot of the base functionality can be run against the Kubernetes cluster. Take a look at these two commands for example:

   - Retrieve the nodes of the cluster:

     ```
     kubectl get nodes
     ```

   - Get the pods in the cluster:

     ```
     kubectl get pods
     ```

4. Next to the preceding commands, you can also try the following Azure CLI command to open up the Kubernetes dashboard. This dashboard is a management interface built on top of the Kubernetes API that can be used next to the `kubectl` command line:

   ```
   az aks browse --resource-group mpn-rg-kubernetes --name mykubernetescluster
   ```

The dashboard is shown in the following screenshot:

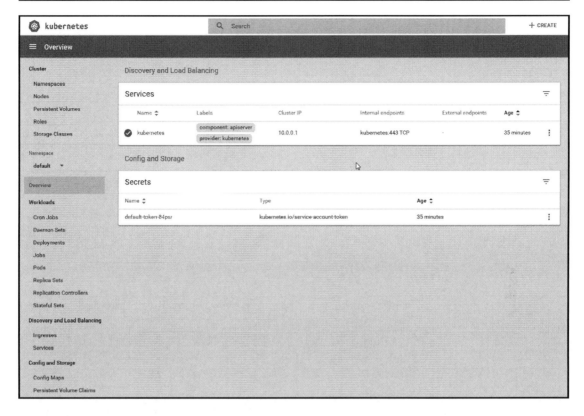

A deployment file needs to be created to be able to run containers within the cluster. So let's see how to do this.

Deploying a container image

We will create a deployment file and deploy it to Kubernetes. To do this, perform the following steps:

1. Make a new file in your favorite text editor and call it `deploy.yaml`. Add the following information to the `deploy.yaml` file:

    ```
    apiVersion: apps/v1
    kind: Deployment
    metadata:
      name: kubernetes-deployment
      labels:
        app: customapplication
    spec:
    ```

```
replicas: 3
selector:
  matchLabels:
    app: customapplication
template:
  metadata:
    labels:
      app: customapplication
  spec:
    containers:
    - name: azuredevops
      image: msftazuredevops.azurecr.io/azuredevops:586
      ports:
      - containerPort: 80
```

In this example, the following is specified:

- A deployment is created with the name `kubernetes-deployment` (`metadata.name`).
- The deployment will create three replicas of the specified container (`spec.replicas`).
- The selector, in combination with the labels tag, is used to specify which components this deployment file will manage within Kubernetes.
- The deployment file will create a container for the `msftazuredevops.azurecr.io/azuredevops:586` image file.

2. To deploy this file to Kubernetes, we will again use the `kubectl` command line and make use of the `apply` command:

   kubectl apply -f deploy.yaml

The `-f` argument is used to specify that a local path is used as a reference to a deployment file. After executing the command, you can open the Kubernetes dashboard to see the status and maybe even observe errors.

 It is possible that you encounter an error stating that pulling the image from your location failed. This could be a security issue. Under the hood, AKS is using a service principal. You should also see this when creating a new Kubernetes cluster. Make sure to give this service principal access rights on the Azure registry.

3. Following a successful execution, try the `get pods` command to see whether there are three pods within the system. If everything proceeded correctly, there should be three pods running within Kubernetes, but the application is still not available to the outside world.

To make it available, we need to add a service to the deployment file.

 If you want to add it to the same file, add a line with these characters, `---`, between the deployments. This is not required when you also define separate files for deployment.

In the `deploy.yaml` file, add the following section:

```
---
apiVersion: v1
kind: Service
metadata:
    name: customapplication-service
spec:
    type: LoadBalancer
    ports:
    - port: 80
    selector:
        app: customapplication
```

This YAML section creates a load balancer and attaches it to the specified selector (`spec.selector.app`), meaning it will be used for the pods as we previously specified.

In the background, Kubernetes will create an Azure load balancer and a public IP for connection to the pods.

4. To retrieve the external IP address of the service, use the following command until it displays the external IP address:

kubectl get service

This will return all services and their external IP addresses if it is present. Also take a quick peak at the additional resource group of Kubernetes to see which Azure resources are created.

Well done! In this section, you learned how to create a Kubernetes cluster and deploy a container image on it via `kubectl` and deployment files. In the next section, we will take this forward and learn how to upgrade these containers.

Upgrading containers

In Kubernetes, applications are very easily updated. For this, Kubernetes uses rolling updates, which means that traffic to a container is first drained before the container is replaced. During an upgrade of the application, Kubernetes will deploy an additional pod and run it through some specified probes.

A probe is a diagnostic that is periodically performed on a pod to check its status. During the upgrading or creation of a pod, Kubernetes brings up the additional pod and makes sure that it passes the liveness and readiness probes.

If the newly created pod succeeds with both probes, the traffic to a single old pod is terminated and traffic to the new pod is opened. For this termination, Kubernetes uses a termination grace period. During this period, the 2 connection to the load balancer is stopped and active connections are processed successfully, and new traffic is routed to a running pod. The default grace period is 30 seconds, during which the pod will be in a termination state and all old traffic to this pod is redirected to the other pods.

This process continues until all pods are replaced with the new version. All of this is default behavior within Azure Kubernetes. A deployment is simply triggered by adjusting the deployment file and applying it with the same command as used previously:

```
Kubectl apply -f [file]
```

By default, `httpGet` probes are added to pods that are being exposed, but they can also be customized by adding the readiness probe or liveness probe to the deployment:

```
readinessProbe:
        httpGet:
            path: /
            port: 80
            initialDelaySeconds: 5
            periodSeconds: 5
            successThreshold: 1
```

This readiness probe performs an `httpGet` request on the pod and has the following options:

- `path`: The path it should call for the `httpGet` request.
- `port`: The port number it should use for the call. This is also configured in our deployment file.
- `initialDelaySeconds`: The seconds it waits before running the probe once the container is started.

- `periodSeconds`: The number of seconds the probe waits before it times out.
- `successThreshold`: The amount of success required for the probe minimum value is 1.

As mentioned, a deployment has a default rolling upgrade scenario configured. The configuration of the rolling deployment can be retrieved by using the following command:

```
kubectl describe deployment kubernetes-deployment
```

 If you are interested in doing so, build a new version of your container and upgrade it within Kubernetes. Before running the upgrade, make sure you have the dashboard open and refresh the page during the update and you will see extra pods coming up and old pods being terminated.

In this section, we learned how to upgrade containers, which will help you stay up to date with the latest version. Moving forward, in the next section, we will look further into the scaling of containers and Kubernetes.

Scaling containers and Kubernetes

As the demand for your application may grow, you will need to scale the application. Scaling the application can be done in multiple ways and different components can be scaled:

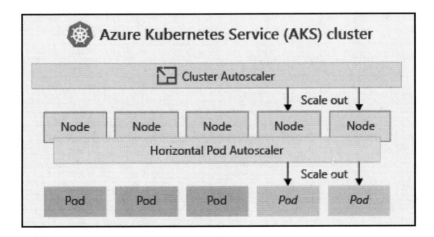

The preceding diagram shows you the different ways to scale your application or cluster, which we will discuss over the upcoming subsections.

Scaling pods manually

Pods can easily be scaled by updating the number of replicas. Try getting your pods by using the `kubectl get pods` command and increase the number of replicas by using the following command:

```
kubectl scale --replicas=[number of pods] deployment/[deploymentname]
```

With this command, the pods are scaled up or down depending on the number of replicas. The up or specified scaling is down as per deployment.

Autoscaling pods

Azure Kubernetes also supports autoscaling. The scheduler will then update the number of pods depending on CPU utilization or other metrics that are available.

Kubernetes uses the metrics server for this. The metrics server collects metrics from the summary API of the kubelet agents that run on the nodes within the cluster.

 The metrics service is available by default if you are using Kubernetes version 1.10 or above. If you are using an older version, you will have to install the metrics server manually.

The autoscale functionality also requires some configuration on the deployment side of Kubernetes. For a deployment, you need to specify the requests and limits for the running container. These values are specified for a specific metric, for example, the CPU.

In the following example, there are requests and limits specified for the CPU metric. The CPU metric is measured in CPU units. In Azure, one unit stands for one core. For different platforms, it can have a different meaning:

```
resources:
  requests:
    cpu: 0.25
  limits:
    cpu: 0.5
```

This part can be added to the container in the deployment file and this will make sure that the pods can be autoscaled when large numbers of requests need to be served.

With the updated deployment file, deploy it and make an autoscale rule within the Kubernetes cluster:

```
kubectl autoscale deployment [deployment name] --cpu-percent=60 --min=1 --max=10
```

This rule will update the deployment with autoscale functionality. If average CPU utilization across all pods exceeds 60% of their requested usage, the autoscaler increases the pods up to a maximum of 10 instances. A minimum of one instance is then defined for the deployment:

After creating the autoscaler, you can check it by running the following command:

```
kubectl get hpa
```

HPA stands for **horizontal pod autoscaler**.

Try creating a CPU-intensive operation within an application and checking automatic pod creation during execution. The Kubernetes cluster will notice the significant amount of CPU usage and will scale out the cluster automatically by creating multiple pods.

Once the intensive operation is finished, Kubernetes will scale the number of pods down to the minimum.

Scaling nodes

Alongside scaling pods, Kubernetes can also scale the number of nodes that run within the Kubernetes cluster. The number of nodes can be scaled using the following commands:

1. First, get the information pertaining to the current environment by requesting the number of nodes:

```
az aks show --resource-group mpn-rg-kubernetes --name
mykubernetescluster  --query agentPoolProfiles
```

2. Then, use this command to update the nodepool. Extract the name of the nodepool from the result of the last command:

```
az aks scale --resource-group mpn-rg-kubernetes --name
mykubernetescluster --node-count 2 --nodepool-name nodepool1
```

Scaling the number of nodes up can increase the performance drastically. This will also make the cluster more expensive. By scaling the number of cluster nodes down, costs can decrease and you are only using the resources that are actually required by your application. To keep track of this, the nodes can also be autoscaled.

Autoscaling nodes

Alongside the manual scaling of nodes, nodes can also scale automatically by updating the Kubernetes cluster. This can be done by using the `az aks update` command. With this command, you can set the minimum and maximum node counts. The autoscaler will then make sure that nodes are created when needed:

```
az aks update --resource-group mmpn-rg-kubernetes --name
mykubernetescluster   --update-cluster-autoscaler --min-count 1 --max-count
5
```

Azure Kubernetes also has the option to scale out with Azure Container Instances. To use this option, a specific configuration needs to be applied when creating the AKS cluster. This is mainly required because Azure Container Instances needs a specific subnet within the virtual network.

In this section, we learned to scale containers and the cluster to drastically increase performance. Next up is deployment from Azure DevOps to facilitate continuous deployment.

Deploying to Kubernetes with Azure DevOps

We have seen a lot of options for deploying and configuring the Kubernetes cluster via the command line. When working with DevOps, however, changes need to be applied in a continuous way.

For this, there is the Kubernetes manifest task within Azure DevOps, which contains a lot of functionalities to manage a Kubernetes cluster:

```
task: KubernetesManifest@0
  inputs:
  action: 'deploy'
  kubernetesServiceConnection: '[service connection name]'
  manifests: '[path to your deployment file]'
  containers: 'msftazuredevops.azurecr.io/azuredevops:$(Build.BuildID)'
```

In the preceding example, the following is configured:

- `action`: The kind of action to we want to perform. In this example, the `deploy` action is used because we want to deploy/apply a deployment file.
- `kubernetesServiceConnection`: The service connection to the Kubernetes cluster.
- `manifests`: The path to the manifest file. As we are using the `deploy` action, this should be a reference to the deployment file.
- `containers`: A special field where you can override the version of the container being deployed. By specifying the above, every image is specified in the deployment manifest with the `msftazuredevops.azurecr.io` reference and the `azuredevops` repository is replaced by the new value as configured in this field.

Using a Kubernetes destination environment within Azure DevOps pipelines also has the advantage of seeing the environment running within Azure DevOps. This will show the number of running pods within the cluster.

Try it out with the following stage configuration for a build that will publish the deployment files to the artifact location of Azure DevOps:

```
stages:
  - stage : Build
    displayName : Build
    jobs:
     - job:
       pool:
           vmImage: 'ubuntu-latest'
       continueOnError: false
       steps:
       - task: Docker@2
         inputs:
           containerRegistry: '[Container Registry service connection]'
           repository: 'azuredevops'
           command: 'buildAndPush'
           Dockerfile: '**/Dockerfile'
           buildContext: '$(System.DefaultWorkingDirectory)/[folder path
for docker]'
         - task: CopyFiles@2
           inputs:
           SourceFolder: '$(system.defaultworkingdirectory)/[path to the
deployment manifest files]'
           Contents: '*'
           TargetFolder: '$(build.artifactstagingdirectory)'
           flattenFolders: true
```

```
          - task: PublishBuildArtifacts@1
            inputs:
              PathtoPublish: '$(Build.ArtifactStagingDirectory)'
              ArtifactName: 'drop'
              publishLocation: 'Container'
```

Next to the build stage, add the following release stage. Following the initial execution of the pipeline, a new environment will be available within Azure DevOps. In the environment created by the release, attach the Kubernetes cluster to see information on the running pods:

```
  - stage : Release
      displayName : Release
      jobs:
        - deployment: KubernetesDeploy
          displayName: Deploy Kubernetes
          pool:
            vmImage: 'ubuntu-latest'
          environment: 'Kubernetes'
          strategy:
            runOnce:
              deploy:
                steps:
                  - task: DownloadPipelineArtifact@2
                    displayName: 'Download pipeline artifacts'
                    inputs:
                      buildType: 'current'
                      targetPath: '$(Pipeline.Workspace)'
                  - task: KubernetesManifest@0
                    inputs:
                      action: 'deploy'
                      kubernetesServiceConnection: '[Kubernetes service
    connection]'
                      manifests: '$(Pipeline.Workspace)[deployment manifest]'
                      containers: '[container registry]:$(Build.BuildID)'
```

In the example, two stages are specified for a multi-stage pipeline. The first stage will build the container image via the Docker task and publish it to a container registry. After publishing the image, it also publishes a number of build artifacts, in this case, the Kubernetes manifests.

The second stage deploys to a specific environment called Kubernetes. This environment will also be created in Azure DevOps if it has not already been added. During the remainder of the process, it retrieves the published artifacts of the build stage and uses the Kubernetes manifest task to deploy the Kubernetes resources.

Summary

In this chapter, you have learned what containers are and how they relate to DevOps. Where DevOps is more of a cultural thing, containers are a way to support it technically. You have also learned how to create container images via a Dockerfile, and specifically by using a multi-stage build file. Finally, we dived into Kubernetes, where we learned a way to host containers and also manage the running containers by using the kubectl command.

Using the knowledge acquired in this chapter, you are now able to deploy applications to Kubernetes and make sure that it scales with the number of requests it receives.

In the next chapter, you will learn more about facilitating the DevOps process by using Azure DevOps. You will learn what works for your organization and team and what doesn't and how to implement that structure and your approach using Azure DevOps.

Questions

As we conclude, here is a list of questions for you to test your knowledge regarding the material covered in this chapter. You will find the answers in the *Assessments* section of the Appendix:

1. What are the benefits of containers for DevOps?
2. True or false: A specific container can be hosted on different platforms (Azure/AWS).
3. Is it possible to add container support to an existing application?
4. What is the RUN command used for within a Dockerfile?
5. Kubernetes can be scaled on different components. What are these components?

Further reading

- Information on installing the Azure CLI: `https://docs.microsoft.com/en-us/cli/azure/install-azure-cli?view=azure-cli-latest`
- Information on installing Docker Desktop: `https://docs.docker.com/docker-for-windows/install/`
- More information on Kubernetes: `https://kubernetes.io/docs/home/`
- You can find more information regarding Azure Kubernetes at the following link: `https://azure.microsoft.com/en-us/topic/what-is-kubernetes/`
- Information on Azure Container Registry: `https://docs.microsoft.com/en-us/azure/container-registry/container-registry-intro`
- More information regarding multi-stage builds: `https://docs.docker.com/develop/develop-images/multistage-build/`

13
Planning Your Azure DevOps Organization

In the previous chapters, you learned about many techniques and practices concerning DevOps. In this chapter, we will take a step back and look at how you can build a strong DevOps organization and what you need to think about when doing so. Next, you will learn what this can bring you with regard to security and traceability. From there on, you will learn how you can consolidate your toolchain, standardizing on Azure DevOps.

We will begin by creating an Azure DevOps organization where you will learn which constructs are available to lay out your products and teams in the tool. You will also learn about licensing and the security implications of the different approaches. Next, you will learn about traceability and how that can be used to create a verifiable software development process. Next up is the consolidation of the tools used. As you progress on your DevOps journey, you may find that each team uses different tools that it is familiar with and enjoys working with. While DevOps is all about empowering people, some level of standardization might be desirable, and you will learn how to go about this. Finally, you will read that you might have to accept that you will never be completely done adopting DevOps.

The following topics will be covered in this chapter:

- Setting up an Azure DevOps organization
- Ensuring traceability
- Consolidating tools
- Accepting there is no end state

Technical requirements

To follow along with the practical parts of this chapter, one of the following is needed:

- A Microsoft Live account, also called a personal account
- A work or school account

Setting up an Azure DevOps organization

To practice with one or more of the technologies and techniques described in the previous chapters, an Azure DevOps organization might have been created specifically for this use, or maybe one was available already that could be used for this purpose. However, creating an organization for a company from scratch takes a little more consideration. Taking the time to properly plan the layout of the organization can save a lot of time later on.

This section describes the components out of which Azure DevOps is built, how you can use this to organize a fitting security model, and licensing options and costs.

How Azure DevOps is organized

The top-level construct in Azure DevOps is called an organization. For most companies, a total of one organization will suffice, but it is allowed to create more than one.

Each Azure DevOps organization is hosted in a specific region. Most of the data (source code and work items) for the organization is guaranteed to be located in the region for the organization, but some information is always stored in other data centers due to the global reach of the service. Having a distributed organization with teams and products in different geographies can be one reason for using more than one organization. For example, if some teams are located in Australia and some in West Europe, it makes sense to create two separate organizations and host all teams in the geography closest to them. This will locate the bulk of the services that are physically close to them, greatly reducing latencies when working with Azure DevOps.

An organization can be linked to an **Azure Active Directory (AAD)**. If this link is enabled, only users that are inside that particular AAD are allowed access to the organization. Using a company AAD is not mandatory; an organization can also be created using a Microsoft account.

In each organization, one or more projects can be created. A project is an isolated container of work items, source control repositories, pipeline definitions, and all other Azure DevOps artifacts. There are only limited sharing and linking possibilities between projects. At the time of writing, only work items can be related across projects and nothing else can. This way, projects can serve as a strong isolation boundary for enforcing rigid security between products or teams if needed. In general, it is recommended to have as few projects as possible, with the goal of having only one if possible.

The following diagram shows a possible organization of Azure DevOps organizations and projects. It shows that there are two organizations connected to the Azure Active Directory. One is located in West Europe, and the other one in Australia. In West Europe, there are two projects in the organization, in Australia just one:

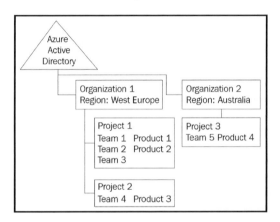

As stated before, the recommendation is to go with as few organizations and projects as possible. But in this example, the latency from Australia to West Europe is a good argument to split into two organizations to have Azure DevOps hosted close to the teams. The split into two projects in West Europe might be due to the need for a high level of isolation for team 4 that is working on product 3.

Combining the teams 1 to 3 and products 1 and 2 into one project has been done on purpose. The reason for this is that within a single project, multiple product areas and multiple teams can be defined. Having all of these in a single project enables easy linking of work items to do portfolio management. This way, working items from one team can also be related to the commits or pull requests of another team on another product. This is helpful if features are spread over multiple products or applications (components).

To make defining all products and all teams in a single project possible, it is important to know about the Azure DevOps security model and how to use this for implementing access control.

Creating an Azure DevOps organization and project

Creating a new Azure DevOps organization and one or more projects is a task often completed by administrators that will also be responsible for managing these environments later. These organizations are most likely connected to an Active Directory. To create an organization for private use or training and learning practices, it might be better to use a personal account.

To create a new organization using a personal account, do the following:

1. Navigate to `https://dev.azure.com`.
2. Choose **Start free**, to start the creation of a new Azure DevOps organization.
3. When prompted with a login dialog, log in using a personal account.
4. After logging in, select the correct country of residence and opt in/out of tips and other service updates using the following dialog:

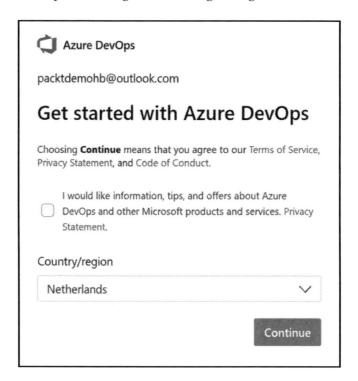

5. Press **Continue** to create a new organization.

Once the organization is created, a new wizard will automatically start creating the first project. To create the project, do the following:

1. Provide a project name.
2. Choose between making the project public or private. Private projects are the default setting and are intended to create software within an organization and not allow anonymous access. Public projects are intended for open source development.

Once a new organization and a new project are created, it is possible to make changes to these choices using the management interface.

 Please keep in mind that renaming the organization or a project will change URLs, so all existing integrations and links may break.

It is even possible to change the location of an organization later. This must be requested and is not as easy as changing other settings. A link to the documentation on how to do this is included at the end of this chapter.

Once an organization and project are available, it is time to set up security.

Azure DevOps security model

Within Azure DevOps, authorizations can be assigned to individual users or to security groups. The security group is either a logical wrapper around an existing AAD group or can be defined within Azure DevOps itself. In general, it is recommended to assign authorizations as much as possible to groups and limit individual user assignments.

To configure the authorizations for a user or security group, two complementary approaches are available:

- Organization- and project-level authorizations
- Object-level authorizations

When working with the on-premises product, Azure DevOps Server, there are also server-level security groups and settings available.

In Azure DevOps services, an organization is called a project collection and a project is called a team project. Sometimes, these names are also visible in Azure DevOps.

Organization-and project-level authorizations: To allow a user to perform a specific action on every object of a certain type, an organization- or project-level authorization can be set. As an example, look at the built-in groups, `Project Collection Build Administrators`, respectively, `[ProjectName]\Build Administrators`, which, by default, have permission to view, manage, and edit build definitions and build resources. The permissions that can be set on the organization and project level are automatically applied to all individual resources in the organization or the project.

Object-level authorizations: On most of the objects in Azure DevOps, individual permissions can be assigned to users or groups. These permissions are set using an **Access Control List** (**ACL**) on the object itself. The following example shows a classic build definition:

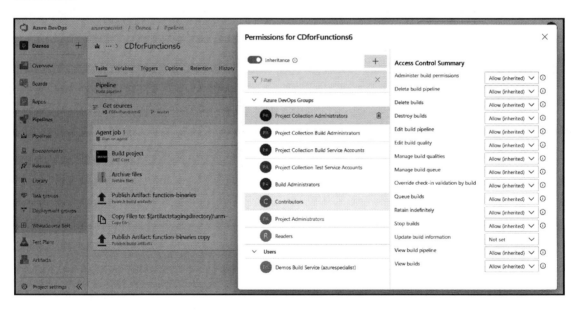

For each group, for each action, it is possible to configure **Allow**, **Deny**, **Not set**, or **inherited**. When an action is configured with **Deny**, access is never allowed, not even if a user is part of a group that has the authorization specified as **Allow.** In other words, when there are two conflicting assignments (**Allow** and **Deny**), **Deny** will take precedence over **Allow**. **Not set** is to be interpreted as an implicit deny that does not take precedence. In other words, when there are two conflicting assignments (**Not set** and **Allow**), the user will be allowed access.

Some artifacts in Azure DevOps are part of a hierarchy. For example, pipelines can be in a folder. Whenever inheritance is enabled, permissions from higher in the hierarchy will propagate to the artifact. This means that, when a user has access to a pipeline folder, all of their rights will propagate to all underlying folders and pipelines, if and only if, there are no more specific authorizations set.

While the security model determines which authorization a user has, user actions are also limited by their assigned access level, which follows from their license.

Azure DevOps licensing

Another aspect of creating an Azure DevOps organization is managing licenses. Within Azure DevOps, every user needs to have an access level assigned before they can log in to the product. There are three access levels defined:

- **Stakeholder**: Stakeholders are free users who can log in to the product but have limited access to its features. Stakeholders can manage work items, manage pipelines, and view dashboards. They do not have access to any of the other product areas, making this license level usable for non-development roles only.
- **Basic**: Basic users have a paid license that gives them access to all parts of the product, except for test management and advanced test execution functionality. A basic user license is priced at € 5.06 per month at the time of writing.
- **Basic and Test plans**: Users of the Basic and Test Plans license option have access to all parts of Azure DevOps. They have the same access as basic users, but are also provided with test management and tools for user acceptance testing, test execution, and test result reporting. At the time of writing, the Basic and Test Plans license option is priced at € 43.86 per month.

The first five basic licenses for every organization are free. This means that experimenting with the product and learning it can be done without incurring any costs. Additionally, Visual Studio subscribers can also get free licenses. Professional subscribers get a free Basic license and Enterprise subscribers get a free Basic and Test Plans license.

Licenses can be assigned and re-assigned at any point, so for a company or team with many joiners and leavers, it is not necessary to buy more licenses then they have people active at any given point.

Licensing costs are not the only costs that come from using Azure DevOps; it is important to also know about the pay-per-use costs.

Consumption-based costs

Licenses give users access to the product and, from there on, they can use all of the services in the product at a fixed cost, except for the following two:

- Azure Pipelines parallel executions
- Azure Artifacts storage

Parallel executions: By default, every Azure DevOps organization is provided with one Microsoft-hosted parallel execution job. This means that, while there can be as many pipelines defined as needed, there can be only one executing at the same time. Of course, this number can be increased, but this comes at the cost of buying more Microsoft-hosted parallel execution jobs, which are currently priced at € 33.74 per month.

As an alternative, it is also possible to buy self-hosted jobs. For these jobs, the execution agents are not provided by Microsoft, but have to be provided by the organization itself. This provides the opportunity (and responsibility) to fully control the hardware. A self-hosted pipeline is currently priced at € 12.65.

Artifacts storage: When working with Azure Artifact feeds, the first 2 GB of storage used is free. Any extra storage used is charged at a rate of € 1.69 per month.

Once more and more of the users of a team have a license for Azure DevOps and perform their work there, this can be used to increase traceability for software development.

Ensuring traceability

One of the advantages of Azure DevOps over some of the other tools covered in this book is that it is a fully integrated suite of tools, each supporting specific DevOps processes. This end-to-end integration allows for detailed and lengthy traceability, from work described on the board to the related binaries being deployed to an environment.

When working with a set of other tools that support only a part of the DevOps process, integrating them is often possible and, of course, this will result in some traceability. For example, when working with Jira and GitHub, it is possible to relate commits, pull requests, and other changes in GitHub back to work described in Jira. When picking merged changes up in Jenkins to build and deploy the product, there will also be traceability from Jenkins back to GitHub. However, there will be no direct visibility on which work item was completed with which Jenkins deployment

The disadvantage of this is that a product owner who works in the Jira tool, cannot see whether a completed user story is associated with a release already. They would have to visit multiple tools to find the answer to that question: in GitHub, they would have to find all commits relating to the story and then see whether those commits have been released already using Jenkins:

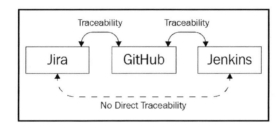

When working with Azure Boards, Repos, and Pipelines, this is different. When using all of the Azure DevOps services, traceability is possible from story to deployment, and the other way around. The following is an example that highlights how to see which commits were deployed for the first time to an environment with a specific deploy:

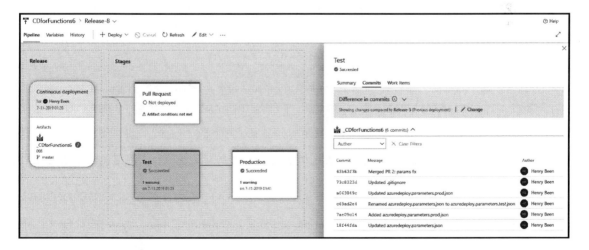

Having this type of end-to-end traceability enables a number of questions to be answered quickly, including the following:

- Has work on this work item already started? (Branches and pull requests can be related to work items.)
- Is this work already part of our nightly build? (Commits and build pipelines can be related to work items.)
- Is this bug already fixed and is the solution available to our customers on ring two already? (Releases and environments show which new commits and work items were part of the latest deployment.)

One thought that is particularly important to reinforce when talking about traceability is that it is not about blame. Traceability is not about finding out who made which mistake, but about finding out what the state of things is and how objects relate. As soon as traceability becomes the basis for blame, engineers will soon find ways to hide their work. This will result in more errors and less visibility, only making problems worse.

With the benefits of traceability clear, let's explore how consolidating tools can help to reap these benefits.

Consolidating tools

One trend that can be observed in the market is that of traceability and DevOps products that extend their offerings to include more than only source control, only pipelines, or just deployments. Examples are GitHub and GitLab, which are adding new services. More integrated **Application Lifecycle Management** (**ALM**) or DevOps suites emerge, while Azure DevOps has been offering this for years now.

However, there are many companies where these integrated suites are not in place. Teams operate in different ecosystems, leading to different tool choices. Or maybe teams just have different preferences or started adopting DevOps practices at different points in time, with other tools to choose from. No matter the reason, there are many companies that have several tools running for the same job.

Unfortunately, several drawbacks are associated with having disconnected tools or multiple tools for the same thing:

- Collaboration between teams is hindered if they are using different tools. No matter the personal preference of developers, it can prove to be a hindrance to productivity when one half of the organization is using Jenkins and the other half is using Azure Pipelines. By extension, switching teams or helping others out is severely impeded when they are using another tool.
- When there are more tools, there are also more costs. Even when all of the tools are open source and free, there are still costs involved. These costs can consist of, for instance, support contracts or requests, training, or the time needed to investigate and overcome specific issues. The same holds for upgrades and maintenance. When there are more tools, the total costs increase.

To overcome these challenges, many large companies decide to standardize which tools are used, either completely or at least to some extent. As an alternative or intermediate solution, it is also possible to use integration between tools as a way of starting a consolidation.

Standardizing tools

To combat these drawbacks, most companies accept one of two strategies:

- Centralized decision making to select one tool (for each DevOps area) for the whole company
- Centralized adoption of a limited set of tools, out of which teams can choose which to adopt

Complete centralization: When completely centralizing, one central team or department decides, on behalf of everyone, which DevOps tools will be used within the organization. Once such a decision has been made and implemented, this reduces costs and makes it easier for engineers to assist in other teams.

The downside is, of course, that one single tool is not necessarily the best choice for everyone while, for the organization as a whole, the selected tool might be the best—such standardization can do damage in a number of edge cases.

Limited centralization: To prevent this, other companies choose to have limited centralization. Instead of just one tool, a group of tools is chosen as the company's standard. Teams are now able to make their own choice out of two or three tools, depending on their specific needs. This limits many of the drawbacks of full decentralization while not sacrificing the productivity of teams with very specific needs.

Adopting one of these two strategies might mean that some existing tools will be deprecated or decommissioned altogether. This can be a slow and painful process, especially in large organizations where there are often conflicting interests. There are many ways to go about this, but there are strategies to make such a migration less painful.

Migration strategies

Reducing the number of DevOps tools in use often means one or more tools must be decommissioned. This can be difficult since often, these tools are used to implement governance and compliance, as required by laws and regulations. In practice, this means that one of two things can be done:

- Old tools are not completely decommissioned but just no longer used, to maintain the change history.
- History must be migrated to the new tools as well before the old tools can be decommissioned.

When choosing to do a migration, there are four ways to go about this:

- Azure DevOps Server to Azure DevOps Services migration
- Big-bang migration
- Synchronization
- Rebuilding

 Azure DevOps Server used to be called **Team Foundation Server (TFS)**. Older versions of TFS need to be upgraded to one of the latest versions of Azure DevOps Server before they can be imported into Azure DevOps Services. The import service always supports the latest two versions of Azure DevOps Server

All three of these are detailed in the following sections.

Azure DevOps Server to Azure DevOps Services migration

For organizations wanting to move from working with Azure DevOps Server to Azure DevOps Services, there is a high-fidelity migration service available. Every project collection that currently exists in the on-premises Azure DevOps Server environment can be migrated to an Azure DevOps organization using the Azure DevOps Server import service. All of the assets currently existing in the on-premises project collection will be migrated to Azure DevOps: work items, source control repositories, and build and release definitions.

The migration of a project collection consists of the following high-level steps:

1. Validating whether a project collection is ready for migration: This step does not make any changes, but only checks whether all preconditions for a migration have been met.
2. Preparing the migration: In this step, a JSON file is generated that describes how the migration should be performed. A second file can also be supplied for linking on-premises identity to AAD identities to ensure that all of the history is still correctly linked to who made the change after the migration.
3. A dry run of the migration is done to verify that the import process will result in the expected outcomes.
4. The actual migration: In this step, the collection is taken offline, a DACPAC is generated from the project collection database, the DACPAC and files from step two are uploaded, and the migration is initiated.
5. After the import, all assets need to be verified and, in specific scenarios, some post-import actions have to be taken.

For using the migration service, a comprehensive guide with checklists and step-by-step instructions is available and linked to at the end of this chapter.

Big-bang migration

The second possible strategy is a big-bang migration. At some point, the old tool is switched off, all data is migrated to the new tool, and the new tool is made available. If there is anything that does not breathe DevOps, it is such a migration. It has a high potential for issues and often there is no turning back. Often, this is not a good migration strategy.

However, one situation where such an approach might make sense is the migration of source control. There are tools available for migrating from different sources to any type of hosted Git solution, including Azure DevOps. Source control also has the benefit that change history is built so deep into the system that migrating with history is often easier than for other types of data.

Synchronization

Another strategy for migration is allowing for a period of time where both tools can be used at the same time.

One way to do this is by using a tool that can be used to sync between the old and the new tool. This can be either in one direction, from old to new, or in both directions. This way, an in-between situation is created where both tools can be in use at the same time. Every team can choose its own time for its migration within a certain window. This avoids a forced migration window. Teams can also opt to use both tools next to each other for a while. This allows them to learn the new tool, while still being able to switch to the tool that they know if they are under pressure. After a period of transition, the old tool can be made read-only or decommissioned completely. This approach often works well for work tracking systems. Between these systems, the concepts are often very similar (epics, features, stories, and sprints), which makes a synchronization a feasible approach.

Rebuilding

A slightly different approach is that of asking teams to rebuild in the new tool. This approach also creates an in-parallel situation, but there is no automated migration or synchronization. Teams will have to redo their process or way of working in the new tool. Since this can take a while, the old tool will remain while teams are working on this. One situation where this is often a good approach is that of build and/or release pipelines.

No matter the strategy that has been chosen, in all cases, it helps to make sure that the new tool or tools are an improvement for the teams over the existing tools. This should improve performance, traceability, ease of use, or integration with other company tools. A positive vibe around any migration can improve the outcomes dramatically.

As an alternative to migrating to a single tool, integrations between tools can be used to bring existing tools together.

Integrating tools

As an alternative to replacing no longer preferred tools, it is also possible to integrate them with the preferred tool. Especially when it has been decided to move to Azure DevOps, this can be a powerful strategy. In many of the chapters before, for each topic, different tools were listed that integrate with Azure DevOps.

When pursuing end-to-end traceability, these integrations can be used as a means to bring tools closer together. Consider the following example.

An organization is using Azure DevOps for managing work items, hosting Git repositories, and executing build pipelines. Deployments are done using Octopus Deploy for historic reasons. Since a full migration is too costly, as an alternative, an integration strategy is chosen. Triggering the Octopus Deploy not manually but automatically from Azure DevOps meets several goals:

- End-to-end automation is achieved.
- Release management can now also be done in Azure DevOps, even though each deployment in Azure DevOps is no more than triggering Octopus Deploy.
- Having release management in Azure DevOps now allows for end-to-end traceability.

When consolidating tools, and really all things regarding DevOps, one thing that you must be ready to accept is that you are never done.

Accepting there is no end state

It is fair to expect that, at any point in time, there will be one or more improvements that teams want to make to their applications, toolchain, or way of working. To cope with this, it is recommended to not keep changing everything all of the time.

Instead, try to implement changes in batches or a series of well-defined steps. Also, note there is a natural order in things. It is impossible to practice continuous deployment without having a proper continuous integration process first. Also, adopting infrastructure as code will deliver the most value when a continuous deployment process for application code is already in place. Next, automating governance and security measures works best when infrastructure and configuration code is common practice. And once all of these practices have been implemented, new things will come up on the radar—future improvements that may be necessary.

Besides this series of improvements, it is also important to realize that not every team is at the same place in this journey and not every team can move at the same pace and that development is not always this linear.

But this does not mean that it is impossible to track and plan future changes and have learnings from one team applied to other teams as well. One oversimplified approach to tracking this can be a table, as shown here.

Here we see the adoption of different DevOps practices or ideas among five teams. All teams are practicing **continuous integration (CI)**. Some of them are practicing **continuous deployment (CD)**, while team 3 is still working on that (**Work in Progress, WIP**) and the fifth team has not started yet. Finally, team 2 is already experimenting with **infrastructure as code (IaC)**. Finally, as there is no end state, it is only a matter of time before the next practice or idea will pop up and a team will start experimenting:

	CI	CD	IaC	next ?
Team 1	✓	✓		
Team 2	✓	✓	experimenting	
Team 3	✓	WIP		
Team 4	✓	✓		
Team 5	✓			

If a table, similar to the one shown in the preceding, is updated, evaluated, and expanded upon frequently, this helps to foster continuous learning and improve the way software is created and delivered. Learning and improving will become the standard and this will help to improve the delivery of value to end users. It also shows that adopting DevOps is never done.

It also provides the means to see which teams are at the forefront and which teams are following along. By giving teams who are in the lead more room for experimentation and knowledge sharing with other teams, organizations can encourage their leader teams to improve even more while, at the same time, accelerating other teams as well.

And with this remark about the need to keep learning, experimenting, and pushing yourself, it is a great time to wrap this book up. Let's recap this chapter in the next section.

Summary

In this chapter, you learned how to configure your Azure DevOps organization and how to create a layout for your products and teams. You learned what the implications are regarding the different configuration options and how to apply those. Next, you learned how you can use Azure DevOps to add traceability to your development process. You learned how to capture ideas and tasks in stories and tasks and how these can be traced all of the way to a deployment and the other way around. The next thing you learned about is how to approach the consolidation of tools used within your organization and when to stop trying to consolidate tools. Finally, you learned that it is important to continuously keep improving.

With the things you learned in this chapter, you are now capable of setting up and configuring Azure DevOps for your team, teams, or organization. You can create a structure that fits your organization and start using it with just one or multiple teams. You are also able to slowly standardize your way of working and consolidate the teams on the same set of tools.

This completes the final chapter of this book. You can refer to this book as a basis for taking the AZ-400 exam, as most of the topics are along similar lines. However, in order to be well prepared for the exam, I recommend reading more about them in other sources as well and try to get as much hands-on experience as you can. As a practice tool, the concluding chapter contains a mock exam to help you prepare for the final exam.

Good luck!

Questions

As we conclude, here is a list of questions for you to test your knowledge regarding this chapter's material. You will find the answers in the *Assessments* section of the Appendix:

1. True or False: All data stored in Azure DevOps by users is guaranteed to be contained within one region.
2. Reorder the following Azure DevOps concepts in such a way that each next element acts as a container for the next concept in the list:
   - Work item
   - Organization
   - Region
   - Project
3. True or False: The general recommendation is to create a new project for every application that is developed by your organization.
4. Which two elements limit the actions any user can perform within Azure DevOps?
5. What is the main benefit of using a single tool for application life cycle management/DevOps as opposed to a suite of tools?

Further reading

- More information on Azure DevOps projects and when to create more than one project can be found at https://docs.microsoft.com/en-us/azure/devops/organizations/projects/about-projects?view=azure-devops#when-to-add-another-project.
- More information about the Azure DevOps security model can be found at https://docs.microsoft.com/en-us/azure/devops/organizations/security.
- Up-to-date information on Azure DevOps pricing can be found at https://azure.microsoft.com/en-us/pricing/details/devops/azure-devops-services/.
- More information about the Azure DevOps Server-import service can be found at https://docs.microsoft.com/en-us/azure/devops/migrate/migration-overview?view=azure-devopsviewFallbackFrom=vsts.

14
AZ-400 Mock Exam

Designing a DevOps Strategy

1. You are tasked with introducing Azure DevOps into your organization. Right now, there are many other tools being used for deployments. You are asked which of the following tools can integrate with Azure DevOps. [There can be any number of answers.]
   1. Octopus Deploy
   2. Jira
   3. Jenkins
   4. App Center

2. You are asked to create a dashboard for your team that displays information about how your team is working. You should focus on displaying metrics and charts that encourage Agile and DevOps ways of working. Which metrics do you choose? [Choose three.]
   1. A widget that shows the average cycle time for work items
   2. A widget that shows the outcome (success or failure) for the most recent deployments
   3. A widget that shows the number of lines of code added per day
   4. A widget that shows the number of pull requests currently open within the team

3. You are asked to implement static code analysis within your project. What is the best time to do this?
   1. During the build stage, just before artifacts are published
   2. During the deployment stage, just before the actual deployment to the target environment

4. You are running Team Foundation Server 2015 on-premises. You are asked to migrate all assets on this server to Azure DevOps using the high-fidelity migration. Put the following tasks in the correct order.
    1. Run the Migration Validation Tool.
    2. Perform a complete end-to-end dry run of the import process.
    3. Create a portable back-up of the TFS servers Project Collection(s).
    4. Upgrade your TFS server to one of the two most recent versions of the Azure DevOps server.
    5. Run the import service for each Project Collection.

5. One of the core principles of DevOps is "to continuously deliver value to our end users". Which of the following is not used to do so?
    1. People
    2. Practices
    3. Process
    4. Products

6. You are working for a large enterprise and have to automate the assignment of licenses to new hires. To do this, you have created a small application that is connected to the HR application. Which type of authorization do you use between your application and Azure DevOps?
    1. User accounts
    2. PAT tokens
    3. OAuth tokens
    4. One-time secrets

7. You need to migrate an existing Git repository to Azure DevOps. Which of the following do you need to do? [Choose two.]
    1. Create an initialized Git repository.
    2. Create an uninitialized Git repository.
    3. Execute `git remote rm origin; git remote add origin <new-repository-url>; git push`.
    4. Execute `git remote redirect origin <new-repository-url>; git push`.

8. You are working in a heterogeneous environment with teams using different DevOps tools through the company. One of your builds is running within Azure DevOps, but another team wants to consume your pipeline artifacts from another tool. Which of the following can you use for staging build artifacts to connect from other tools?

    1. Pipeline artifacts
    2. Artifactory
    3. Octopus Deploy Binary Server
    4. Artifact feeds/universal packages

9. You are tasked with configuring source control for your team in Azure DevOps. Which of the following requirements can only be fulfilled by using TFVC?

    1. You need to enforce the four-eyes principle.
    2. You need to configure access to specific folders for one user only.
    3. You need to configure access to specific files for one user only.
    4. You need to connect to classic build pipelines.

10. You need to execute and record exploratory testing sessions. In addition to executing tests, you should also be able to automatically report bugs on your Azure Boards backlog. You plan to use the Test & Feedback extension for this and assign all testers a Testing license. Does this complete the goal?

    1. Yes
    2. No

11. You need to execute and record exploratory testing sessions. In addition to executing tests, you should also be able to automatically report bugs on your Azure Boards backlog. You plan to use the Test & Feedback extension for this and assign all testers a Basic+Test license. Does this complete the goal?

    1. Yes
    2. No

12. You need to execute and record exploratory testing sessions. In addition to executing tests, you should also be able to automatically report bugs on your Azure Boards backlog. You plan to use the Test & Feedback extension for this and assign all testers a Basic license. Does this complete the goal?

    1. Yes
    2. No

13. You are tasked with identifying metrics that can be used to measure the impact of adopting DevOps. Which of the following do you advise to be used? [Choose two.]

    1. Amount of work in progress at the same time
    2. Velocity

    2. Cycle time

    3. Sprint duration

9. Which of the following is not a DevOps habit?

    1. Team autonomy and enterprise alignment

    2. Maximizing the amount of work not done

    3. Hypothesis-driven development

    4. Live-site culture

10. You are tasked with creating a test strategy for the new application that you are creating with your team. Which of the following recommendations should you make?

    1. For verifying that the most critical user scenarios are still working correctly, one or more system tests should be written.

    2. For verifying that the most critical user scenarios are still working correctly, a stress test should be performed before every deployment.

    3. For every ten unit tests, there should be at least one integration test.

    4. Before enabling a new feature in production, a final smoke test should be performed on the production environment.

11. Source code is one of the most valuable assets for your company. You want to implement multi-factor authentication for access to Azure DevOps when users are not connecting through the corporate network. Which of the following can you use to do this?

    1. Azure Active Directory Conditional Access

    2. Azure Active Directory Network Allowance

    3. Azure DevOps Network Controls

    4. Azure Active Directory Account Groups

12. You are working in a team that provides Azure subscriptions and resource groups to other teams. As part of your work, you want to monitor whether all teams implement recommended Azure best practices for security. Which of the following do you use?

    1. Azure Policy

    2. Azure Security Center

    3. Azure Key Vault

    4. Azure Security Monitor

18. You are tasked with providing the means for starting SonarCloud scans from within Azure DevOps. Which of the following steps create a complete solution? [Choose two.]
    1. Update the Sonar Cloud configuration in your Azure DevOps Project.
    2. Create a new Sonar Cloud Service Connection.
    3. Activate the Sonar Cloud Integration Pack.
    4. Install the Sonar Cloud Extension.

19. You need to apply an update to a deployment within Kubernetes—which command should you use?
    1. `kubectl apply`
    2. `kubectl deployments`
    3. `kubectl get services`
    4. `kubectl deploy`

20. What are the basic tools you need to use when managing an Azure Kubernetes cluster? [Choose all that apply.]
    1. Azure CLI/PowerShell
    2. kubectl
    3. Azure DevOps

Implementing DevOps Development Processes

21. You are developing a Microsoft .NET Core application and want to analyze the application to check whether there are any open source libraries with known security vulnerabilities being used. Which of the following products can you use for such an analysis? [Choose two.]
    1. Jenkins
    2. Whitesource Bolt
    3. Snyk
    4. App Center

22. You are currently using (i) JIRA, (ii) GitLab, and (iii) Octopus Deploy for some of your DevOps processes. You want to consolidate your DevOps tools and have chosen to go with Azure DevOps. Which Azure DevOps services should you use to replace these? Choose the correct service to replace these three services. [Match three pairs.]
    1. Azure Pipelines
    2. Azure Repos
    3. Azure Boards
    4. Azure Artifacts

23. You are evaluating different options for build agents. What are valid arguments for opting for private agents over Microsoft Hosted Agents? [Choose two.]
    1. You need custom software to be available on the agent before any job is executed.
    2. You need to ensure that the same environment is used for executing only one pipeline job, before being destructed.
    3. You need direct network connectivity from the build agent to your on-premises network.
    4. You need to ensure that you are always running on up-to-date images.

24. You are responsible for managing the settings of the applications your team deploys to an Azure App Service. Which of the following offerings cannot be used to achieve this?
    1. Azure App Configuration
    2. ARM templates
    3. Azure Policy
    4. Azure Key Vault

25. You are tasked with creating a large number of build pipelines for your team. Almost all pipelines need to have the same structure. Which Azure DevOps Pipelines construct can help you?
    1. Branch Policies
    2. Task Groups
    3. Azure Artifacts
    4. Deployment Groups

26. You are using Entity Framework as the database access layer from your application. You are responsible for managing database upgrades and want to use Entity Framework for this as well, to manage the database schema from code. Which type of schema migration should you use?
    1. Migrations-based
    2. End-state based

27. You need to save your local changes to a Git repository. Which commands do you need to use?

    1. `git clone` and `git push`

    2. `git commit` and `git push`

    3. `git add`, `git commit`, and `git push`

    4. `git add` and `git commit`

28. You need to prevent anyone from merging changes to the master branch if the changes do not compile or any of the unit tests fail. Which of the following can you use to accomplish this?

    1. Branch protection center.

    2. Azure Repos branch policies.

    3. Azure Repos branch security.

    4. This is not possible in Azure DevOps; you need to use another product, for example, GitHub.

29. Your company uses GitHub Enterprise on-premises for hosting source control. For implementing continuous integration and deployment, you are looking to use Azure DevOps. Which of the following components form a complete solution to make this possible? [Choose two.]

    1. An external Git service connection

    2. Opening the firewall for HTTPS connections from Azure Pipelines to GitHub Enterprise

    3. A Git sources proxy for HTTP

    4. On-premises agents

30. A new team joins the company and they have to start work on a new application. They ask you to recommend a branching strategy that allows them to work on multiple features in parallel and deploy a new version at any time, and minimizes the need for merging changes late. Which of the following do you recommend?

    1. Create an eternal branch per team member and cherry-pick commits to merge.

    2. Create a branch per feature and merge this branch upon completion.

    3. Create a branch per task and merge this branch upon completion.

    4. Create and merge a branch as often as possible when a shippable piece of work has been completed.

31. You are tasked with configuring source control for your team in Azure DevOps. Which of the following source control systems do you choose preferably?
    1. TFVC
    2. Git

32. Which of the following is true?
    1. You can have as many Git and TFVC repositories in an Azure DevOps project as you want.
    2. You can have at most one Git repository and at most one TFVC repository in an Azure DevOps project.
    3. You can have at most one TFVC repository and as many Git repositories as you want in your Azure DevOps project.
    4. You can have either Git repositories or TFVC repositories in an Azure DevOps project, but not both at the same time.

33. Your team is creating a mobile application and wants to use App Center for distributing that application to both the App Stores and the testers within the team. Which of the following should you use? [Choose two.]
    1. Invitation-only pre-release groups
    2. Push-to-store integration
    3. Store Connection
    4. Distribution Groups

34. You are creating a series of microservices for a new project. You are looking for a way to manage configuration from a centralized point. There are many configuration settings shared between microservices. Which of the following solutions best fits this use case?
    1. Azure Key Vault
    2. Azure App Configuration
    3. Azure Configuration Center
    4. ARM templates

35. You have to ensure that code cannot be checked into the master branch of a repository when it has not been viewed by at least two people. Which of the following is a complete solution for this? [Choose three.]
    1. Enforce the use of a pull request for merging changes to the master.
    2. Reset approval votes on the pull request for a branch when a new commit is pushed to that branch.
    3. Have a minimum of at least two reviewers, but allow everyone to merge their own changes.
    4. Have a minimum of at least one reviewer, not being the person who opened the pull request.

36. You have to sign the binaries (DLLs) that your team produces so that other teams that consume them can verify the binaries are not altered and really are the binaries originating from your team. You have to store the certificate used for signing securely. Where can you do this and still have the file available for use in your pipeline? If multiple answers fit, choose the simplest solution.
    1. Azure Pipelines Library
    2. Azure Key Vault
    3. Encrypted in source control
    4. Azure DevOps Certificate Store

37. You have to ensure that every build pipeline contains a task group that is pre-shared by your team. Which of the following Azure DevOps constructs can you use to do this?
    1. Pipeline Decorators.
    2. Pipeline Verificators.
    3. Pipeline pre-execution tasks.
    4. This is not possible—you have to implement a manual auditing process.

38. Your sources are stored in a Subversion source control system. You want to move to Azure DevOps Pipelines for continuous integration. You do not want to move your sources and connect from Pipelines to Subversion. Is this possible?
    1. Yes
    2. No

39. The development team is creating a containerized application. The solution needs to be deployed to a Kubernetes cluster in Azure. You need to create the cluster and ensure that the application is running as it should. Select which commands you should perform and place them in the correct order of execution.
    1. `kubectl apply`
    2. `az group create`
    3. `az aks create`
    4. `az appservice plan create`
    5. `kubectl get deployments`
    6. `az aks get-credentials`
    7. `kubectl get hpa`
    8. `az create group`
    9. `kubectl get services`

40. A great advantage of running containers instead of virtual machines is that containers share the operating system kernel. This makes container images also smaller than virtual machine images. Is this correct?
    1. Yes
    2. No

Implementing Continuous Integration

41. Order the following types of tests based on the size of their scope. Start with the test types with the smallest scope.
    1. Integration tests
    2. Unit tests
    3. System tests

42. Which of the following are true? [Choose more than one.]
    1. Stress tests are performed by applying an ever-growing load onto a system, to identify the breaking point of the system.
    2. Integration tests always include the database.
    3. Performance tests are performed to measure how quickly the system can perform a given task.
    4. Usability tests are performed to identify use cases where the system is too slow to respond.

43. You are creating an Azure DevOps dashboard to provide the team with insight into the quality of the code being written. Which of the following widgets does not belong on such a dashboard?
    1. A widget that shows recent deployments and whether they were successful or not
    2. A widget that shows the number of check-ins per day
    3. A widget that shows how the unit test code coverage changes over time
    4. A widget that shows whether the latest build has failed or not

44. Which of the following is not a valid merge strategy?
    1. Squash commit
    2. Rebase
    3. Interleave
    4. Merge commit

45. Which of the following is not part of the OWASP Top 10?
    1. Injections
    2. Sensitive Data Exposure
    3. Least Privilege Principle violations
    4. Using dependencies with known vulnerabilities

46. Your team is creating container images that should be deployed into Azure later on. Which of the following can you use to store your images? [Choose two.]
    1. Azure Container Instances
    2. Azure Container Registry
    3. Azure Kubernetes Service
    4. Docker Hub

47. You want to be notified whenever any integration build fails. You configure an email subscription on your Azure DevOps project. Will this complete this goal?
    1. Yes
    2. No

48. You want to trigger a YAML pipeline whenever a new version of an artifact hosted in an Azure Artifact feed becomes available. Is this possible?
    1. Yes
    2. No

49. You want to use a mix of hosted agents, private agents in the cloud and an on-premises agent in the same stage of a multi-stage YAML pipeline. Is this possible?
    1. Yes
    2. No

50. You want to create a release pipeline that is triggered at the same time every day of the week. You also want to exclude Sunday. Is this possible?
    1. Yes
    2. No

51. The developer team is creating a container-hosted application and wants to share the image on the internet. The team builds the image via Docker and tries to host it via Kubernetes. Is this the correct way?
    1. Yes
    2. No

52. Which of the following are places where you can store the container images? [Choose all that apply.]
    1. Azure Container Instance
    2. Docker Hub
    3. Azure Container Registry
    4. Azure Container Storage

Implementing Continuous Delivery

53. The company you are working for is using ServiceNow as the change management system. There is a rule that ServiceNow should be used to track every deployment to production environments. You are responsible for ensuring that your application is not deployed to the production environment if there is no valid change registered in the change management system. Which of the following will accomplish this? [Choose two.]
    1. You implement a deployment callback that checks for a valid change in ServiceNow.
    2. You add a deployment gate as a precondition to deployment to the production stage.
    3. You add a deployment gate as a postcondition for completing deployment in the QA stage.
    4. You create an environment and call it Production-ServiceNow check.

54. You need to deploy an application to twelve on-premises virtual machines, grouped into three subnets. Which of the following actions should you perform to have a complete, working solution to do this? [Choose three.]
    1. Create a new deployment group and add the correct agents to that group.
    2. Download and install the Private Agent on all of the virtual machines that you need to deploy to.
    3. Add a Selection Job to your release pipeline to select which deployment group to use.
    4. Download and install the Private Agent on precisely one virtual machine in every subnet.
    5. Add a Deployment Group Job to your release pipeline to execute the tasks necessary for deploying the application.
    6. Configure a username and password on your deployment pipeline to configure how to connect to the agents.

55. You need to configure a release pipeline to meet several conditions before a deployment to the production environment can be started. These conditions are (i) that at least two out of four members of an approval board should approve of the deployment and (ii) that Azure Monitor should be checked for any alerts in the first hour after the release. Can this be done using Azure DevOps Pipelines?
    1. Yes
    2. No

56. You are using **SQL Server Data Tools** (**SSDT**) for describing your database schema as code. You want to use SSDT for schema upgrades as well. Which type of schema migration should you use?
    1. Migrations based
    2. End-state based

57. You are working with a schema-less database. Does this remove the issue of schema management completely?
    1. Yes
    2. No

58. Your team must follow regulations that state that every new version has to be approved by the test manager manually before it can be deployed to production. Which of the following changes fulfills this requirement in the most meaningful way?
    1. You add a pre-deployment gate to the production stage that verifies the sign-off in a home-build system where all application versions that are signed off can be recorded.
    2. You add a post-deployment gate to the QA stage that sets the test managers' approval in the designated system if all automated tests have succeeded.
    3. You add a post-deployment approval to the QA stage that must be given by the test manager.
    4. You disable automated approval to the production stage and instruct everyone to only start a deployment after consulting the system that contains all sign-offs by the test manager.

59. You are creating several release pipelines for your team. Many of the pipelines will use the same configuration values for some tasks. Which of the following can help you to repeat their values as a complete solution?
    1. Variable groups
    2. Task groups
    3. Variable containers
    4. Azure Key Vault

60. You want to automatically generate release notes out of the stories completed in a deployment. You want to do this without using any extensions or add-ons—only the built-in capabilities of Azure DevOps should be used. Is this possible?

    1. Yes
    2. No

61. You want to deploy an application to the Azure Service Fabric from Azure DevOps. Do you need to install an extension for tasks to do this?

    1. Yes
    2. No

62. You need to apply an update to a deployment within Kubernetes. Which command should you use?

    1. `kubectl apply`
    2. `kubectl deployments`
    3. `kubectl get services`
    4. `kubectl deploy`

63. What kind of task is used within Azure DevOps to deploy containers to Azure Kubernetes?

    1. Kubernetes Manifest
    2. Kubernetes
    3. Kubernetes General Task
    4. Kubectl

64. What kind of file is most appropriate to deploy resources to a Kubernetes cluster?

    1. ARM template
    2. Terraform document
    3. PowerShell script
    4. YAML deployment file

Implementing Dependency Management

65. You are using Azure Artifacts for hosting NuGet packages that your team creates. You have a new requirement for making one (and only one) of the packages that you create available to all other teams in your organization. Which of the following are valid solutions? [Choose more than one.]
    1. You create a new feed and allow any user in your Azure Active Directory to use packages from this feed. You move the package to be shared to this feed.
    2. You allow all users within your organization to use your existing feed.
    3. You create a new feed and allow any user in your organization to use packages from this feed. You move the package to be shared to this view.
    4. You create a new view in your existing feed and publish the package to be shared to this view. Next, you configure that all members of your organization can read packages from this view.
    5. You add your existing feed as an upstream source to the feed that is used by any other team so they can pull your packages as well.

66. Which of the following are valid arguments for splitting your solution into multiple smaller solutions and using shared packages or libraries for assembling the complete application from these smaller solutions? [Choose two.]
    1. You have over 25 C# projects in a single solution.
    2. Your code base is becoming so large that compilation and/or running unit tests is starting to take too long.
    3. Your team is becoming too big and is split into two. Splitting the solution as well will establish clear ownership: one solution per team.
    4. You are approaching the Git limit of 10,000 files in a single repository.

67. For which of the following does Azure Artifacts support upstream sources? [Choose two.]
    1. Composer
    2. Python
    3. Gems
    4. Maven

68. You are working with Azure Artifact feeds for dependency management. You are taking a new dependency on a library that is publicly available through NuGet. Which of the following can you use to consume this package through an existing feed?
    1. Upstream sources
    2. External views
    3. Upstream views
    4. Dependency views

69. You have a library that is used in two applications but only within your own team. Which of the following strategies is the best way for sharing this library?
    1. Link the shared library as a shared project into the two consuming solutions.
    2. Have the library in a separate repository and use a build pipeline for building the library and upload it as a NuGet package to Azure Artifacts. Consume it from here in your two applications.

70. You want to use universal packages for distributing application components from Azure DevOps to different deployment orchestrators. Is this possible?
    1. Yes
    2. No

Implementing Application Infrastructure

71. You are working on an application that will be deployed in two different Azure Regions to allow for failover scenarios. Which of the following together make a valid solution? [Choose two.]

    1. You create one ARM template with two parameter files. The first parameter file corresponds to the first Azure region, and the second parameter file to the second Azure region. You use the ARM templates to update the infrastructure.

    2. You create an ARM template and parameter file to update the infrastructure in one region only. In the other region, you update the infrastructure manually to prevent configuration drift.

    3. You first update the infrastructure in both regions. Only when the infrastructure is updated successfully do you deploy the application to both regions.

    4. You first update the infrastructure in one region, followed by a deployment of the application. Only when this succeeds do you update the infrastructure in the other region and deploy the application to the other region.

72. You need to deploy an Azure Resource Manager template to an Azure Resource group using an Azure DevOps pipeline. Some of the parameters that you need to use are stored in Azure Key Vault. Which of the following options combined is not a necessary part of a complete solution?

    1. Create a new Variable Group and link it to the correct Key Vault using a Service Connection.

    2. Give the Azure Active Directory Service Principal a Reader RBAC role on the correct Azure Key Vault.

    3. Configure a new Azure Resource Manager Service Connection in your Azure DevOps Project and create a new Azure Active Directory Service Principal that way.

    4. Give the Azure Active Directory Service Principal the following Access Policies on the correct Key Vault: list and get.

73. You are tasked with creating and configuring several virtual machines in Azure. Which combination of tools should you use? [Choose two.]
    1. Azure Automation DSC
    2. Azure Runtime Runbooks
    3. ARM templates

74. You are configuring the Azure resource group where your application will be deployed later. You are provided with a pre-created service principal for doing the deployment from Azure DevOps Pipelines. Which RBAC role assignment should you give to this service principal to deploy resources?
    1. Reader
    2. Contributor
    3. Deployer
    4. Owner

75. You have to set up the RBAC role assignments for your teams. You want to follow the principle of least privilege. You also need to ensure that access to your team resources is available to whichever needs it. Which of the following solutions is best?
    1. You add the principal used for deployments and all team members to an Azure Active Directory group. You assign this Azure Active Directory group the contributor role on your Azure resource group.
    2. You give the principal that is used for deployment contributor rights on the resource group and all team members the reader role.
    3. You create two new Azure Active Directory groups: reader and writer. You add the service principal used for deployments to writer. You add all team members to reader. You assign the reader role to the reader group and the contributor role to the writer group.
    4. You create a new Azure Active Directory group. You add the service principal used for deployments to this group. You assign the group the contributor role. You create an escalation procedure for team members to be temporarily added to this Azure Active Directory group.

76. Which of the following tools cannot be used for managing Azure Resources?
    1. Terraform
    2. Azure DevOps CLI
    3. Azure PowerShell
    4. CloudFormation

77. You are practicing infrastructure as code and want to deploy an ARM template from Azure DevOps as part of your deployment process. Which of the following solutions does this in the simplest way?
    1. You execute an Azure CLI script from a Cmd task in your deployment pipeline.
    2. You execute a PowerShell script from your deployment pipeline.
    3. You use the built-in task for deployment of the ARM template.
    4. You upload the template to an Azure Storage account and use an HTTP REST call to start the deployment of the ARM template.

78. You are transforming the way your team delivers its application by practicing *everything as code*. Which of the following cannot be created using Azure Blueprints or ARM templates?
    1. Azure Subscriptions
    2. Azure Active Directory Security Groups
    3. Azure RBAC custom roles
    4. Azure RBAC role assignments

79. You are working in a team that provides Azure subscriptions and resource groups to other teams. As part of your work, you want to limit the types of Azure resources a team can create. Which of the following do you use?
    1. Azure RBAC roles and role assignments
    2. Azure Policy
    3. OWASP Zed Attack Proxy
    4. Azure Security Center

80. What is not a benefit of working with infrastructure and configuration as code?
    1. Minimizing configuration drift
    2. Peer-review support
    3. Lower lead time on configuration changes
    4. Source control history of configuration changes

Implementing Continuous Feedback

81. You have to gather crash reports from the applications that your team creates. Which tools can you use to do this? [Choose two.]

    1. Snyk
    2. Raygun
    3. App Center
    4. Azure Automation

82. You are configuring many alerts. Some alerts need to result in a warning per email, others are critical errors and need to result in an SMS text message that's sent out. Regardless of the alert being a warning or an alert, you also need to update a home-build system with the alert being fired.

    You create the following solution: One action group for warnings both sends the email and calls a WebHook on the home-build system. One action group for errors both sends the SMS text message and calls a WebHook on the home-build system. For alerts that are a warning, you configure action group one. For alerts that are an error, you configure action group two.

    Is this a complete and correct solution?

    1. Yes
    2. No

83. You are configuring many alerts. Some alerts need to result in a warning per email while others are critical errors and need to result in an SMS text message being sent out. Regardless of the alert being a warning or an alert, you also need to update a home-build system with the alert being fired.

    You create the following solution: One action group sends an email, sends an SMS text message, and calls a WebHook on the home-build system. You configure this alert group on all alerts and add an alert condition configuration to only send emails for warnings and to only send SMS text messages for errors.

    Is this a complete and correct solution?

    1. Yes
    2. No

84. You are configuring many alerts. Some alerts need to result in a warning per email while others are critical errors and need to result in an SMS text message that's sent out. Regardless of the alert being a warning or an alert, you also need to update a home-build system with the alert being fired.

    You create the following solution: One action group for warnings sends an email. A second action group for errors sends the SMS text message. A third action group calls a WebHook on the home-build system. For alerts that are a warning, you configure action groups one and two. For errors, you configure action groups two and three.

    Is this a complete and correct solution?

    1. Yes
    2. No

85. You want to invite your users to provide ideas and suggestions on your product. This should be in a public place so that other users can comment and vote on those suggestions. Which of the following tools can be used to do this in the simplest way? [Choose two.]
    1. Azure Blob Storage Static Site
    2. GitHub Issues
    3. Uservoice
    4. Azure Boards Public Views Extension

Answers

1: 1, 2, 3, 4	2: 1, 2, 4	3: 1	4: 4, 1, 3, 2, 5	5: 2
6: 2	7: 2, 3	8: 4	9: 3	10: 2
11: 1	12: 1	13: 1, 3	14: 2	15: 1, 4
16: 1	17: 2	18: 2, 4	19: 1	20: 1, 2
21: 2, 3	22: 1(3), 2(2), 3(1)	23: 1, 3	24: 3	25: 2
26: 1	27: 2	28: 2	29: 1, 2	30: 4
31: 2	32: 3	33: 3, 4	34: 2	35: 1, 2, 3
36: 1	37: 1	38: 1	39: 2, 3, 6, 1, 8	40: 1
41: 2, 1, 3	42: 1, 3	43: 2	44: 3	45: 3
46: 2, 4	47: 1	48: 1	49: 1	50: 1
51: 2	52: 3	53: 2, 3	54: 1, 2, 5	55: 1
56: 2	57: 2	58: 3	59: 1	60: 2

61: 2	62: 1	63: 1	64: 4	65: 3, 4
66: 2, 3	67: 2, 4	68: 1	69: 2	70: 1
71: 1, 4	72: 2	73: 1, 3	74: 2	75: 4
76: 4	77: 3	78: 2	79: 2	80: 3
81: 2, 3	82: 1	83: 2	84: 1	85: 2, 3

Assessments

Chapter 1

1. True. In traditional organizations, development is often tasked with creating changes to software, while operations is responsible for maintaining the stability of the target systems for these changes. Since changes inherently carry risk and may disturb stability, operations is often resistant to change.
2. False. While, in theory, it is possible to practice the different DevOps practices in isolation from on another, the real value comes from combining them. For example, continuous deployment without continuous integration and test automation does not only make very little sense; it is even dangerous to continuously deploy changes without the quality assurances that continuous integration and test automation offer.
3. The incorrect answer is number 4. DevOps is not a job title, but a cultural movement. Actually, creating a new DevOps team in between development and operations is often at loggerheads with the DevOps philosophy. Instead of two teams or departments with their separate goals, there are now three.
4. Fastlaning is an approach to expediting unplanned, high-priority work over planned work, all while maintaining a single sprint board for the whole team.
5. There are many definitions of DevOps. Some of the main elements that are frequently included are business value, end users, continuous deployment, automation, and collaboration.

Chapter 2

1. The main difference between centralized and decentralized source control is that in a decentralized source control system, every user of the system has the full history of the sources. In a centralized system, only the server has the full history. Decentralized systems work best when working disconnected from the server, whereas centralized systems often allow for more detailed access control.
2. True. Git is the best known decentralized source control system.
3. The correct answer is number 3. Rebasing is not a branching strategy, but a merging strategy.

4. When working with Git, a pull request is used to request the merging of changes from one branch with another. Pull requests can be reviewed, approved, or denied. To enforce the use of pull requests, Git policies can be used.

5. The correct answer is number 2. Trunk-based development is not a merging strategy, but a branching strategy.

Chapter 3

1. False. Continuous integration is about integrating the work of every developer with that of their colleagues at least daily and building and testing the integrated sources. Just running a daily build does not constitute continuous integration.

2. True. A classic build pipeline is always connected to a source code repository. It might be that the sources are not used in the build pipeline, but the connection is always there.

3. False. It is possible to create a YAML pipeline that starts directly with a stage. A link to a source control repository is no longer mandatory.

4. The correct answer is number 1: a service connection. Service connections are configured in the organization or project that contains the pipeline that needs to call into the external tool. Once a service connection is configured, it can be used from one or more pipelines.

5. The correct answers are numbers 1 and 3: access to closed networks and the ability to install extra software. Self-hosted agents are deployed on infrastructure owned by you. This means that you can deploy them on networks that you control, giving them network access to that network. Since the agents are deployed on your infrastructure, you can also decide on which software is installed (and which is not). Tasks and extension tasks are automatically downloaded to the agent before it executes a job. You can have as many parallel pipelines as you want without using self-hosted agents. However, you will need to buy extra parallel executions from Microsoft for this purpose.

Chapter 4

1. False. It is also possible to trigger a new release on a schedule or manually.

2. All of the answers are correct.

3. Numbers 2 and 3 are correct. Both ring-based deployments and canary deployments expose only a limited group of users to the new version of your application. Feature toggles are also used for progressive exposure, but are not used to limit the risks of a deployment but that of a new feature release.

4. True. Deployment groups are used to perform tasks from a release pipeline not on one agent in the group, but on all agents. Deployment groups are intended to be used to deploy software on the machine that is also running the agent.

5. One possible advantage is that end-to-end traceability of all steps is retained in Azure DevOps. If you also manage your work items and source code in Azure DevOps, you will keep end-to-end traceability from the work item to release within Azure DevOps, and all this while still using the App Center for actual deployments.

Chapter 5

1. False. A version of a package can be visible in more than one view.

2. False. Pipeline artifacts can only be consumed from within other pipelines within Azure DevOps.

3. True. Azure Artifact feeds can be used to share universal packages to other products. This allows you to compile an application in Azure DevOps, upload the binaries as a universal package, and download it again in another product. This is useful when using another deployment tool, for example, Octopus Deploy.

4. The correct answers are numbers 2 and 4. Answer number 1 is incorrect since the package references (either in a `.csproj` file or in a `nuget.config` file) should only reference packages by name and version. Answer number 3 is incorrect since `consumer` is not a valid access level in Azure Artifact feeds. The correct access level is reader (or higher), making answer number 2 correct. Answer number 4 is also correct. You need to add the package location to your NuGet configuration.

5. One motivator can be the size of the solution. If compiling and testing the solution is taking so long that developers have to wait for feedback in relation to their work, it can be better to split the solution into smaller parts. This will shorten the feedback loop for developers, thereby increasing speed. Another motivator can be that multiple teams are working on an application and they want to increase the amount of isolation between teams.

Chapter 6

1. True. ARM templates allow you to specify the end state for all resources in an Azure resource group. Applying an ARM template will always result in the creation of missing resources and updates for existing resources. If a deployment mode of `complete` is specified, even resources not in the template will be removed.

2. The correct answer is number 2. Modules, Run As accounts, and variables are all constructs that were discussed in `Chapter 6`, *Infrastructure and Configuration as Code.*

3. False. ARM template parameters allow the referencing of values in an Azure Key Vault, so as to prevent users from having to enter secrets or other sensitive information in source control. At the time of deployment, the secrets are retrieved and used within Azure, provided the identity that starts the operation has access to that key vault.

4. True. You can define one or more schedules within an Azure Automation Account and then link these to a Runbook.

5. Many benefits can be expected when practicing infrastructure as code. Two oft cited examples are the prevention of configuration drift and the ability to create new environments on demand. Configuration drift is prevented by reapplying the same infrastructure specification to an environment at a schedule. Environments on demand can be used to quickly create a new test environment, performing tests and then removing the environment again. This allows for more repeatable test results and, possibly, savings in terms of testing infrastructure.

Chapter 7

1. True. Entity Framework and Entity Framework Core both have built-in support to generate a migration after changes to the schema definition have been made.

2. False. Most migration-based approaches use an extra table to keep track of which migrations have already been applied to the database.

3. True. End state-based approaches work by comparing the current schema to the target schema. This results in the generation of a one-time SQL script that is run against the database to update the schema. There is no state stored between runs.

4. The correct answers are numbers 1 and 2. Running side by side, if done correctly, reduces change risks dramatically. If there are issues, you can always remove all new code, along with the database copy, and restart afresh from a working situation. Having both situations working correctly also allows for very precise performance measurements regarding the production workload. However, one of the disadvantages is that the cycle time is actually very likely to increase. You have to move multiple smaller changes to production one by one, which increases the total time taken.

5. False. Your schema (either implicit or captured in data objects) still changes. However, this only becomes visible when reading an object back from the database that was persisted with a previous version of the object. In essence, you are only delaying coping with the issue of schema changes.

6. You can choose to not use database-level coding techniques, such as stored procedures and triggers. The more of your logic you capture outside of the database, the smaller the total number of database changes you have to make.

Chapter 8

1. True. In a unit test, a individual component is tested in isolation. In an object-oriented language, this is often a single class.

2. False. In an integration test, the correct working of a group of components is verified, and not the entire assembled system. If the entire assembled and deployed system is tested, this is referred to as a system test.

3. Answer number 2 is correct. The testing pyramid prescribes a large set of unit tests that verify as many requirements as possible. Integration tests are added only for those risks that cannot be covered using unit tests, resulting in a lower number of integration tests. Even fewer system tests are added, only to cover the risks not covered by either unit or integration tests.

4. Answer number 3 is correct. All other types of testing are covered in this chapter.

5. Two techniques that can be mentioned here are code reviews and pipeline gates. Code reviews allow developers to review the work of their colleagues to help each other keep quality high. Pipeline gates can be used to not allow a build or version of an application to propagate further down a pipeline if certain conditions are not met. Example conditions can include certain quality metrics, or minimum standards for test coverage or test results.

Chapter 9

1. False. To securely create and deliver software, the whole process, and especially the pipeline, needs to be secured. Just adding security at the end will not work, as security has to be woven through all different steps of the delivery process.
2. The OWASP **Zed Attack Proxy (ZAP)** can be used for this type of testing.
3. True. In modern applications, up to 80% of the code can be from open source libraries or frameworks.
4. The correct answers are 1, 2, 4, and 6. There is no such thing as Azure DevOps Secure Variables or Azure DevOps Key Vault.
5. Azure Policy can be used to prohibit or list undesired Azure configurations, often relating to infrastructure provisioning or configuration. Azure Security Center can be used to identify and remediate runtime security risks.

Chapter 10

1. False. The platform metrics that are emitted by Azure are defined by every individual service and cannot be changed.
2. 93 days. This number guarantees that there is always at least 3 months of history.
3. True. Custom metrics can be calculated in your own application code and emitted to Application Insights through the SDK or REST API.
4. Alert fatigue.
5. True. Azure allows for the creation of action groups that can contain webhooks to be called in response to an alert being raised.

Chapter 11

1. False. One possible downside is losing a competitive edge in the market. If competitors know what you are going to develop next, they may anticipate in that regard.
2. Possible concerns are that some users or groups of users are more vocal than others, which might result in a difference between the general opinion and the opinion that is heard. Also, feedback on a public roadmap is most likely coming from existing users only. While it is important to retain those, prospects might not comment on your roadmap with features they are missing.
3. Two examples that are discussed in this chapter are sentiment on social media channels and the number and severity of support requests.

4. Answer number 3 is correct. A hypothesis states a belief that a certain feature is needed – the hypothesis. The second part is a measurable user response that is to be observed before the belief is confirmed. This is called the confirmation threshold. A hypothesis does not yet have a conclusion.

5. Possible benefits of user interviews or focus groups are that they are often conducted at a smaller scale, allowing not only for the measuring of feedback, but for also understanding the reasons behind it. Another benefit is that participants can be carefully selected to be representative of all users or a particular segment.

Chapter 12

1. The benefits of containers for DevOps are consistency, the separation of concerns, and platform portability.

2. True: Depending on the host operating system, it does not matter where the container is hosted.

3. Yes, this is possible. This can be done by adding Docker support and a project level.

4. The RUN command is used for the installation of components or for performing operations during the process of building the container image.

5. Nods and pods can be scheduled within Azure Kubernetes Service. Both of these components can be scaled manually or automatically.

Chapter 13

1. False. Some information can travel to other regions or is available globally. For example, sometimes, agents are running in other regions when capacity in the chosen region is low.

2. **Work item | Project | Organization | Region**. An Azure DevOps organization is the top-level construct that can be created by users. Every organization is in precisely one region, which is maintained by Microsoft. Within an organization, one or more projects can be created. In turn, a project can contain many work items, such as user stories, features, or epics.

3. False. The general recommendation is to have just enough projects: the fewer the better. Isolation and very strict authorization boundaries may be reasons for choosing to use multiple projects.

4. Authorizations and licensing. Authorizations can be set up to the limit that can be accessed by every individual user or a group of users. The license assigned to a user can also prohibit the use of certain features. For example, users with a stakeholder licence cannot work with source control.

5. End-to-end traceability. When executing work management, source control, building, artifacts, and deployments from a single tool, it is possible to trace the deployment in which a user story was delivered to users.

Other Books You May Enjoy

If you enjoyed this book, you may be interested in these other books by Packt:

Azure for Architects - Second Edition
Ritesh Modi

ISBN: 978-1-78961-450-3

- Create an end-to-end integration solution using Azure Serverless Stack
- Learn Big Data solutions and OLTP–based applications on Azure
- Understand DevOps implementations using Azure DevOps
- Architect solutions comprised of multiple resources in Azure
- Develop modular ARM templates
- Develop Governance on Azure using locks, RBAC, policies, tags and cost
- Learn ways to build data solutions on Azure
- Understand the various options related to containers including Azure Kubernetes Services

Azure Networking Cookbook
Mustafa Toroman

ISBN: 978-1-78980-022-7

- Learn to create Azure networking services
- Understand how to create and work on hybrid connections
- Configure and manage Azure network services
- Learn ways to design high availability network solutions in Azure
- Discover how to monitor and troubleshoot Azure network resources
- Learn different methods of connecting local networks to Azure virtual networks

Leave a review - let other readers know what you think

Please share your thoughts on this book with others by leaving a review on the site that you bought it from. If you purchased the book from Amazon, please leave us an honest review on this book's Amazon page. This is vital so that other potential readers can see and use your unbiased opinion to make purchasing decisions, we can understand what our customers think about our products, and our authors can see your feedback on the title that they have worked with Packt to create. It will only take a few minutes of your time, but is valuable to other potential customers, our authors, and Packt. Thank you!

Index

A

Access Control List (ACL) 360
access levels, Azure DevOps
  basic 361
  Basic and Test plans 361
  Stakeholder 361
agent capabilities
  finding 88
agent jobs
  about 57
  types, reference link 79
agent pools, types
  about 83
  built-in agent pools 83
  private agent pool 84
agent queues 83
agent selection 87
agent-based deployment 103
agentless jobs 57
agents
  about 83
  adding 85
  removing 86
Agile work management
  about 11, 12
  fastlaning 13
  flow-based methodology 12
  work items, synchronizing to one system 13
  work management tools, decommissioning 14
Agile
  and DevOps 11
Ansible 184
application code vulnerabilities
  automated vulnerability scanning, implementing 259
  detecting 258

OWASP Top 10 259
OWASP Zed Attack Proxy, using 260
application crashes
  investigating 278
Application Insights and Azure Monitor, integrating with tool
  about 302
  Azure Boards 303, 304
  Grafana 304
  IT service management applications 302
Application Lifecycle Management (ALM) 364
application settings
  managing 177
ARM templates
  Azure App Service settings, managing 178
  Azure Blueprints 167
  deploying 162
  functions 161
  generating, with Export template 164, 165
  generating, with Resource Explorer 166
  outputs section 160
  parameter files 157, 158
  parameters section 156, 157
  resources section 159
  reverse engineering 164
  subscription level templates 166
  updates 168
  variables section 158
  working with 155, 156
artifactory 150
artifacts 73
artifacts storage 362
automated functional tests, types
  integration tests 213, 214, 215
  system tests 215, 216
  unit tests 211, 212, 213
automated functional tests

types 210
automated UI tests 100
Azure Active Directory (AAD) 179, 356
Azure App
  configuring 180, 182
Azure Artifacts
  supported ecosystems 132
Azure Automation resources
  about 169
  connections 172
  credentials 172
  modules 171
  run as account 169
  schedules 170
  variables 171
Azure Automation
  about 169
  PowerShell DSC 174
  resources 169
  runbooks 172
Azure Blueprints
  supported artifacts 167
  versus ARM templates 168
Azure Boards 303, 304
Azure CLI
  used, for downloading universal packages 149
  used, for uploading universal packages 149
Azure Container Instance 330
Azure Container Registry (ACR) 150, 330
Azure DevOps licensing
  about 362
  access levels 361
  consumption-based costs 362
Azure DevOps organization
  about 356, 357
  creating 358, 359
  project, creating 358, 359
  setting up 356
Azure DevOps releases
  approvers 102
  artifacts, creating 96, 97, 98
  deployment groups, working with 103
  gates, adding 102
  release deployment stages, specifying 99
  stage triggers 100, 101

stages, in pipeline 100
  triggers, releasing 96, 97, 98
  working with 95, 96
Azure DevOps security model 359
Azure DevOps security model, approaches
  about 359
  object-level authorizations 360
  organization-and project-level authorizations 360
Azure DevOps, images
  building 330
  pipeline, creating for 332, 333, 334, 335
  running, in Azure 330
  service endpoint, creating for 330, 331
Azure DevOps
  build definition, creating 55
  improvements, working on 369, 370
  Kubernetes, deploying with 350, 352, 353
Azure Key Vault 66
Azure Kubernetes Service (AKS)
  about 340
  functionalities 340
Azure Pipelines
  universal packages, downloading from 147, 148
  universal packages, uploading from 147, 148
Azure Resource Manager (ARM) templates 251
Azure role-based access control (Azure RBAC) 254

B

binary management, tools
  Artifactory 150
  Azure Container Registry (ACR) 150
  exploring 150
  MyGet 150
Black Duck 271
blue-green deployments
  about 111
  immutable servers 112
branch 37
branch policies 46, 48
branching 37
branching by abstraction 40, 41
branching strategies
  about 37
  GitFlow 38

GitHub flow 37
Release Flow 39
bugtrackers 311
build artifacts
    accessing 73, 74
build definition
    build, triggering 66
    creating, in Azure DevOps 55
    history 69
    options 68
    source control, connecting to 56, 57
    task groups 69, 70
    using, as code 75, 76
    variable groups 65, 66
    variable groups, creating 64, 65
    variables, creating 64, 65
build results
    viewing 71
builds
    pull request, building 72, 73
    running 71
built-in agent pools 83

C

centralized source control 30
chaining builds 67
Checkmarx 271
Chef 183
classic builds 55
classic releases 241, 242
CloudFormation 182
Cluster IP 338
code review 236
complete centralization 365
Configuration as Code (CaC) 154
configuration drift 154
consolidating tools 364, 365
container image, application
    creating 323
    Docker support, adding 324, 325, 326
    images, creating with 326, 328
container image
    building 322
    running 329
container registry 322

containers
    about 320, 321
    benefits 321
    hosting options 322
    scaling 347
    upgrading 346, 347
continuous delivery 94
continuous deployment (CD) 94, 370
continuous deployment strategies
    blue-green deployments 111
    failing forward approach 116
    feature flags 114, 115
    implementing 110
    progressive exposure 112
    versions, rolling back 115
continuous feedback
    about 308
    used, for making decisions 308
continuous integration (CI) 54, 370
continuous integration, fundamentals
    about 55
    automated build process 55
    continuous integration system 55
    package management system 55
    version control system 55
CredScan 256
cycle time 14, 15

D

database changes
    testing 199
database schema changes
    applying 192
    process, adding 193, 195
    upgrading, as part of release 192
    upgrading, by application code 192
database schema, as code
    end-state approach 190
    managing 188
    migration approach 189
databases
    dealing with, approaches 198
    influence, minimizing 198
decentralized source control 30
declarative approach 154

dependencies
  working with 260
deployment group job 103
deployment groups
  managing 104
  used, for creating release pipeline 105
  working with 103
desktop applications
  crash reports, obtaining 281, 282
Develop 38
DevOps evolution
  stages 25, 26
DevOps habits
  about 22
  enterprise alignment 23
  evidence gathered, in production 24
  exploring 17
  focus, on flow of customer value 23
  hypothesis-driven development 24
  infrastructure, managing as flexible resource 25
  live-site culture 24
  rigorous management, of technical debt 23
  team autonomy 23
DevOps organization
  creating 16, 17
DevOps practices
  about 18
  application performance monitoring 22
  configuration management 18, 19
  continuous deployment 20
  continuous integration 19
  exploring 17
  infrastructure as code 21
  release management 19
  test automation 22
DevOps principles
  applying, to security and compliance 248
  developers, merging with security engineers 249
  security concerns 250, 251
DevOps
  about 9, 10, 11, 321
  and Agile 11
  benefits 14
  goals 14
direct feedback

focus groups, using 311
gathering 309
in-product feedback 309
interviews, using 311
public roadmap, sharing 310

E

end-state approach
  about 190
  advantages 191
  disadvantages 191
exploratory testing 223, 224

F

failing forward strategy
  risks 116
feeds
  access, securing 135, 136
  creating 132, 133
  setting up 133, 134, 135
  types 132
  upstream sources, configuring 137, 138
  views, managing 136, 137
four-eyes principle
  enforcing 75
full side-by-side deployment approach 199
functional tests, types
  strategies, for selecting 224, 225
  testing pyramid 226, 227
  testing trophy 227, 228

G

Git repositories
  migrating 34
  working with 32
Git-to-Git migration
  steps 34
Git
  about 32
GitFlow 38
GitHub 48
GitHub flow 37
GitLab 49
GitLab CI 89
GitLab CI/CD 123

Grafana 304

H

horizontal pod autoscaler (HPA) 349
hypothesis-driven development
  implementing 313, 314

I

imperative approach 154
in-product feedback
  disadvantages 310
indirect feedback
  gathering 312
  sentiment analysis 313
  support requests 313
Infrastructure as Code (IaC) 154
infrastructure compliance
  audit results, fetching 267, 268
  Azure Policy, assigning 263
  Azure Policy, writing 264, 266
  ensuring 263
  initiatives, assigning 266
integrating tools 369
integration tests 213, 214, 215
IT Service Management (ITSM) 302
IT service management applications 302

J

Jenkins 90, 123
Jenkinsfile 90
JSON schema
  reference link 168

K

Key Performance Indicators (KPIs) 14
Key Vault
  settings at runtime, loading 178, 180
knife 183
Kubernetes cluster
  creating 340
Kubernetes, core components
  about 336
  deployment 338
  master node 337

  pods 337
  regular nodes 337
Kubernetes, services
  about 338
  Cluster IP 338
  load balancer 338
  node port 338
Kubernetes
  about 336
  container image, deploying 343, 344, 345
  deploying, with Azure DevOps 350, 352, 353
  functionalities 336
  infrastructure 341
  managing 342
  operation 338, 339
  scaling 347
  working with 340
Kusto Query Language (KQL) 286

L

Large File Storage (LFS) 33
lead time 15
limited centralization 366
load balancer 338
load test 100
load testing 229

M

Managed Identity 179
manual functional tests, types
  about 216
  exploratory testing 223, 224
  manual test results, reporting 224
  scripted testing 217, 218, 219, 220, 221, 222
master branch 37
mean time to recovery 16
Mean Time To Repair (MTTR) 14
merge commit 42
merging strategies
  about 41
  Git 41, 42
  Team Foundation Version Control (TFVC) 41
migration script
  editing, considerations 189
migration strategies 366

migration strategies, ways
  Azure DevOps Server to Azure DevOps Services
    migration 367
  big-bang migration 367
  rebuilding 368
  synchronization 368
migrations
  about 189
  disadvantages 190
  without retaining history 36, 37
mobile applications
  App Center, integrating via Azure Pipelines 122
  app store, connecting to 118, 119
  crash reports, obtaining 278, 279, 280
  creating 117
  deploying 116
  distribution groups, using 119, 120
  publishing 120, 121, 122
monolithic repository (monorepo)
  about 43
  advantages 44
multi-job pipelines
  about 79
  control options 80
multi-stage pipelines 55, 242, 243, 244
multi-stage YAML pipelines
  approvals 108, 109
  approvers, adding 109
  approvers, defining 110
  artifacts, downloading 107
  stages, adding 106, 107
  writing 106
multiple repositories
  advantages 44
MyGet
  about 150

N

n-product feedback
  examples 309
  gathering, advantages 309
node port 338
node
  about 183
  autoscaling 350

scaling 349
non-functional tests, types
  about 228
  load testing 229
  performance testing 228
  usability testing 230

O

object-relational mapper (ORM) 195
Octopus Deploy 124
Open Web Application Security Platform (OWASP) 259
OWASP Zed Attack Proxy (OWASP ZAP)
  about 259
  baseline scan mode, running in 260
  full active scan mode, running in 260

P

packages
  consuming 144
  consuming, from pipeline 146
  consuming, from Visual Studio 144, 145
  publishing 139
  publishing, from pipeline 140, 142
  uploading, by hand 139, 140
  versioning 142, 143, 144
parallel executions 362
performance testing 228
pods
  autoscaling 348, 349
  scaling, manually 348
PowerShell DSC
  about 174
  applying 175
  compiling 175
  using, with Azure Automation 175, 177
private agent pool
  creating 84
progressive exposure
  about 113
  canary deployments strategy 113
  ring-based deployments 113
public roadmap
  sharing 310
  sharing, pros and cons 310

pull mode 175
pull server 175
Puppet 183
Puppet Master 183
push mode 175
push-based deployments 103

Q

quality gates
  about 241
  classic releases 241, 242
  multi-stage pipelines 242, 243, 244
quality metrics
  obtaining, automatically 237, 238, 239
quality
  defining 204, 205
  metrics 205, 207
  metrics, examples 206
  technical debt 207, 208
  visualizing 239, 240, 241

R

rebase 43
Red Hat Package Manager (RPM) 150
relational mapper (ORM) 188
Release Flow 39
release notes
  automating 122, 123
releases 55
repositories
  creating 44
  managing 43
  removing 45, 46
  securing 46
resource 183
resources section, ARM templates
  about 159
  dependent resources 159
  nested templates 160
results, measuring
  about 14
  amount of work in progress 15
  change failure rate 16
  change rate 16
  cycle time 15

lead time 15
mean time to recovery 16
Role-Based Access Controls (RBAC) 304
runbooks
  about 172
  executing 173
  execution, ways 173
  gallery 174
  jobs 173
runtime security risks and threats
  detecting 268, 270
  monitoring 268, 270

S

scaffolding 189
schema-less database
  about 195
  objects, reading from 197, 198
  objects, writing to 195, 196
scripted testing 217, 218, 219, 220, 221, 222
secrets
  handling 251
  storing, in service connections 252, 253, 254
  storing, invariable groups 254, 255
  unsecured secrets, detecting 256, 257
security concerns
  at branch-master merge stage 250
  at build stage 250
  at cross-cutting stage 251
  at deployment environment (target systems) 251
  at release stage 251
service endpoint
  creating 330, 331
shared components
  identifying 130, 131
source control connection, build definition
  build artifacts, publishing 61
  job, configuring 57, 58, 59
  Task Marketplace 63
  tasks, adding to jobs 60
  tools, integrating with pipeline 61, 62
source control systems
  about 31
  Git 32
  migrating 33

Team Foundation Version Control (TFVC) 31
source control, tools
  about 48
  GitHub 48
  GitLab 49
  Subversion 49
source control
  centralized source control 30
  decentralized source control 30
  types 30
squash commit 42
standardizing tools 365, 366
Subversion
  about 49
  migrating, to Azure Git repository 36
system tests 215, 216

T

Team Foundation Server (TFS) 31, 366
Team Foundation Version Control (TFVC) 31
  migrating, to Git repository 35
technical debt 207, 208
Terraform 184
test
  categories 209
  types 208, 209
testing pyramid 226, 227
testing trophy 227, 228
tests, in pipeline
  executing 231
  external tests, running 235
  integration tests, running 234, 235
  unit tests, running 231, 232, 233
time to market 15
tools, for ARM templates deployment
  Azure CLI 163
  Azure Pipelines 163, 164
  PowerShelll 162
tools, for maintaining application quality
  about 236
  code reviews 236
  quality gates 241
  quality metrics, obtaining automatically 237,
    238, 239
  quality, visualizing 239, 240, 241

tools, for managing infrastructure and configuration
  through code
  Ansible 184
  Chef 183
  CloudFormation 182
  Puppet 183
  Terraform 184
traceability
  ensuring 362, 363, 364
trunk-based development
  about 39, 40
  reference link 37

U

unit tests
  about 211, 212, 213
  code coverage, recording 233, 234
  running 231, 233
universal packages
  downloading, from Azure Pipelines 147, 148
  downloading, with Azure CLI 149
  uploading, from Azure Pipelines 147, 148
  uploading, with Azure CLI 149
  working with 146
usability testing 230
UserVoice 311

V

Veracode 271
Visual Studio
  packages, consuming from 144, 145

W

web applications, alerts
  fatigue 298
  metrics, selecting to capture 299, 300
  optimizing 298
web applications, logging
  altering 286, 287, 288, 289
  emitting 284, 285
  searching 286
web applications, metrics
  alerting 293, 294, 295
  emitting 290, 291
  graphing 292, 293

web applications
  alerting, optimizing 297
  instrumenting 282, 283, 284
  live site reviews 301, 302
  logging 284
  metrics 289
  on-call schedule 300, 301
  requests, investigating 295, 296, 297
WhiteSource 271
WhiteSource Bolt
  working with 261, 262, 263
Work in Progress (WIP) 370

YAML file
  writing 76, 77
YAML pipelines
  about 55
  artifacts 81
  build definitions, using as code 75, 76
  creating 78
  multi-job pipelines 79
  variables 81
  working with 75
  writing 76
  writing, tips 82, 83
Yet Another Markup Language (YAML) 55

Y

Made in the USA
Las Vegas, NV
09 February 2021

17410910R20238